NEW IDEAS
ON
WHAT COULD HAPPEN WHEN...

Mommie is bad...
The galaxy is being pulled in by the
      Strange Attractor...
A bag lady's money never runs out...
A spaceship tangles in a fishing line...
The best-laid plans of mutant men are
      very good...
An alien with a clipboard knocks at the door...
DaVinci-drive packets ply among the stars...
A combat-weary veteran befriends
      the Mouselady...
A second splits...
The Bering Sea rolls above your past life...
Evil saunters handsomely through the city...

...and more. And marvelous.

BRAND-NEW TOP-FLIGHT SF STORIES!
From The Latest Hot New Talents
discovered by

L. Ron Hubbard's Writers of The Future®
Contest!

WHAT'S BEEN SAID ABOUT THE *L. RON HUBBARD Presents WRITERS OF THE FUTURE* ANTHOLOGIES

"... one of the best collections of new SF I've ever seen."
ARTHUR C. CLARKE

"These stories represent the best of the fresh talent in the field..."
GENE WOLFE

"Opening new trails into the worlds of SF..."
JACK WILLIAMSON

"What a wonderful idea—one of science fiction's all-time giants opening the way for a new generation of exciting talent! For these brilliant stories, and the careers that will grow from them, we all stand indebted to L. Ron Hubbard."
ROBERT SILVERBERG

"There's an explosion of talent in these pages."
ROCKY MOUNTAIN NEWS

"All the stories are provocative, imaginative, and entertaining..."
DELAND (Florida) NEWS

"A double success for science fiction fans—it encourages new talents in the field, and it provides readers with some very good stories." BUFFALO (New York) NEWS

"... these stories present imaginative situations and solid literary skill." THE OTTAWA (Canada) CITIZEN

"... recommended as literally being the best, the very best, available to the public today."
MIDWEST BOOK REVIEW

"Writers of The Future *brings back some of the science fiction reminiscent of* Twilight Zone *and* The Outer Limits. *But it also brings a modernized innovativeness and mystery unmatched by its forerunners.*"

THE UTAH STATESMAN

"... *not only is the writing excellent ... it is also extremely varied. There's fantasy and adventure fiction ... humor ... and mainstream SF ... Don't miss this anthology. There's a lot of hot new talent in it.*"

"... *the best-selling SF anthology series of all time.*"

LOCUS MAGAZINE

"... *packed with raw talent ... a must buy for everyone who wants to write science fiction.*"

FANTASY REVIEW

"... *drop whatever you're doing and run to the nearest bookstore. This book is more than worth the effort.*"

THE LEADING EDGE

"*This is a remarkable collection ... in its content and scope.*" THE JOHNS HOPKINS UNIVERSITY NEWS-LETTER

"*The varied style and consistent quality lead to a reading experience beyond belief.*" PLANETARY PREVIEWS

"... *an exceedingly solid collection, including sf, fantasy and horror ...*" THE CHICAGO SUN-TIMES

"*If you buy only one paperback in the SF field this year, make it this one.*" MEMPHIS COMMERCIAL APPEAL

L. RON HUBBARD

PRESENTS

WRITERS

OF THE

FUTURE

VOLUME V

The Year's 14 Best Tales from his
Writers of The Future
International Writing-Talent Program

With Essays on Writing and Art by
L. RON HUBBARD
ALGIS BUDRYS
MARTA RANDALL
JANE YOLEN
HAL CLEMENT
FRANK KELLY-FREAS

Edited by Algis Budrys
Frank Kelly-Freas, Director of Illustration

Bridge Publications, Inc.

Introduction: Copyright © 1989 Algis Budrys
Daddy's Girls: Copyright © 1989 K. D. Wentworth
The Nomalers: Copyright © 1989 Jamil Nasir
Blue Shift: Copyright © 1989 S. M. Baxter
Just don't: Copyright © 1989 Eolake Stobblehouse
Rachel's Wedding: Copyright © 1989 Virginia Baker
The Wallet and Maudie: Copyright © 1989 Dan'l Danehy-Oakes & Alan Wexelblat
Dear Mom: Copyright © 1989 Stephen C. Fisher
A Little Womanly Advice: Copyright © 1989 Marta Randall
Prosthetic Lady: Copyright © 1989 Paula May
Despite and Still: Copyright © 1989 Marc Matz
A Walk by Moonlight: A Folktale of the Present Day: Copyright © 1989 Mark Anthony
Wisdoms & Warnings: Writing SF for Younger Readers: Copyright © 1989 Jane Yolen
Starbird: Copyright © 1989 J. Steven York
A Ghost in the Matrix: Copyright © 1989 Steve Martindale
Under Ice: Copyright © 1989 C. W. Johnson
The Magic Picture: Copyright © 1989 Hal Clement
The Disambiguation of Captain Shroud: Copyright © 1988 Gary W. Shockley
Writing for the Future: Copyright © 1989 Algis Budrys
Illustrating for the Future: Copyright © 1989 Frank Kelly-Freas
Illustration on page   4: Copyright © 1989 Jean Elizabeth Martin
Illustration on page 15: Copyright © 1989 Patrick Wynne
Illustration on page 44: Copyright © 1989 Mark Maxwell
Illustration on page 66: Copyright © 1989 Bob Giadrosich
Illustration on page 79: Copyright © 1989 David Dorman
Illustration on page 110: Copyright © 1989 David Dorman
Illustration on page 142: Copyright © 1989 Todd Hamilton
Illustration on page 171: Copyright © 1989 Alan Gutierrez
Illustration on page 192: Copyright © 1989 Dell Harris
Illustration on page 223: Copyright © 1989 Dell Harris
Illustration on page 236: Copyright © 1989 Lawrence Stewart
Illustration on page 282: Copyright © 1989 Denis Beauvais
Illustration on page 308: Copyright © 1989 Ed Kline
Illustration on page 343: Copyright © 1989 Carolly Hauksdottir
Illustration on page 367: Copyright © 1989 Stu Shepherd
Illustration on page 407: Copyright © 1989 David Lee Anderson
Cover Artwork: Copyright © 1989 Author Services, Inc.

ISBN 0-88404-379-7

Library of Congress Catalog Card Number: 84-73270
First Edition Paperback 10 9 8 7 6 5 4 3 2 1

Printed in the United States of America
Cover Artwork by Frank Frazetta

WRITERS OF THE FUTURE and ILLUSTRATORS OF THE FUTURE are trademarks
owned by L. Ron Hubbard Library.

CONTENTS

ACKNOWLEDGEMENTS

The judges for L. Ron Hubbard's Writers of The Future Contest serve at a cost in time and attention taken from their own prestigious careers. In the Contest year of this anthology, they were:

Gregory Benford	Algis Budrys
Ramsey Campbell	Anne McCaffrey
Larry Niven	Frederik Pohl
Andre Norton	Robert Silverberg
Jerry Pournelle	John Varley
Jack Williamson	Gene Wolfe
	Roger Zelazny

Serving as instructors in the WOTF invitational writers' workshop were Michael R. Collings, Ph.D., of Pepperdine University, and Orson Scott Card.

For their participation and their support of the discovery of exciting new talent, we thank

Hal Clement, teacher, novelist and master of the "hard-science" story;

Marta Randall, social critic, novelist and past-President of the Science Fiction Writers of America; and

Jane Yolen, storyteller to the young, master of fantasy and past-President of the Science Fiction Writers of America.

Our cover illustration is an original commissioned painting by Frank Frazetta

Mr. Frazetta's career as a master in his field has spanned decades and aroused worldwide admiration for his works. Our cover painting, "Encounter," is a sequel to his "Dreamflight" cover for *Writers of The Future III*.

The original art may be seen at the L. Ron Hubbard Gallery, 7051 Hollywood Boulevard, Hollywood, California.

Introduction
by
Algis Budrys

The *L. Ron Hubbard Presents WRITERS OF THE FUTURE* series is one of master storyteller L. Ron Hubbard's proudest creations, and all of us who work on it have a share in that pride. As befits its source in an SF-writing legend, the emphasis is on stories, stories, stories. Like the previous volumes, this book is full of very good short science fiction and fantasy. It ranges across almost the entire board of possibilities in speculative fiction, and it will meet very high standards for readability and satisfaction.

The stories here will take you from some new twists on the here-and-now to the farthest reaches of the Universe. They'll also do amazing things to the idea of time. They delve into hidden aspects of the past, and they go into *the* probable future. Beyond that, they'll lift you into the barely imaginable but still "real" future . . . and they also swing out to *an* imaginable but "unreal" time, and then a "real time" in the *exact* sense of that term.

They're ingenious, powerful, and packed with the kinds of entertainment that only science fiction and fantasy can offer their readers.

They're effectively written. Some of them are funny; some are not. Some are longer and some are shorter. One is very short . . . a striking example of that most difficult of all forms, the SF short-short story. Every one of them is special—literally, a discovery.

You'll find they're all by names unfamiliar when the book first appears. Once you've read them, though, I think you'll understand why so many increasingly well-known and much-liked writers have emerged from this series. This series gets you in at the launch-point of careers that deserve launching. The reputation of these unique and highly popular anthologies testifies that the stories, and their authors, will be impressive from the outset. They will meet with approval from meticulous critics . . . and they will be very good reading, too, which is what really matters.

This is the fifth such annual volume of new stories by new writers. The *L. Ron Hubbard Presents WRITERS OF THE FUTURE* series continues to be the best-selling SF anthology series of all time.

In the back of this book, in my essay, ''Writing for the Future,'' you'll find complete information on how these good things came to be: the book, the Contest, and the total program, and L. Ron Hubbard's uniquely effective creation of them. You'll see why a roster of the top names in SF lends its active support to this anthology and the program it springs from.

But there's no good reason to keep you from the stories a moment longer.

Enjoy the book!

—Algis Budrys
EDITOR

Daddy's Girls
by
K. D. Wentworth

About the Author

K. D. Wentworth has been an elementary school teacher for a dozen years, an experience she says provides a lot of instruction in human nature.

A cum laude *graduate in Liberal Arts*, she lives in Tulsa, Oklahoma. Her primary recreation is dancing. Having studied tap and ballet as a child, she now, in her thirties, performs with folk-dancing groups.

She belongs to no writers' groups, apparently does not know that northeastern Oklahoma houses many active SF fan groups as well as professional and apprentice writers. Thus, she typifies the sort of novice who thoroughly follows the folk-wisdom that writing is a lonely profession.

It is and it isn't, but never mind that. What she has learned, at some point, is that the way to write is to sit down and do it. In her case, three pages a day, every day, no matter what. And here are some of those pages. . . .

Illustrated by Jean Elizabeth Martin

Brushing a black curl out of the way, Ariel fits the tiny snooper into her ear and leans back on her bed.

"...don't know, Carlos," her mother's voice is saying in that controlled contralto Ariel knows so well. "Maybe we should just terminate and start over again. I don't like this sudden fascination she's developed with scribbling and— "

Her father cuts her off. "For God's sake, Lanya, this is your third go-round with Ariel. By now I'd think you could get it right!"

There is a long, painful silence. While she listens, Ariel studies the holocube she found packed away in the storage space two days ago. Inside the cube's frozen moment, Ariel, Carlos, and Lanya ride a duraplas raft down the white water rapids of a beautiful river. Ariel's face is joyful and free, her black hair flying back in the river spray. Carlos and Lanya lean forward, hugging their arms tightly around her.

Ariel's fingernails dig into the cool, unscratchable plas. She has never been on a raft with her parents. That was one of the *others*.

She hears a scrape as her father pushes back his chair and leaves the table. Ariel knows it is him even though she can't see the dining room. Her father always leaves when he doesn't know what to say. Her mother will just sit there.

The front door slams. Ariel removes the snooper and thrusts it under her mattress where the Hazel 2000 won't find it. Pulling out her sketch pad, she balances it on her knees and works on her light-pencil drawing of an Arabian mare, shading in the mane with delicate strokes.

"Ariel?" her mother's voice demands over the intercom.

Ariel transfers the pencil to her other hand and works on the proud, arching tail as she depresses the button. "Yes, Mother?"

"Don't 'yes, Mother' me! You know very well what time it is, young lady!" Her mother's voice sounds very brittle, almost like it might break.

Ariel glances at the glowing chronocrystal up on the wall: four o'clock. With great precision she lines the sketch pad up with the square corner of her desk. Then she walks through her wing into the main house.

Her mother sits in the living room with her long legs crossed and her red mouth clamped in nervous disapproval. Her mother is actually mad at her father, but he has left.

"You're already three minutes late for your music lesson." Her mother's sharp red fingernails beat an insistent, angry rhythm on the plastiglass tabletop. "You will practice your scales an extra thirty minutes to make up for it."

Ariel slides into her seat at the synthesizer and slips the Mozart into her ear. While her mother looks on, she practices the notes over and over, but sometimes her fingers slip and hit the wrong keys.

At the end of the hour and thirty minutes, Ariel lays the Mozart aside.

"I don't know what's wrong with you," her mother complains, then sips at a clear tumbler of syntha-gin. "You should be playing much better by now."

Ariel thinks that means one of the *others* was much better at piano by this age, but her mother will never say that.

"Don't look at me that way." Her mother stirs the

drink with the tip of her little finger, clinking the ice cubes around. "Go finish your homework."

Ariel retreats to her room, sealing her door before she pulls out the box of old pictures, holos, and letters she found in the storage space several days ago. Lying on her stomach, she thinks about what her friend Lisa told her.

"You mean you're ten and your parents haven't told you which one you are yet?" Lisa's freckled face had been both surprised and superior. "*My* parents told me eons ago!" Lisa had opened her bag and pulled out several smudged prints. "I'm a Four. That's real good because now my parents have had lots of practice and they know exactly what to do. They know I'm a keeper. My dad said so."

Ariel had looked carefully at the old photographs Lisa passed her. In one, a much younger Lisa was sitting on a baby elephant at the circus. In another, an older Lisa with short hair was smiling in an out-of-fashion dress at least a foot too short.

"But these are all pictures of you." Ariel had handed the prints back. "I don't get it."

"Those are the *others*, dummy. *I've* never been to the circus or had short hair." Lisa had shaken her head, making her ginger-colored braids fly. "God, you're such a baby. Your parents don't tell you anything!" She had flopped backwards on Ariel's bed and bounced for a moment.

"What others?"

"The ones that came before me." Lisa had sat up and stared at her solemnly. "The ones that didn't work out."

Ariel had just looked at her, not wanting to say more and sound even dumber.

"You know," Lisa had said, "like when your dad gets a new Hazel and it puts soap in the meatloaf, and he sends it back and gets another. Like that."

Ariel had begun to understand then. "Like a trade-in."

"Yeah," Lisa had said. "Which one do you think you

are? I know you're not a First 'cause my mom said your parents should have lots of practice by now. That's real good, though, 'cause no one ever wants to be a First. My dad says they hardly ever work out.''

After Lisa had gone home, Ariel had searched the storage area up under the roof and brought down a box of pictures and holos of herself doing things she'd never done, wearing clothes she'd never worn.

All the Ariels in the pictures look just like her except —they aren't her. She can't tell how many there have been from the pictures, but one had evidently gotten older than ten before she had been traded in. There are clothes and letters and pictures to prove it.

The letters intrigue her the most. Most are from someone named Tommy and he seems to like Ariel a lot. The letters are real mushy and there is even a picture of an older Ariel standing next to a boy with light-brown hair. She wonders if that is Tommy but there is no way to be sure.

At seven o'clock, she reports to the dining room for dinner. Her father has come back. He almost always returns by dinner.

Ariel slides into her seat and bows her head for the blessing. Her mother always says it real fast so it doesn't take very long. The Hazel 2000 sets chicken soup on the table and Ariel tries to hold her spoon just right so her mother won't get mad.

After the soup, they wait in silence for tonight's turkey. Ariel looks at her father and he doesn't look mad anymore. She decides that maybe now is a good time to ask him.

"Daddy," she begins quietly, staring at her folded hands in her lap. "Which one am I?"

"What?" Her father's voice sounds funny, kind of hollow.

"Which number am I in our family?" She looks at his

face framed in dark curly hair like her own. "You know, how many Ariels were there before me?"

"Who told you that?" Her mother's face matches the white of the new plas chairs they bought last week.

Ariel picks at the turkey and dressing Hazel sets in front of her. "Lisa says she's a Four."

Her mother rises convulsively, looking angrily at her father and throws her white napkin on the floor as she leaves the room. The Hazel picks it up, folds it neatly, and lays it in her mother's place at the table.

"Lisa says she's a keeper, Dad." Ariel sneaks a look at her father. "Am I a keeper too?"

Her father just sits there, staring at Ariel's face, but Ariel doesn't feel like he's really seeing her.

Ariel eats another bite of her turkey and dressing. Then she makes a face. "This has too much salt in it," she says. "Are you going to trade Hazel in?"

Her father's eyes drop down to his plate. "No," he replies softly, "I can adjust that."

"What happened to the other Ariels? Did they go to live with other families?"

Her father looks very pale. "They went back to the same hospital they came from. Then we got you."

"Are you going to trade me in?"

"No."

Ariel decides that she isn't really hungry. She slides out of her seat and walks around to her father, but he doesn't look up. "I guess that's good, isn't it?"

Suddenly her father's arms reach out and encircle her, crushing her to his chest. "Yes," he whispers fiercely. "That's very good." His face is wet.

Ariel strokes his black hair. "I'm sorry, Daddy. I didn't mean to make you sad."

Her father straightens up. "You didn't make me sad, Baby."

She smiles. It's been a long time since he called her that. "Do I have to eat the turkey?"

He pats her on the back and releases her. "No. You get a nutrition bar out of the kitchen and take it to your room. I'll reset the Hazel before I go to bed."

"Okay."

"And, Ariel?"

She stops on her way to the kitchen and looks over her shoulder.

"Stay in your room tonight. Your mother and I have to talk."

Ariel nods and goes on to the kitchen. She finds a peanut butter-and-jelly bar in the pantry.

Her mother always says peanut butter and jelly is "putrid."

In her room, she nibbles on the nutrition bar after she retrieves the snooper from under her mattress. Slipping it back into her ear, she sits at her desk and studies her drawing. The Arabian mare's coat glows up at her with a rich chestnut color.

"... don't want another clone of this one! I want to scrap this one and start over with a totally different embryo! This one is never going to amount to anything!" Her mother's voice ends on a rising tone.

Ariel picks up the light-pen and sets it for a darker brown so she can put in some shading.

"People are not disposable!" Her father sounds furious.

"You know the rules. You can't keep one once it starts to go wrong." Ariel hears the clink of ice cubes.

The snooper relays an ominous silence. Ariel switches to black for the hooves, hoping her father isn't going to leave again.

"There's nothing wrong with her!"

Ariel hears footsteps pacing around the living room. That will be her father.

"We'll see about that!" her mother says. "I'm going up to the hospital tomorrow!"

After that there is only silence. Ariel puts the last touches on her picture of the mare and hangs it on her wall. She steps back, admiring the way she managed to fit the mare's neck into its shoulders this time. Of course, her mother will take it away from her tomorrow.

Her mother prefers music.

"Well," her father says, "we'll miss her, of course, but she won't be gone forever."

Ariel nods. "How long does it take?"

"About a year." He looks up from the Hazel's control panel. "First she has to grow to full size. Then they'll check her out and make sure that nothing's wrong this time."

"Do I have to practice music while she's gone?"

Her father winks. "Not as far as I'm concerned."

Ariel thinks about that and decides that she might practice a little anyway. She moves closer to look over his shoulder into the Hazel's complicated insides. "You never did tell me which one I am."

He makes a final adjustment on the cooking circuit. "You're a Three, Ariel."

"Oh." She hands him the control panel cover. "That's good, isn't it?"

He smiles at her and clicks the cover into place. "It's perfect."

The Nomalers
by
Jamil Nasir

About the Author

The following story came into existence as the product of an extended combination of seemingly unlikely factors. Jamil Nasir was born in Chicago in 1955; his father is a Palestinian college professor and his mother qualifies for membership in the Daughters of the American Revolution. Her father, incidentally, invented the forklift truck.

Nasir grew up in Jerusalem; Amman, Jordan; and Ann Arbor, Michigan, among other places, and once made the Dean's List in chemistry before graduating magna cum laude in law. He's currently working as a lawyer in Washington, D.C., meticulously assessing major liability claims, with his firm's leave to write fiction part-time.

And for more data on long-chain causation, we now introduce you to. . . .

On a bright October morning Ralph Jennings and I, wearing gray pinstripe suits, rattled over the rolling brown fields of Southeastern Iowa in an airport rental car.

Ralph was driving and giving me instructions: "Remember not to stare. The clients are self-conscious about being different, and they don't like strangers. Let me do the talking. No matter what strange things you may see, *don't stare*." He added as an afterthought: "And don't let the Old Nomaler fool you. He's a smart old bird."

I tried to look grave. Meeting The Client is the first tiny step they let you take toward being a real lawyer.

A town posted "Priopolis Speed Limit 25" came and went in a flash of hamburger joint, gas station, and trailer-size white houses. A few miles later we turned on a bumpy road with a sign that said "Private—Keep Out" and stopped at a shack with a wire fence stretching into the distance in both directions. A man came out of the shack.

He was on the short side of medium height, thin, with lank brown hair. His nose dropped in a thin, straight line from forehead to lip, and his eyes were so close together he looked cross-eyed. Big teeth stuck out crookedly between thin lips. He was like something you would see in an aquarium, on the other side of the glass.

"Ralph Jennings and Blaine Ramsey to see Mr. Nomaler," Ralph said, and gave the man his driver's license. The man looked at me. I dug out my driver's license. He took both of them into the shack.

"Security," Ralph explained.

A few minutes later the man brought our licenses back. "OK," was all he said.

A few miles on we came over a rise, and there was an enormous three-story farmhouse with a jumble of additions, wings, annexes, enlargements, connecting buildings, barns, outbuildings, garages, even a shingled tower, all weathered into a gray fortress that looked like it would hold a hundred people. Smoke drifted from several chimneys. Ralph pulled up to a leaning porch darkened by fir trees and stacked with boxes and junk. Two young men came out onto the porch. They looked like twins of the man at the security shack.

"Mr. Jennings?" one asked, and they led us into a big front hall without shaking hands.

Comfortable domestic things were going on in the hall. An aproned woman chased a baby who was running away with someone's shoe. Three ten-year-olds made a terrific noise playing cards on the threadbare carpet. A middle-aged man smoked a pipe in a greasy armchair. There was a smell of lunch cooking.

Everyone, from the baby to the man, had the same thin, flat nose, squeezed-together eyes, buck teeth, lank hair.

I tried not to stare. Everyone was staring at us. The baby started to cry and dropped the shoe, and the aproned woman swept him away to another room.

"The Old Nomaler's busy," said one of the young men. "He wants you to wait."

"We'll be glad to," said Ralph, who hates waiting for anything.

They led us up some stairs and down a narrow passage to a small, dim room. Ralph set his briefcase on a swaying coffee table with a strip of formica missing, and asked: "Can you show me the bathroom?" They led him off like a prisoner. I sat on a bloated vinyl sofa and tried not to breathe a sour smell. After a minute, I opened a window

Illustrated by Patrick Wynne

and leaned out of it. Fir trees growing almost against the house gave me a breath of cool, aromatic air.

Down in the yard, a boy was yelling: "Train coming! Train coming!"

Train tracks ran two hundred yards behind the house. Seven or eight little boys, some almost babies, quickly gathered by a rusted tractor below my window. An older boy, about twelve, balanced on the tractor's seat. As the train rumbled past, he called out numbers. It took me a minute to figure out that they were the four- and five-digit identification numbers painted on the sides of the train's boxcars. The little boys sat on the ground rigid with concentration.

When the fifty-odd cars had passed, the older boy yelled: "Total!"

"Five hundred and twenty thousand, two hundred and twenty-three!" hollered back the little boys almost in unison.

Steps in the passage announced the two Nomalers marching Ralph back from the bathroom. Both of them stared at the open window, then at me. One brushed past me and shut it severely. Then they stalked off without a word.

"You shouldn't touch anything," Ralph murmured, sitting on the sofa with a creak. "They don't like it." He pulled his briefcase next to his feet like a protective talisman.

Half an hour later the two Nomalers led us through a maze of halls, rooms, stairways, foyers, ramps, basements, balconies, and passages. When we finally reached the Old Nomaler's room there was no way to tell what part of the house we were in.

The room opened off a landing at the top of a dark, creaking staircase. A confused babble came from half a dozen TVs ranged around an old man propped in a king-size bed. When he saw us he nodded to another man, who started turning the TVs off. The old man looked like all the other Nomalers except that he was wrinkled and bald, with a winglike fringe of white hair. He wore dirty pajamas, and a quilt was pulled up to his middle. Around his bed were cardboard boxes full of papers, broken lamps, old bicycle parts, moth-eaten stuffed animals, and other things. Piles of papers lay on ancient desks pushed against the walls. Three worn black rotary telephones sat on one desk next to an obsolete desk-top calculator. A dozen folding chairs were set around.

"Lawyer Jennings," the old man honked, ducking his head and waving. "Brought somebody with you, I see." He held a pair of bifocals against his vertical nose.

"This is Blaine Ramsey," said Ralph, patting my shoulder warmly, "one of our most competent and trusted associates." I had been the only associate not busy when the Nomaler matter came in.

"How do you do, sir," I said.

"How de do, how de do. Well, sit down, sit down. You remember Derek Dan, there, Lawyer Jennings." He nodded at the middle-aged Nomaler who had turned off the TVs.

"Of course. Hello, Derek," said Ralph.

"Lawyer Jennings," said the man.

We took two folding chairs. I got out a note pad and tried to look competent and trustworthy. Derek Dan Nomaler sat where he could read what I wrote down.

"You've heard about this here new rulemaking up in St. Paul," said the old man. "The shipping insurance regulation for the Mississippi River?"

"I hadn't before you directed my attention to it," said Ralph. "I read it before we flew out of Washington last night."

"What do you make of it?"

Ralph gave him a couple of paragraphs of jargon that sounded good without meaning anything. When he was done, the Old Nomaler said: "I want you to get rid of that regulation, put things back to the way they were before."

Ralph appeared judicious. "Well, there may be grounds for doing that. Federal pre-emption, perhaps other jurisdictional problems. The difficulty, of course, is standing to appear before the Minnesota Commission. Since the rule by its terms affects shipping interests only, we would effectively have to own a Minnesota shipping company to be an aggrieved party under the appeals statute."

"We'll buy one," said the Old Nomaler.

Ralph took that like a man, even nodding as if he had thought of it first.

"Of course, we could handle such a purchase for you. However, may I point out that the Nomalers have no conceivable interest in overturning a Minnesota shipping rule. You don't own any concerns that could possibly be affected by it. What do you hope to gain?"

The Old Nomaler gave a honking laugh.

"You always ask the same question, Lawyer Jennings, and I always give you the same answer: you just let me take care of that and you see to your own side of it."

II

The Nomalers' shipping company purchase went through a month later, Ralph hinting darkly that they had overpaid almost a million dollars to close the deal that fast, and in February our appeal came up for hearing before the Minnesota Public Service Commission, Docks Division. The sky in St. Paul was like dirty snow propped just out of reach, the sidewalks cordoned off below twenty-foot ice stalactites that loomed from the parapets of tall buildings. But the streets were almost deserted: everybody with sense walked in their shirtsleeves through the glassed-in "skyways" that ran at second-story height between most of the buildings. There was even a roundabout way to walk all the way from our hotel to the Public Service Commission, which Ralph took, I puffing behind with two bursting litigation bags. An hour later I sat next to him in a small, dingy hearing room as he spoke emotionally about the great waterways of our nation, the free commerce that had always moved on those waterways, the humble men whose dreams created that commerce, the dangers of governmental strangulation of free enterprise . . . my attention wandered after awhile. The regulation we were seeking to overturn was about as far as you could get from interesting: it simply required shipping using Minnesota docks to carry a particular kind of liability insurance. The only interesting thing about the whole case, as far as I was concerned, was why the Nomalers cared about it in the first place. I glanced idly around the hearing room.

From the last row of seats provided for interested members of the public, someone was staring at me. A woman.

Ralph got done with his argument and sat down, and an Associate Commission Counsel stood up and launched into an even more boring argument supporting the rule. I studied the woman out of the corner of my eye. She seemed to watch me with a weird, hungry stare. She was an interesting specimen herself: in a perfect world she might have been beautiful, with a mane of black hair and large, burning eyes, but some stress or sorrow of this world had streaked her hair gray, hollowed out her cheeks, eaten away the flesh of her bone-thin body.

The Associate Commission Counsel's voice finally droned away to silence. There was a pause, during which the few retirees in the public seating dozed and the room's radiators could be heard faintly ticking out heat; then Administrative Law Judge Sneed roused himself to turn over a sheet of paper and clear his throat and say: "Finally, on behalf of the Council Against Domination, a consumer group

certified under Commission Rule 846.C.ii.(j), we will hear
from Mr. Timothy Nolan.''

The hungry-looking woman pulled a sheaf of papers
out of a black vinyl case and handed them to the man next
to her. He came forward. He was fat, with jiggly cheeks, a
bulbous nose, and hair worn in a kind of Afro. His face had
an injured, anxious look, like a boy spanked for things he
didn't do. Something about him was oddly familiar.

He stood awkwardly in front of Judge Sneed's table,
shuffled through his papers for an uncomfortable time, then
started in a high, quavering voice: ''Yes, your Honor. I'm
coming before this Commission, because it's my painful
duty to . . . to correct the gross, distorted view of this case
offered by the appellants.'' He glanced at Ralph and me with
a mixture of wrath and apprehension.

''This issue is nothing like what they say it is. They
have mischaracterized it. They are wrong on every single
point they have brought out. This rule ought to stand just
the way it is. It's an abomination—it's a shameful— But *why*
do you think these appellants have come before this Commission to try to strike down this rule? Mr. *Jennings*,'' the
word was spat out with much quivering of the cheeks, ''has
made a lot of fancy arguments which—which— But let me
tell you the *real* reason, your Honor, the *real* reason.''

He shuffled through his papers with trembling hands,
then started in a dramatic voice: ''Your Honor, the shipping
insurance rates are going up. Yes, the only two companies
offering the exact kind of insurance required by this rule
have taken big losses in a harbor accident in the mosquito-
infested area of Malaysia. Only a few people know that. Mr.
Jennings' clients know it, but they aren't telling. No, your
Honor. They haven't presented it to this honorable
Commission. The insurance rates will go up by a factor of
ten in the next few months.''

I was uncomfortably aware of the thin woman's eyes on me.

"If their insurance rates go up that much, barge companies using the Mississippi River will have to raise their freight tariffs. To avoid the higher tariffs, farmers will start moving their produce by rail instead of barge, as a result of which the Minnesota and Southern Railroad Company will start making a profit for the first time in 24 years, prompting a consortium of Australian investors who are looking for railroads to buy, to try to acquire a controlling share in it, causing the Federal Government, which has to approve sales of railroads to foreign interests, to require Australia to lift trade barriers on U.S. farm produce in return; when Australia does that, the selling price of U.S. corn will rise 2½ cents a bushel, making it profitable for Southeastern Iowa farmers to switch from wheat to corn as their preferred crop, slowing the chromium phosphate depletion of their soil and thus making their crops less vulnerable to a grain blight that *is spreading now from Mexico.*" He looked up to shake his fist. Judge Sneed watched him, wide-eyed. "If the Southeastern Iowa farmers keep growing wheat, the blight will wipe them out in five years, and they'll have to sell their land at bankruptcy prices. To Mr. Jennings' clients— the *Nomalers!*"

He stalked back to his seat, quivering.

Judge Sneed let go of the edge of his table and took a breath.

"Thank you, Mr. Nolan," he said. "Any rebuttal?"

"No, your Honor," Ralph said sweetly.

III

After the hearing adjourned, Ralph made important noises into a pay phone in the lobby, then said to me:

"We've located a potential Minneapolis buyer for the Nomalers' shipping company. I have to do a hearing in Florida tomorrow on the *Hess* matter; I want you to stay here for a day or two so you can ferry the papers down to the Nomalers if this Minneapolis company makes us an offer."

He was already reading the *Hess* pleadings when a cab took his gray profile off in the direction of the airport.

I got lost in the skyway maze on the way back to the hotel. After I had gone through the second-floor lobby of the First Bank Building for the third time, I put my litigation bags down in front of a fast food place to get my bearings. That was when I saw Timothy Nolan of the Council Against Domination.

He didn't see me. He was sitting by the window of the fast-food place, gorging himself and crying. As I watched, he stuffed a hamburger, yogurt, fried chicken, chocolate cake, french fries, cole slaw, a pickle, and a grilled cheese sandwich into his mouth until his cheeks ballooned, tears streaming from eyes that stared into a fearful distance.

IV

Later I slouched on my hotel bed and tried to read a science fiction magazine. The gray light outside my window was getting grayer when someone knocked at the door.

It was the Council Against Domination woman, gray eyes burning in a gaunt face, long, bony hands twitching on the same black vinyl case she had brought to the Docks Division hearing.

After I had stared at her for a good long time, she murmured: "Can I come in? I have something to discuss with you."

I got out of the way, closed the door and my mouth behind her.

"Sure," I said stupidly. "Come in."

She gave me what was probably supposed to be a smile, threw her coat on the bed, and walked stiffly to look out at where snow was starting to filter out of a gray sky onto the gray city of St. Paul.

I cleared my throat. She whirled in alarm, then gave me another emotionless smile, tossed a lock of graying hair out of her eyes.

"I'm hungry," she said. "Can you buy me dinner?"

She looked hungry. I fumbled with room service menus, the telephone, ordered dinner for two. When I finished, she was leaning against the wall, hugging her vinyl case against her skinny chest.

"I can tell you about the Nomalers," she said. "I know you're curious about them."

"What about them?" I asked stiffly, aware of the rules against Discussing Client Confidences.

"Everything. How they're planning to drive all the other farmers out of business, dominate the whole country. Everything."

"You don't really believe that fairy tale Nolan told at the hearing?"

"It's the truth."

"Come on—everyone in the room was trying not to laugh. Not the biggest MIT genius with the fastest computer is going to tell you things like that an insurance rule in Minnesota will cause a grain blight in Iowa."

"Computers can only think about numbers. Nomalers can think about *things*."

The telephone on the bedstand rang. She answered it before I could move.

"Hello?" she murmured in a languid, steamy voice. "I'm sorry, he's—busy. Can you call back?" Then: "Oh." She held the phone out to me.

It was Ralph, in Florida. He sounded a little funny, but he only said: "I just heard from our Minneapolis buyers. They're going to make us an offer. You can pick up the papers tonight. The Kristensen Transport Company." He gave me the address. "I'll call the Nomalers to set up a time when you can take the papers down."

When I hung up, the woman went on talking as if nothing had happened: "We know the grain blight is what the Nomalers are counting on in challenging the rule. Tim figured it out, replicated their analysis."

"Uh-huh."

"Yes. You see, he used to be one of them."

That stopped me. I suddenly realized why Nolan looked familiar: the narrow forehead, close fish-eyes, bobbing Adam's-apple—but force-fed fat, with a cheap nose job and a permanent.

"They sent him to college as an experiment. Their young don't go to school—they bribed some state education officials to certify a home program. Tim was one of their best—trainees. But in college he found out how evil they are, turned against them. He's been fighting them ever since."

The pride in her voice made me wonder: "He met you in college?"

She shrugged.

"I think you're both a couple of nuts," I said. "How—"

"Tim calculated that you would be wondering about the Nomalers," she broke in. "How do you explain that I knew that?"

There was a knock at the door and a muffled voice said: "Room service."

The woman had a sudden urge to use the bathroom.

I opened the door and a cheerful kid wearing pink and gold with epaulets wheeled in a hot cart and set the little table by the window. He was taking the covers off the plates when he stopped in the middle of asking me had I seen the basketball game, and his face got red. The Council Against Domination woman had come out of the bathroom wearing nothing but a towel. A small towel.

"Darling, is dinner—oh, excuse me," she said, and smiled winningly at the kid. When he had left, still red, I closed my mouth far enough to ask: "What are you—?"

The phone rang. We both dived for it. I got it, but not before she had delivered a very sexy giggle into the mouthpiece.

"Hello, Blaine Ramsey? This is Derek Dan Nomaler," came a statickey, faraway voice.

"Hello, Mr. Nomaler!" I said, trying to sound cordial and businesslike. The woman was crawling on me, breathing like a locomotive. Her towel had gotten lost. She put her mouth near the telephone and panted: "Come on, baby, let's do it some more—"

I got my hand on her face and pushed. She bit me.

"Ramsey," came the distant, crackly voice. "Are you there?"

"Yes, sir!"

"The Old Nomaler 'll be ready to see you at eight o'clock tomorrow night to sign them papers. You hear me, Ramsey?"

The woman was doing her best to kick a hole in my rib cage, laughing wildly.

"I'll be there! Thank you, sir!"

I hung up and let go of her. She backed away, rubbing her neck, which I realized I had been squeezing. Her naked body wasn't bad looking, if you like them gray and gaunt. Her eyes were shining.

"I have to dress," she said, and ran into the bathroom, slamming the door.

In thirty seconds I went through a range of emotions, settling finally on wild curiosity. The woman's black vinyl case was lying on the bed. I unzipped it.

An inner ID tag said: "If Lost, Please Return To: Ms. Jessica Ann Leighton, 301 Elm Street, Minneapolis, Minn. 52217," written small and neat. Nolan's notes from the hearing were in a different hand, wavering and scribbly. The only other thing in the case was a big diagram made of pieces of note paper scotch taped together. I unfolded it and laid it on the bed.

It was some kind of flow chart, drawn in ball-point pen, with hundreds of square, round, triangular, and diamond-shaped boxes connected by lines, arrows, and symbols. I read the writing in some of the boxes. One said: "Piedmont 351, vel. 345 mph, alt. 18500 ft., acc. .05 g, vect. 87/108/??" and a lot of other even less comprehensible stuff. Another said: "Precip. 82%, vis(alt)=" and ended in something like the General Theory of Relativity. In the very center, with many lines and arrows leading to it, was a big red magic marker star.

The bathroom door opened, there was a sharp drawn breath, and then the woman was between me and the diagram, pushing me away with one hand and folding it up with the other. When she had it and Nolan's notes back in the case, she tossed back her hair and looked me in the face. She was breathing hard, and in her eyes was exultation and hatred.

"Goodbye, Mr. *Ramsey*," she spat, and ran out of there.

V

I paced the room a little, watching dinner for two congeal on the table by the window and trying to make any sense at all of Ms. Jessica Ann Leighton. Finally, I figured

I needed professional help. I called the firm's Washington number. It was pretty late, but one of the paralegals, Edward Bolingbroke III, was still in the office. He wasn't happy about the assignment I gave him, but an hour later he called back.

"There's a lot in the Nomaler files," he told me. "I haven't been able to review all of it, but I can give you a start. First thing we handled for them was a tort case— wrongful death. About twenty years back. One of the Nomaler boys had a car accident with a gasoline truck that made weekly deliveries to a gas station down there. Freak impact flipped the truck into somebody's wheatfield. Both drivers got out, nobody hurt, but some gas spilled and caught fire, started a pretty bad brush fire. It was late summer—dry. The wind was blowing in such a way that the fire burned up to a big chemical storage tank owned by a local company, full of methy— methy-iso— no, methyl iso— anyway, something poisonous they use for making pesticides. The tank caught fire and blew up, and a cloud of poison smoke blew almost a mile and settled smack onto a local farmer's house. Killed the farmer and most of his family. It just happened that he was a big wheel around there, had organized local opposition to the Nomalers, boycotting their wholesale outfits, refusing to sell them land and so forth. Survivors brought suit in county court. Your friend Jennings got the venue changed, and the jury denied liability for lack of proximate cause: unforeseeable freak chain of events. The case of *Leighton v. Nomaler,* affirmed by the Iowa Court of Appeals at—"

"Leighton?"

"Samuel Arthur Leighton was the farmer's name."

I was silent until Eddie said: "You still there? Want to hear the next one?"

"Yeah."

"This might have been luck, but . . . It was an acqui-
sition we handled for them—a series of acquisitions. In the
spring of 1973 the Nomalers mortgaged everything they
had, took out business loans, sold off land, and invested ten
million dollars in guess what? Unprofitable Texas oil wells.
A few months later the OPEC oil embargo hit and Texas oil
wells got very profitable. They sold out their holdings a
couple years ago, just before prices dipped again. Jennings
handled the sales. Overall, they made more than eighty million on the deal. I'll tell you, Blaine, either these folks are
damn lucky, or . . . "

"Or what?"

"Or nothing. They're just damn lucky. That's as far as
I've gotten so far."

The next afternoon I flew to Iowa City with the Kristensen purchase contract papers and rented a car. I took
Interstate 80 west, turned south on state highway 149, and
west again on a county route. Between country songs and ads
for hog wormer and feed corn, the radio weatherman was
predicting light snow and twenty degrees below zero.

The twenty degrees below zero I could believe, but by
the time I reached Priopolis it was pitch dark and the light
snow had turned heavy. I could barely see the "Private—
Keep Out" sign marking the Nomaler's road. I crawled
along at 10 mph past the dark guardhouse. By the time I saw
the lights of the main house, it was almost nine-thirty. A hundred yards away, my car stuck in a snowdrift and I couldn't
get it unstuck. I trudged to the porch Ralph and I had used
before. The wind through my overcoat was numbing. I
pounded on the door with a hand that felt like a piece of
wood.

The door cracked wide enough for yellow light to show
swirling snowflakes and a narrow, cross-eyed woman's face
that shrilled: "Go away! You're at the wrong place!" She
tried to close it, but I stuck my foot in the crack.

I worked my frozen lips. "I'm the lawyer—"

She was screeching at someone inside. A second later the door jerked open and a shotgun barrel hovered in front of my nose.

"What do you want?" rasped the skinny, fishlike man holding it.

"I'm the lawyer—from Minneapolis—I brought the papers—"

"Where's your car?"

"Got stuck—up the road."

"Let's see your I.D."

I pulled out my license with foot-thick fingers and gave it to him. Another man took it away somewhere.

"Can I come in?"

"Not yet."

Heat flowing out of the door brought some feeling back into me. By the time the other man came back with my license, I was warm enough to be mad as hell.

But since these folks were Ralph's clients, I limited my remarks to "I appreciate your hospitality," as they let me in. They ignored me. The one with the shotgun locked it in a closet, bolted and chained the porch door. Then they all went off without a word. The hall was still, empty, warm, and smelled of dust and firewood. Now and then a floor-board creaked somewhere. I stood on the doormat, snow melting off my coat and hair. I noticed the mat didn't say "Welcome" on it.

Finally two Nomalers came down the hall. One said: "The Old Nomaler 's ready to see you." We took the scenic route to his room, and soon I was again basking in his bene-ficient gaze, Derek Dan hanging around behind my chair close enough to pick my pockets.

"No offense," honked the Old Nomaler, waving a hand at me. "Folks got to be careful who they let in these days."

I got the Kristensen papers in order and handed him a

set, explained the details of the purchase offer. I could feel
Derek Dan's eyes over my shoulder, could hear the moaning
wind banging something loose against the side of the house.
I felt suddenly alone and vulnerable, like a diver in the kingdom of the fish-people. I missed Ralph, with his gray head,
opaque eyes, careful hands, his steadfast refusal to believe
in anything but winning cases.

After I explained the deal, the Old Nomaler signed
each paper in exactly the right place.

"Mr. Nomaler," I said as I put them away, "I'd like to
ask a favor. The weather's pretty bad out. My car's stuck
in the snow, and I don't think I could possibly get back to
Iowa City tonight anyway. Could you put me up for the
night?"

He thought about it for a long time, eyes rolling up to
look at the ceiling. Finally he said: "Well, I suppose so, I
suppose so. Be murder to turn a feller out on a night like
this." He honked with laughter. "Derek Dan, see to it."

I followed Derek Dan onto the dark landing, where my
two escorts stood against the wall. He took one of them into
a small side room and closed the door. The other watched
me like he might miss something important if he blinked.

A low-voiced argument started in the side room. As it
got heated, I caught a few words: "responsibility," "never," "Nomaler," and "murder."

But they came out deadpan as ever. Derek Dan went
back into the Old Nomaler's room. The other two walked
me through the house to a small, dim room.

"Woman's coming to make the bed," one of them
said, and shut the door. A key turned in the lock.

I took off my coat and sat in a deep, smelly armchair.
A leaning night-table and a metal bed frame with lumpy mattress made up the rest of the furniture. Wind gusted
strongly outside a small window.

There was a knock, the key turned, and a young Nomaler woman poked her head in.

"I come to make the bed," she said, and flushed deeply, as if that might give me ideas.

"I won't watch."

But I did, while she worked rapidly and expertly with the sheets and blankets. A homemade dress—purple with little white flowers—hung on her as on a clothes rack. Her thin hair was parted in the middle and tied behind with a drooping ribbon. Her close-together eyes had a look of timid sincerity.

"I'll get you your dinner," she said when she had turned back the cover and smoothed it.

"It's very kind of you."

"Well—the Old Nomaler said to do it. I wouldn't dare on my own account."

She flushed again and went out, and a little while later came back with a tray. She set it on the night-table, which rocked drunkenly.

"My name's Emily Del," she said. "I'll be back to clear away when you're done."

"Blaine," I said, and held out my hand. She shook it inexpertly, went out quickly.

The food was odd: thin, lukewarm broth, unfamiliar vegetables, and home-baked bread, all spiced heavily with something strange. After I ate it, I felt peculiar. I was trying to pin down the feeling when Emily Del came in again. She closed the door and leaned her back against it.

"Where are you from?" she asked.

"Washington, D.C."

"Is that far away?"

"About a thousand miles."

"Still in Iowa, though, isn't it?"

"No. But it's still in America."

She nodded thoughtfully, as if weighing that. Then she came over to where I was sitting on the bed.

"If I asked you to do something," she said, "would you promise not to tell anyone?"

"I guess so."

She undid the top button of her dress and pulled out a tattered, years-old *People* magazine, sat down beside me, too excited now to be shy, and opened it to a well-worn page with a color photo of a movie star.

"Can you read her name?" she breathed, her finger on the caption.

"Natassia Kinsky."

It took a few tries for her to get it right. "I think she's *so* pretty," she sighed, gazing at the picture. "I wish I looked just like her."

I studied her narrow face, snaggled teeth.

She got up and moved away timidly. "Thank you for reading her name to me."

"Can't you read?"

"'*Course* I can read. But not hard words like that. And I couldn't show it to any of the boys—they'd take it away." She slipped the magazine back inside her dress.

"The boys read better?"

"Well, yes. They have to because they're the Calculators. We're the Breeders. There's plenty of things we do better than them. That's called Division of Labor. The famous Henry Ford Nomaler invented it."

"But what's the point of it?"

"To spread the Nomaler way of life all around the world, of course. Don't you think the Nomaler way of life is superior to any other you've seen?" It sounded like a quotation.

"Sure."

"There you are, then." She came close again, looking

anxiously into my face. "You won't tell anybody, will you? We aren't supposed to talk to outsiders."

I said of course I wouldn't.

VI

It was almost midnight when I got undressed, got between the covers that Emily Del's deft, skinny hands had made up; but I couldn't sleep. I lay and listened to the wind shake the house. The strange feeling from the Nomaler food had crept into my brain, making it strangely clear, thoughts ranged neatly in rows like pieces on a chessboard. After awhile I nudged one of them tentatively: my wondering about Jessica Ann Leighton and Timothy Nolan. Thought patterns built effortlessly around it.

Unless Jessica Ann was just crazy, she had been trying to advertise yesterday that she was in my hotel room naked. She had given her pitch to anyone who would listen, but had stopped pitching right after Derek Dan Nomaler's phone call. That made it look like her public relations effort was aimed at the Nomalers. But why? Thoughts whirled like jig-saw puzzle pieces, settling finally into an odd pattern. Jessica Ann had told me that Nolan had "calculated" I was curious about the Nomalers. If you believed that, silly as it sounded, and believed that Nolan used the same methods the Nomalers did, then the Nomalers could also "calculate" my curiosity, perhaps could "calculate" that Nolan had "calculated" it and had sent Jessica Ann to take advantage of it. Derek Dan Nomaler had heard a woman in the throes of passion in my room yesterday, and could confirm who it was if he checked with the hotel and ran across a certain bell-boy. With me staying in their house, the Nomalers would surely wonder whether I was loyal, or whether Jessica Ann Leighton, whose father they had killed, had turned my head with her emaciated charms. But how had Nolan known I would be staying in the Nomaler house? Could he have "calculated" the snowstorm? One of the boxes on the diagram in Jessica Ann's vinyl case had said "Precip. 82%"; did that symbolize light snow turned unexpectedly heavy? The same diagram had a big red star in the middle; what—or who—was that? Some calamity the Council Against Domination had prepared and sent into the Nomaler household with me? Was I a messenger of doom to my own clients? I leapt up, ran from the room and down narrow, twisting corridors. I had to see the Old Nomaler, warn him about the Red Star, tell him—

I woke up with a start, wind howling faintly outside the window. I lay in the dark for awhile, trying to get the dream out of my head, cursing the Nomalers' strange food. Gradually I became aware of an uncomfortable pressure in my bladder. I got out of bed and dressed without turning on the light.

Emily Del had forgotten to lock the door. I stepped into the hall and tried to remember whether I had passed a bathroom on my trip down from the Old Nomaler's room.

"Hello?" I said to no one.

There was a dim light at one end of the hall. I went that way, floorboards squeaking faintly. There was no other sound but the distant gusting of wind. I went down some stairs, along another hall, looking through open doors for a bathroom. One doorway showed a small, plain chapel with pews and an altar below a crucifix flanked by candles. For no particular reason, I went in.

The crucifix was carved wood, and there was something strange about it: as I got closer I saw that the figure of the Messiah was dressed in farm boots, overalls, and a hat. The face was thin, with a long perpendicular nose, eyes so close together they looked crossed, buck teeth jutting at different angles between thin lips. Underneath the crucifix was a plaque: "Jacob John Nomaler, Murdered January 9, 1919." That gave me a funny feeling. I backed away, backed into the first row of pews so hard I sat down. A hymnal lay open on the pew, a rough, handsewn book crudely printed. It was open to a hymn called "Rivers of Their Blood." The first verse went:

> We will swim in
> Rivers of their blood,
> We will soar in
> Regions of the sun,
> We will show them
> What is meant to be.
> We will drown them
> In righteousness' sweet sea.

I got up and walked as fast and quietly as I could in the direction of my room. It took me three or four minutes to realize I was lost. When I stopped to get my bearings, I heard voices coming faintly down a flight of stairs.

I started to hurry in the other direction, but stopped myself. I was these folks' *lawyer,* for God's sake. If they wanted to practice bizarre religions, I should be glad. I would just go up and ask whoever was there to show me the bathroom. I started up the stairs.

I stopped again almost at once. I recognized one of the voices. It was the Old Nomaler's, and I was on the staircase below his room.

His voice was doing strange things. It droned with a stream of words, like an auctioneer singing a Gregorian chant. It was punctuated by mechanical clicking, rustling of paper, and monosyllables in other voices.

I poked my head cautiously above the top stair. In dim yellow lamplight the Old Nomaler sat in his bed, an I.V. in one arm, face flushed and eyes flashing. On each side of

him sat a middle-aged Nomaler, holding him by the hand.
One was Derek Dan. A dozen others sat in a crowded circle
around the bed, rifling through cardboard boxes of papers.
A younger Nomaler sat a little way off talking into a telephone; another was writing furiously on a thick tablet; a
third was tacking pages from the tablet onto a corked wall.
An old-fashioned desk-top calculator rested on Derek Dan's
lap, and his free hand flew over the keys.

" . . . Ramseyum cognation Leightonee Nolanor in ho-
mology, apposition, cause, proportion, context," the Old
Nomaler's voice droned, "opportunity, confidence factor,
relation Jenningsum Jenningsee—"

"Innocence pathway," rapped Derek Dan.

"Guilt pathway," rapped the middle-aged Nomaler on
the Old Nomaler's other side.

"—rapport, intersection, eliminate below-ten, above-
ten, ignore Leightonum Leightonor—"

The Nomalers with the cardboard boxes, shuffling papers rapidly, began weaving words into the Old Nomaler's
canticle: "libidinous," "financial," "eighty-three," "ad-
verse," "input need hotelus," "inhibitor guilt pathway."

"Maximum destructive," said Derek Dan.

"Projection," said the other middle-aged Nomaler.

The one at the telephones was dialing.

A few inches behind me, a voice screamed: "Emergency stop!"

Wiry hands grabbed me, hustled me up the stairs and
into the room. Two dozen fish-faces stared without expression.

"Is there a bathroom around here?" I quavered, pulling my collar straight.

The Old Nomaler laughed feverishly.

"Listening?" he demanded.

The three Nomalers who had grabbed me nodded.

"What else?"

"I was just looking for the bathroom," I said feebly. "I got lost, and—"

The Old Nomaler laughed again, loud and long and crazy. "Take him to the bathroom!" he screamed savagely, veins in his neck and forehead distended. Then he started his crazy laughing again, his eyes on my face staring and murderous, jagged, rotten teeth bared.

The three Nomalers marched me to a windowless bathroom with an old-fashioned toilet you pulled a chain to flush, a bathtub standing on enameled claws, and a mirror with the silver flaking off the back. I stood over the toilet for five minutes, but nothing would come out. My face in the mirror looked wild. When I opened the door, the three Nomalers were standing in a row. They marched me through the house in dizzying spirals, and my room appeared when I least expected it. I went in meekly, the door was closed and locked, and their footsteps went away.

It was 3:00 a.m. I sat in the armchair without turning on the light, thinking about the Old Nomaler's crazy, murderous face. I sat there an hour before I heard rapid footsteps in the hall. I did a silent back-flip, and crouched behind the armchair.

The key turned and a dark streak hit the bed with a maddened keening.

I dived on the streak.

It was like fighting a bale of wire and sharp elbows.

It whimpered "Help!" in a woman's voice. I pulled the face close to mine. Emily Del was sobbing with fear.

"They're going to kill us," she sobbed. "They're coming! We have to get away!"

"Who?" I hissed.

"The Calculators! They were whispering outside my door. I talked to you, and you saw the Central Processor,

and they're coming! They'll fry us and eat us like they did
to—!"

I put my hand over her mouth, held still. I thought a
floorboard had creaked in the hall. I jumped to the door,
reversed the key, locked it from the inside.

The knob turned silently.

"Come on," I whispered. I grabbed my coat off the
chair, opened the window and storm window as quietly as
I could. A gust of snowflakes swirled in. The tops of young
fir trees were within diving distance of the window.

"Come on," I whispered again, and dived onto one.

It bent almost double, and I slid feet-first into snow
above my knees. Emily Del came down the same way, her
dress over her head. Bitter wind cut deep into me. My hands
were already numb. Emily Del was wearing only her purple
housedress.

"Come on!" I yelled above the storm. I grabbed her
hand and dragged her in the direction I thought my rental
car must be. Fifty yards from the house she fell in the snow.
When I picked her up, she was stiff with cold. I unbuttoned
my coat, wrapped half of it around her, and we stumbled
on. The snow cleared for a second between gusts, and I saw
the car, snow drifted to the roof.

My car keys weren't in the coat pocket where I had left
them. The car doors were locked. I hadn't locked them. Suddenly I knew what had happened.

Emily Del was slipping to the ground. I held her. "We
have to get back to the house," I yelled in her ear.

Her face was still, preoccupied, eyes almost closed.

"I can't," she murmured.

"We have to! They tricked us, to get us outside. They
wouldn't have killed us—that would mean trouble. They
don't do things that way. They analyze, calculate, manipu-
late—they can't get in trouble for this—we snuck out, forgot
the car keys. How do they do it? And without computers!"

A smile of pride came into her sleeping face. "Computers can only think about numbers," she slurred, "Nomalers can think about *things*. Nomalers—"

And she was gone.

I held her cold body in my arms. I could faintly see the dark hulk of the house in the snow. "You bastards!" I screamed against the wind.

That seemed to get results. A metal shriek drowned the roar of the storm. A fiery mass plummeted from the clouds straight onto the house, and the walls burst outward in blinding flames, hurling streamers of fire and debris like a Fourth of July rocket, throwing weird shadows in the snow.

I dived behind the car just in time to escape a shower of hot metal and burning wood that broke the windows and thudded into the snow, hissing and steaming. When I poked my head out to look, only splinters of the house were standing, and the whole area was burning fiercely, hissing and sparking.

I picked Emily Del up and slogged nearer the fire. There was no need to get in the car now. There was plenty of heat.

VII

I woke up next afternoon in an Iowa City hospital—in a private room, bought with the firm's group health insurance. There was nothing much wrong with me. Emily Del was recovering from acute hypothermia in another room.

An orderly brought me some stuff that was supposed to be lunch, and a newspaper. Banner headlines on the front page said: AIR CRASH KILLS HUNDREDS IN IOWA.

"A commercial airliner collided with a private plane over Southeastern Iowa early this morning, crashing into a crowded farmhouse in what aviation officials are calling a freak accident. Blizzard conditions kept rescue teams from reaching the crash site for nearly two hours. Of the estimated two hundred people aboard Piedmont 351 and in the farmhouse, only two are known to have survived.'' There were gruesome details of the carnage, and descriptions of the disaster workers' heroic battle with the elements, then: ''The tragedy began when Timothy A. Nolan, a Minneapolis resident, flew a rented aircraft out of a small airfield near Minneapolis. While flying conditions were marginal, according to Elstien Wiggs, flight controller at the airport, Nolan, a licensed pilot, was determined to reach Priopolis, Iowa that evening. An unexpectedly heavy snowstorm interfered with transponders carried by Nolan's plane and the airliner, devices normally enabling air traffic controllers to track planes and warn them of danger.''

The telephone by my bed rang. It was Ralph Jennings, full of questions.

''I hope you managed to save the Kristensen purchase papers?'' was the first one.

I admitted that I hadn't.

''Damn it, Ramsey—Does Ms. Nomaler still want to sell the company?''

''I don't know.''

''Damn it, Ramsey, what have you been *doing* up there?''

I got him off the phone with promises to straighten everything out. Directory assistance gave me Jessica Ann Leighton's Minneapolis number.

''Hello, this is Blaine Ramsey,'' I said when she answered.

There was silence at the other end of the line.

''I just wanted to tell you that I'm inclined to believe your story about the Nomalers,'' I went on. ''And I wanted to ask whether you and Nolan set up that whole charade with me at the hotel to divert their attention, so they would be too busy to calculate what someone like Nolan might do with an airplane and a freak snowstorm . . .''

Her voice was icy. ''I have no idea who you are or what you're talking about,'' she said. ''Please don't bother me again.'' And she hung up.

I stared at the telephone. Its expression revealed nothing.

Anyway, we won our appeal. You can use Minnesota docks as much as you want without state liability insurance.

Blue Shift
by
S. M. Baxter

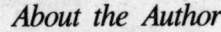

About the Author

Stephen M. Baxter, a computer systems analyst for a bank in the City of London, lives in Buckinghamshire. His wife, Sandra, is a chartered accountant. In his early 30s, he has behind him a doctorate in engineering as well as a mathematics degree from Cambridge, and a textbook titled Angular Distribution Analysis in Acoustics.

"Blue Shift" is his third professionally published SF story. It's been followed by sales to various UK publications. Those include the prestigious SF magazine, Interzone, which had already published his first sale, "The Xeelee Flower." "Blue Shift" is part of what he calls "the Xeelee sequence."

What he brings to SF is his own touch on the vastness and wonder of the Universe. That's one of the prized effects of SF, and prize it we did. . . .

Blue shift!
My fragile ship hovered over the sparkling surface of the strange attractor. From across a billion light-years worlds and galaxies were tumbling into the attractor's monstrous gravity well, arriving so fast they were blue-shifted to the color of fine Wedgewood.

I could have stared at it all until my eyes ached, but I had a problem. Swirling round me like assassins' hands were a hundred Xeelee ships. They would close on me within minutes.

My hand hovered over the control that would take me home—but I knew that the Qax, who had sent me to this fantastic place, were waiting there to kill me.

What a mess. And to think it had all come out of a sentimental journey to a breaker's yard in Korea. . . .

Of course I should have been looking for a job before my creditors caught up with me, not getting deeper into debt with travel costs. But there I was on the edge of that floodlit pit, watching gaunt machines peel apart the carcass of a doomed spaceship.

A wind whipped over the lip of the pit. The afternoon light started to fade; beyond the concrete horizon the recession-dimmed lights of Seoul began to glow. It was a desperate place. But I had to be there, because what they were breaking that day was the last human-built spacecraft. And my life . . .

A shadow moved over the pit; workmen paused and

Illustrated by Mark Maxwell

looked up as the kilometer-wide Spline ship drifted haught-
ily past the early stars. There was a Spline ship looming
over every Earth city now, a constant reminder of the power
of the Qax—the ships' owners and our new overlords. Just
when we'd got back out into space . . . just when we'd begun
to compete on equal terms with the rest of the galaxy . . .
the Qax had walked in, flattened a few cities, closed down
our shipping lines and put us right back where we started.

The shadow moved on and the wrecking machines
worked their way further into the ship's corpse. The only
way any human would leave Earth in the future was in the
alien belly of a Spline. I began to think about finding a bar.

"Like watching the death of a living thing, isn't it?"

I turned. An elegant stranger had joined me at the pit's
guardrail. Gray eyes glittered over an aquiline nose, and the
voice was rich as velvet.

"Yah," I said, and shrugged. "Also the death of my
career."

"I know."

"Huh?"

"You're Jim Bolder." The breeze stirred his ash-tinged
hair and he smiled paternally. "You used to be a pilot. You
flew these things."

"I don't know you. Do I?" I studied him warily; he
looked too good to be true. Did he represent a creditor?

He spread uncalloused palms in a soothing gesture.
"Take it easy," he said. "I don't want anything from you."

"Then how do you know my name?"

"I'm here to make you an offer."

I turned to walk away. "What offer?"

"You'll fly again."

I froze.

"My name's Lipsey," he said. "My . . . clients need a
good pilot."

"Your clients? Who?"

He glanced about the deserted apron. "The Qax," he said quietly.

"Forget it."

He exhaled sadly. "Your reaction's predictable. But they're not monsters, you know—"

"Who are you, Lipsey?"

"I . . . was . . . a diplomat. UN. I helped negotiate our treaty with the Qax. Now I try to do business with them." The low light deepened the lines on his impressive face. "I know it's hard to sympathize, but I believe we have to be pragmatic. They're just like us, you see. Looking out for number one, scrabbling for Xeelee artifacts. . . ."

I jammed my hands in my pockets and turned away once more. "Maybe, but I don't have to fly one of their damn Spline ships for them."

"You don't fly a Spline ship. Such strong opinions, and you don't even know that? Spline ships fly themselves."

"Then what's the ship? Squeem? Centauran?"

"Xeelee," he said softly. "They want you to fly a Xeelee ship." He smiled again, knowing he'd hooked me for sure.

The Xeelee own the universe.

They are everywhere, throughout our Local Cluster of galaxies and beyond. Aloof, they move past our stars on their unimaginable business.

Humanity is one of a hundred junior races struggling to survive in the Xeelee shadow. We fight over discarded Xeelee artifacts, dribbled miracles that can change the future of a race overnight. No human will ever forget that the Qax weaponry that had left Earth cratered had been Xeelee-based.

As for their ships . . . among pilots, Xeelee nightfighters are legends.

"I don't believe you," I said.

Lipsey shrugged, turning his face from the rising breeze. "The Xeelee fighter was found derelict—a long way from here. The Qax paid well for it."

I laughed. "I'll bet they did."

"And they'll pay you well for flying it."

"Prove it exists."

Furtively he dug inside his coat of soft leather and produced a plastic-wrapped package. "This was found aboard," he said. "Take a look."

I peeled back the packaging. Inside was a delicate hand-gun sculpted from a marble-like material. The butt was wrapped in a hair-thin coil. Fine buttons were inlaid into the barrel, too small for human fingers.

"Xeelee construction material." Lipsey's gray eyes were fixed on my face. "Controls built to the Xeelee's usual small scale."

"What is it?"

"We don't know. There is synchrotron radiation when the thing's operated at its lowest power setting, so the Qax think the coil round the butt is a miniature particle accelerator. They haven't had the courage to try the higher settings." His face lit up briefly at that. He put away the artifact and pulled his coat tight around him. "The ship's in orbit around the Qax home sun. The Qax will tell you the rest when you get there. I've a shuttle waiting at Seoul spaceport; we can leave straight away."

"Just like that?"

He studied me with a frank knowledge. "You have someone to say goodbye to?"

". . . No. I guess you know that. But tell me one thing. Why don't the Qax fly the damn ship themselves?"

He stared at me. "Have you ever seen a Qax?"

A million years ago the race we call the Spline made a strategic decision.

They were ocean-going at that time, great whale-like creatures with articulated limbs. They'd already been space travelers for millenia.

Then they rebuilt themselves.

They plated over their flesh, hardened their internal organs . . . and left the surface of their planet, rising like mile-wide, eye-studded balloons. Now they're living ships, feeding patiently on the thin substance drifting between the stars.

Since then they've hired themselves out to fifty races, including the Qax; but since they're not dependent on any one world, or star, or type of environment, they're their own masters—and always will be.

But there are drawbacks . . . mostly for their passengers.

Our cabin was a red-lit hole scooped out of the Spline's gut. Our journey to the Qax home world meant three days in that stinking gloom. It was like being swallowed.

As a precondition of accepting our commission, the Spline sold us each an emergency beacon. It was a sort of limp bracelet. "You work it by squeezing its midportion," Lipsey said. "The Spline guarantee your rescue, anywhere within the galaxy. Of course, the price of the rescue's negotiable."

"I don't want it."

He shrugged. "Have it on credit. You might need it one day."

"Maybe." I wrapped the bracelet around my wrist; it nestled into place like a living thing.

Disgusting. I missed human technology.

We entered orbit around the Qax planet.

Our air and water were reabsorbed by the cabin walls, then an orifice dilated and we passed through a bloody tube to space. The stars were clean and cold. I felt free for the first time since we'd left Earth.

Lipsey's two-man shuttle was extruded from another sphincter, and we spiraled over the Qax world. Under the murky atmosphere I saw a planet-wide ocean. Submerged volcano mouths glowed like coals. There were no cities, no lights. "It's a goddamn swamp," I concluded.

Lipsey nodded cheerfully, intent on his inexpert piloting. "Yes. It's like the primeval Earth."

"So where are the Qax? Undersea?"

"Wait and see."

We landed and stepped out onto a spaceport, a metal island in a bubbling quagmire. Steam misted up my faceplate. Lipsey lifted a suitcase-sized translator box down from the shuttle. "Meet our client," he said.

"Where?"

He smiled. "Here! All around you."

The translator box woke up. "This is the human pilot we discussed?"

I jumped, whirled around. Nothing but swamp.

"Yes," said Lipsey, his tone deep and reassuring. "This is Jim Bolder."

"And this is really one of your best?" boomed the Qax grumpily.

I bristled. "Lipsey, what is this?"

He smiled, then stood beside me and pointed. "Look down there. What do you see?"

I stared. "Turbulent mud." Hexagonal convection cells a hand's breadth across, quite stable: the ocean was like a huge pan of boiling water.

Lipsey said: "All known forms of life are based on a cellular organization. But there are no rules about what form the cells have to take. . . ."

I thought it over. "You're telling me that those convection cells are the basis of the Qax biology?"

I stared at the sea, trying to perceive the limits of the

mighty creature. I imagined I could see thoughts hopping over the rippling meniscus like flies. . . .

"Can we proceed?" the Qax broke in. The box gave it an appropriate voice: deep-bellied, like an irritable god.

I tried to concentrate. "Show me the Xeelee ship," I said.

"In time. Do you know what we want of you?"

"No."

"What do you know of galactic drift?" the Qax began. "Your astronomers first detected it in your twentieth century. . . ."

The galaxies are streaming.

Like a huge liner our galaxy is soaring through space at several hundred kilometers a second. That's maybe no surprise—until you learn that all the other galaxies, as far as we can see in any direction, are migrating too. And they're all heading for the same spot.

Standing there on that shiny island in a mud sea, I struggled with the scale of it all. Throughout a sphere a billion light-years wide, galaxies are converging like moths to a flame.

But what is the flame? And—who lit it?

"We call it the strange attractor," said the Qax. "We know something about its properties. It is three hundred million light-years from here. And it's massive: a hundred thousand times the mass of our galaxy, crammed into a region about half the diameter of a galaxy."

A cold mist settled over us; the Qax restlessly stirred its oceanic muscles. I felt like a flea on the back of a hippopotamus.

"We need to understand what is happening out there," the Qax went on. "Now: we have trading contacts throughout the Local Cluster, and we've been analyzing sightings of Xeelee ships. We had the idea of trying to track down the

Xeelee prime radiant—their source and center of activities.
We have done so."

I thought that through . . . and my mouth dried up.
"You're not suggesting," I asked slowly, "that the Xeelee
are responsible for the strange attractor? That they're building it?"

"We plan to send a probe to find out," said the Qax.
"Our captured Xeelee ship is the technology we need to
cross such distances."

"Which is where I come in?"

"Do you accept the commission, Bolder?"

"Yes," I said immediately, staring fixedly at the translator box. To fly a Xeelee fighter to the center of everything
. . . my only fear was that I'd be turned down.

Lipsey interrupted smoothly: "Subject to a suitable
fee, of course." He smiled like a good agent.

Surrounded by the primeval murk, we began discussing
powers of ten.

We returned to Lipsey's shuttle.

"Lipsey . . . why do the Qax care? What turns them
on?"

"Short term profit," he said simply. "This is a young
planet, not all that stable. Hot spots come and go, and individuals tend to be broken up quickly.

"As a result they don't have a strong sense of self, and
they find it hard to plan for—or even imagine—the future."
His face creased with wonder. "There are only a few hundred of them, you know, each of them miles across . . . but
thanks to their peculiar biology their awareness and material
control go right down to the molecular level. They've developed a high, miniaturized technology; it's the basis of their
commercial power. Of course," smiled, "they trade by
proxy."

I frowned. "We're millions of years from a crisis over

this strange attractor. If they're so short-lived, why spend so much on gathering data about it?''

"Profit. With a secret as big as this they can name their own price.''

We rendezvoused with a Spline craft, orbiting the Qax star. The Spline was a gunship. We scurried around huge walls covered with ten-meter-wide scales, and I peered curiously into hundreds of weapon emplacements—and then, drifting through the Spline's long shadow, we found the Xeelee ship.

A Xeelee nightfighter is a hundred-meter sycamore seed wrought in black. The wings sweep back from the central pilot's pod, flattening and thinning until at their trailing edges they are so fine you can see the stars through them.

Lipsey caught me gawping. "Save it. You've seen nothing yet. . . .''

The pilot's pod was an open framework about my height. A human crash couch had been cemented inside it. I clambered through the skeletal hull and into the couch. The hull became a mesh of blackness around me that barely excluded the stars. "Kind of open,'' I said.

Lipsey, watching from outside, laughed a bit unsympathetically. "Evidently the Xeelee don't suffer from vertigo. Do you?''

I clamped the translator box to a strut above my head. Now the Qax spoke. "Study your controls, Bolder.''

"Right.'' Set ahead of me and to my sides were three control panels, each briefcase-sized. Magnifying monitors showed me sequin-like control studs. Waldoes would let me work the panels by my sides, but there was no waldo for the third.

"The panels to your sides are for in-system flight,'' said the Qax. "The third, before you, is for the hyperspace drive. The three panels were the only equipment found in this ship—apart from the synchrotron handgun.''

"I'm not getting that back?"

"They think you're dangerous enough as it is," Lipsey said quietly.

The Qax continued: "We've worked out a setting to take you out to the strange attractor. Just hit the red button, on the left of the third panel. Hit it again to come home."

I ran a gloved finger over the surface of the third panel. Apart from the red button the panel was half-melted . . . unusable. I asked why.

"Of course," the Qax explained acidly, "you'd never be tempted to steal a treasure like this, but . . ."

I slipped my hands into the waldo manipulators. The ship woke up. "So tell me how I fly this thing."

The wings of the sycamore seed billowed out, a shaken blanket a hundred kilometers wide.

"The motive force comes from the structure of space itself," the Qax explained. "The wings are sheets of discontinuity in space. The—healing up—of space drives the ship forward."

I squeezed minutely. The wings trembled and the pod jerked. Lipsey and his shuttle disappeared. "Try to restrain your monkey impulse to meddle," said the Qax. "You've just traveled half a light-second."

I let go, fast.

"Now," said the Qax. "A controlled pressure with your right index finger . . ."

All I've ever wanted to do is fly. I've given up everything else in life for it, I suppose . . . and now my wings pulsed like sheets of shadow as I flew around the Qax star at half the speed of light. I stared into the eye of a vacuole and, whooping, whizzed under the blue-shifted arch of a stellar flare.

Blue shift! I was traveling so fast that light itself seemed as sluggish as the Doppler-shifted noise of a passing train.

The Qax gave me my head. Probably the ship was fairly immune to accidents . . . even if I wasn't.

"The Xeelee hyperdrive works on unconventional principles," the Qax told me. "On your return, we're not sure precisely where in our system you'll arrive—but we know it will be a fixed distance from the sun.

"The mass of the ship and sun are the deciding factors. The more mass the ship has, the closer to the sun you'll be placed."

I flew out to that critical return orbit. I wasn't surprised to find a Spline gunship, pitted with weapons that tracked me like eyes. Around the curve of the orbit was another gunship, and another. I swept out of the ecliptic plane, only to find more gunships. The Qax sun was encased by a sphere of them, completely staking out my return radius. "This must be costing you a fortune," I said. "Why?"

Lipsey said elegantly: "Oh, they're not scared of you, Bolder. But they wouldn't like a hundred armed Xeelee to come swarming out of that ship instead of you, now would they?"

After two months' training I felt ready. I skimmed out to the Spline-guarded radius and closed up my wings. Lipsey, once more alone with the Qax, said gently: "Godspeed."

"Yah." I hit the red button—

—and gasped as the hyperdrive jump made the Qax sun wink to nothingness. Below my feet appeared a compact yellow star, set in a sky crowded with stars and dust. I became aware of a trickle of clicks and pops as instruments clustered around me began to study the hurtling wonders.

"Wow!" I said.

"Bolder," said the Qax, "skip the epithets and report."

"I think I'm near the center of the galaxy."

"Good. That is—"

—another jump—

"—according to plan."

"Jesus." The yellow sun had disappeared; now I hovered below a dumbbell-shaped binary pair. Great tongues of golden star-stuff arced between the twin stars. The sky was darker; I must be passing through the galaxy and out the other side—

—jump—

—and now I was suspended below the plane of the galaxy itself; it was a Sistine ceiling of orange and blue, the contrasts surprisingly sharp—

—jump—

—and these jumps were coming faster; I watched a dwarf star scour its way over the surface of its huge red parent and that dim disc over there must be my galaxy—

—jump—

—and now I was inside a massive star, actually within its pinkish flesh but before I could cry out there was another—

—jump—

—and—

—jump—jump—jumpjumpjumpjump—

I closed my eyes. There was no inward sensation of motion; only a flickering outside my eyelids that told me of skies being ripped aside like veils.

" . . . Bolder! Can you hear me? Bolder—"

I took a breath. "I'm okay. It's just—fast." I risked another look. I was passing through a frothy barrage of stars and planets; beyond them sheets of galaxies moved past as steadily as roadside trees. I said slowly: "I must be making a megalight, or more, an hour. At this rate the journey will take about two weeks—"

And then I tumbled into the creamy plane of an elliptical galaxy. I wailed and closed my eyes again.

Ten days later, the popping stars no longer bothered me. I guess you can get used to anything. Even the growing gray patch ahead of me—a cloud of objects around the strange attractor—seemed less important than the itchy confines of my suit. In fact, I felt fine until a disc of sky directly behind me turned china-blue. . . .

"I don't get it," I said. "Objects that I'm leaving behind should be red-shifted."

"It's nothing to do with your motion, Bolder," the Qax explained. "The blue shift is gravitational. You're now close enough to the strange attractor that light from the outside universe is beginning to fall more steeply down its gravity well."

I checked my instruments. "But that's ridiculous . . . I'm still millions of light-years away."

The Qax didn't bother to respond.

Two more days. The light became a hail of hard blue as it plummeted after me into this pit of space. I entered the outskirts of the mist around the attractor; it resolved into individual stars and what looked like bits of galaxies.

The muddled starlight bathing my cage began to flicker. I felt my heartbeat rising. The skies riffled past me like the pages of a great book, ever slower. Finally the ship stuttered to a halt.

"I've arrived," I whispered. "I'm still inside the star mist." I looked around, clutching the arms of my couch. "I'm in orbit round what looks like a small G-type star. But the sky's crammed with streaming stars, hundreds of them close enough to show discs. It's blue-tinted chaos.

"And—I can see something ahead. A bank of light beyond the mist." My breath caught at the sheer scale of it all. "That's the attractor, right?"

"Don't touch your controls until we tell you, Bolder," the Qax murmured.

"What? Why not?"

"You've got company. To your left . . ."

A horde of night-dark ships came soaring away from the attractor and out into the star cloud. There were small fighters like mine, swirling in flocks like starlings. And here and there I saw cup-shaped freighters kilometers wide, cruising like eagles. The sky was black with ships.

"Xeelee," I breathed. "There must be millions of them. Well, you were right, Qax . . . but I don't believe in coincidence. I haven't stumbled across the only Xeelee fleet in the area. This star cloud must be swarming with them."

"Follow them," said the Qax.

"What?"

"Activate your drive. You're a lot less likely to be noticed as one of a flock than as an individual."

". . . Yah." I spread my wings and banked sideways into the flock. Soon I was waddling along, a self-conscious duck among swans. Inside the waldoes my sweating fingers began to cramp up with the effort.

The fleet was heading for a young star. Through the crowd ahead of me I could see the star's disc, its violet light diamond-hard. As we neared the star the torrent of ships abruptly splashed sideways, as if encountering an invisible shield. When I reached the braking radius I banked left and set off after the herd.

Twenty hours after my arrival the Xeelee completed their formation. With wings folded like patient vultures they completely surrounded the star.

"What now?" I asked uneasily.

"No doubt we'll find out."

I wished I could rub my gritty eyes. "Qax . . . I haven't slept since coming out of hyperspace, you know."

"Take a stimulant."

Sudden as an eyeblink, blood-red threads of light snaked into the star from every ship in the fleet.

Well, from every ship except one. Mine.

It was a poignant sight: a stellar Gulliver, pierced by a million tiny arrows. The star's light flickered, oddly. And I became aware of a stirring in the ranks of the Xeelee nearest me.

"They're starting to notice me," I whispered. "How do I turn on my beam?"

"You don't," said Lipsey. "Remember that Xeelee handgun? This must be what happens at the highest setting."

A purple arch of tortured gas erupted from the star. Soon flares covered the star's surface; clouds of ejecta drifted through the cherry-red beams. Cup freighters moved in, placidly swallowing the star flesh.

It was like watching the death of a magnificent animal. "They're destroying it," I said. "But how?"

"The handgun must be a gravity wave laser," the Qax said slowly. "The coils on the butt of that handgun are small synchrotrons. Subatomic particles move at fantastic velocities in there; the thing emits a coherent beam of gravity waves which—"

"I thought you needed large masses to get significant gravity waves."

"No. As long as you move a small mass fast enough . . . The energy must come from the same source as your ship's—from the structure of space itself."

"Handguns to break stars, eh?"

A shadow moved across my vision. I glanced about quickly. A dozen Xeelee slid across the blue-shifted sky and gathered into a close sphere around me.

"They've rumbled me." Rapidly, I thought over my options. Before me was the reassuring red glow of the hyperspace button: my escape hatch, if things got too hot . . . but,

I quickly decided, I'd come too far to go home without seeing the attractor itself.

I spread my wings as far as they would go and dragged them downward in one mighty swoop. I shot head-first out of the closing trap and kept going, heading deeper into the blue-tinged star cloud. My breath was loud in my helmet.

"What now?" I gasped.

"Run!" said Lipsey.

I ran for hours. I dodged stars only light-minutes apart, their surfaces distorted into surreal shapes by their proximity to each other. The bank of grayish light beyond the mist grew remorselessly brighter and wider—and all the time the Xeelee formation was a spear pointing at my shoulder-blades.

At last, abruptly, I burst out of the star mist. The naked light ahead was dazzling. Heart thumping I wrenched at the wings and skidded to a halt. I found myself in a region clear of stars and debris that must have been ten thousand light-years wide . . . and the curtain of stars on the other side was tinged blue.

So I was at the center. The bottom of the pit; the place all the stars were falling into. And at the heart of it all, flooding space with a pearly light, was the strange attractor itself.

It . . . sparkled. It was like a monstrous wedding ring, rotating visibly. "Qax," I croaked. "Speak to me."

"A massive rotating toroid," murmured the Qax. "More than a thousand light-years across. A made thing."

"But—why? What's the point?"

The Qax paused. "Well, this fits one of our hypotheses. Look in the central region, Bolder."

The hole in the ring hurt my eyes. It was a sheet of space that was somehow . . . tilted. I saw muddled space, stars streaked like cream in coffee.

"Do you know about the Kerr metric?" asked the Qax. "No? The attractor is a massive toroid rotating extremely

quickly. Your own theory of relativity predicts some odd
effects with such a structure. Closed lines in space and
time, for instance—"

"Come again?"

"Time travel. And more. . . . Bolder, all the physical
constants that define our universe—like the speed of light,
the charge on the electron—are reflections of properties of
space itself. Symmetries in higher order dimensions. And if
the attractor is disturbing those symmetries—"

"New constants. New physical laws. The Xeelee don't
like this universe, so they're building another."

"Or a way out of this one."

Facets of the ring's whirling surface sent shafts of light
back to the doomed stars; the shafts showed like sunlight in
a dusty room. I focused my monitors on that dust and saw
ships—an aviary of all shapes and sizes, uncountable tril-
lions of them.

A few light-minutes from me I made out a particularly
monstrous ship, a disc that must have been the size of the
moon. Hundreds of cup freighters nestled into neat pouches
in the disc's upper surface, dumping out stolen star material. Vents in the underside of the main ship emitted a constant rain of immense crystalline shafts, as if it were some
huge sieve leaking rainwater.

Peering deeper into the midst of the craft I could see
fantastic bucket-chains of the disc ships descending to the attractor, dwindling to pinpoints against that vast carcass.
Returning ships, I saw, were diverted to clouds of cup
freighters for reloading.

I began to see the pattern. "So the disc ships are huge,
ah, dumper trucks," I said. "They descend to the attractor
and plate over its surface with crystalline star-stuff. They're
growing the thing layer by layer, with a patience that's
lasted billions of years. . . ."

There was a flicker in my peripheral vision. My posse.

They whirled around me and began to close in once more.

I closed up my wings and prepared to punch the red button. "Lipsey, I've seen enough. We've got to spread this news around all the races in our region—find a way to stop the Xeelee before they wreck our universe. We've time to plan—"

He coughed apologetically. "Ah—look, Bolder, this information is Qax commercial property. You know that."

I hesitated. "You're kidding. We're doomed if the Qax keep this knowledge to themselves."

He sighed. "The Qax don't think on those time scales. They can't, remember. They think about profit, today."

I forced my hand away from the escape button; a cold knot in my stomach started to tighten. Suddenly this wasn't a game. If I tried to go home after what I'd just blurted out, the Qax wouldn't hesitate to use their Spline warships to blast me out of the sky. Abruptly my isolation telescoped into a vivid reality, and the cage around me seemed absurdly fragile. . . . And the Xeelee whirled tighter, reminding me that hanging around here wasn't an option either.

I had to find more time. To my right, obscured now by the fog of fighters around me, was that dumper truck with its attendant freighters. I opened up my wings, clutched at space and lurched out of the trap. Soon I was thrusting my way into the crowded freighter formation, my wings tucked tight. The fighters blurred after me.

I rammed thoughts through my sleep-starved brain as I flew. Could I evade the waiting Spline? Maybe I could divert the ship's hyperspace flight—but how? Prize open the melted control box? Change the ship's mass, to change the distance I arrived from the Qax sun?

Of course I could abandon ship before I reached the Qax system, at one of the later jump points. I had that Spline emergency beacon; I'd be picked up. And if I kept quiet I could hide from the Qax, for years maybe. . . .

But, damn it, if I did that humanity and a few hundred other races would one day end up falling into the Xeelee pit. Hiding wasn't good enough.

I dipped under the lip of the dumper truck and dodged the processed attractor material sleeting from the truck's base. The huge icicles fell a few thousand kilometers and then broke up into a fine mist . . . and as I stared abstractedly at that mist I realized there was a way out of this. It was stupid, crazy, nearly unworkable. And my only chance.

"All right, Qax," I said. "I'll come home. But first . . . "

I dropped, spread my wings as far as they would go and whirled like a seagull through the crystal rain. The wings plated over rapidly and grew stiff and cumbersome.

"Bolder, what the hell are you doing?"

"Wrecking this beautiful ship," I told Lipsey with real regret.

The Xeelee fighters finally closed around me, shutting out the rain.

I pressed the button.

The Xeelee trap disappeared; I'd jumped back to the blue-tinged light of the star cloud. And then—

Jump. Jump. Jump—jump—jump—jumpjumpjump—

The skies became a blur. The air sighed out of my body.

I fell toward the welcoming pool that was my home galaxy. I peered out of my glazed-over cage as the stars' flickering began to slow. For the first time in a month I unbuckled the straps that bound me to my couch, and prized the translator box free of the strut over my head.

Lipsey and I said our goodbyes. "Do me a favor," I said. "Whatever happens, keep talking. Tell me what you see."

"Whatever you say." I imagined his noble face gazing

out over the seething Qax ocean. "Bolder . . . I want you to know I'm sorry."

"Yah." The ship—jumped—to the dumbbell binary system. It was dazzling; I'd arrived much closer than I remembered from my visit on the way out. I bunched a gloved fist in triumph. This was going to work—

—jump—

A compact yellow star at the heart of the galaxy, searingly close to the ship. Last stop. Time to get out.

I climbed onto my seat, put my shoulders against the pod's crystalline plating, and pushed. For a heart-stopping moment I thought the shell was too strong—then it crumbled and I popped into space, clutching my translator box. Below me glittered the crusted wings of the ship I'd taken so far.

My plan had worked. The attractor substance had added enough mass to the ship to shift its arrival points significantly closer to the system centers. Now I had to rely on the Qax to do the rest—

—jump—

—and the ship disappeared and I was left alone in a cloud of fragments; they sparkled in the light of the compact star.

I drifted there for a while, rotating slowly. Then I squeezed the Spline distress bracelet. It turned rigid and cold.

Lipsey began to speak out of the translator box. His voice was hoarse, forced. I listened, absently picking sparkling fragments out of the space around me and stuffing them into a suit pocket.

"You haven't come out where we expected, Bolder. What have you . . .

"You're causing the Qax a lot of confusion, I can tell that much. . . ."

A pause. "I think they've found you . . . but what the hell are you doing there?"

The Spline warships rotated like eyeballs, scouring space. . . .

Then they found my ship, inexplicably close to the Qax sun.

The Qax panicked. They sent their shell-shaped armada roaring in toward the sun. Waves of energy pounded the Xeelee ship; the great wings sagged like melting chocolate. And in the middle of that torrent of energy was a thread of cherry-red light that arrowed through the wreck and into the sun.

As I'd hoped, in their anxiety and confusion the Qax had thrown at my ship all they had—including their only Xeelee weapon. Of course, it was only a single star-breaker. I'm told it took a couple of days before the flares started.

Lipsey died alone, surrounded by their rage. But he died laughing at them. I heard him.

A Spline freighter ingested me after a day.

The Spline sold me access to an Earth news channel. I figured, what the hell. Since I was still broke, in spite of everything, I wasn't going to be able to pay them anyway. . . .

Earth was rejoicing. Qax-owned ships were disappearing from the skies of Earth—and from all over the Local Cluster, come to that. The Qax were going to need every cubic meter of carrying capacity to get themselves off their home world before their sun blew up. They were going to be occupied for a long, long time, and much too busy to hunt me down.

And once I released my news about the Xeelee, we'd be busy too. One day we'd go back to the strange attractor, take on the Xeelee star-breakers—

But in the meantime I'd have to find a job. My adventure was over and I faced the dreary prospect of spending the rest of my life paying off the Spline—among others. I reached for my suit and dug out my handful of attractor fragments. Cold as ice, and just as worthless, they sparkled even in the Spline's blood-tinged light—

Worthless?

Suddenly I imagined these stones set in platinum and resting against tanned flesh: Xeelee-made gems from half a billion light-years away.

Maybe I had a way to pay off my debts after all. I could buy my own ship, start a small line. . . .

I put away the stones and began to dream again.

Illustrated by Bob Giadrosich

Just don't

by
Eolake Stobblehouse

About the Author

Certainly it's not his real name; his real name is more complex. A Dane in his twenties, Stobblehouse never finished his secondary schooling and is a self-taught fine-arts painter. He'll probably be entering L. Ron Hubbard's Illustrators of The Future™ Contest with the same frequency he shows in trying for a prize from WOTF.

He lives in Copenhagen. He's our first published entrant whose daily language is not English. And that's enough of that, or this introduction will be longer than his story. . . .

One fine day on Planet Earth, I was sitting in my own comfortable home in my own comfortable chair in my own comfortable body. And just as I had leisurely turned a page in my book, and was about to leisurely take a sip of my coffee, the doorbell rang.

I raised my body, squinting at the sunshine outside, and went to the door.

Having opened it, I found myself looking at a spaceman. I knew immediately that he was a spaceman from his different looks and his suit.

Now, I was quite dumbfounded. I had a funny feeling in my stomach, and didn't know what to make of the situation. But this spaceman seemed quite as cheerful as any sergeant handling civilians.

He looked up from his clipboard, said, "Follow me, please," and turned around.

I hesitated, looking back into my comfortable home, and then stumbled after him. "Hey," I asked. "What gives? What's happening?"

"Oh," he said, "they are going to give you guys another treatment. Some of you are regaining your memories."

"What memories!?"

"Don't think about it," he said.

Circulate

by

L. Ron Hubbard

About the Author

L. Ron Hubbard (1911–1986) is frequently described as the most widely-read SF author of all time. And it's true that he is. What's more important to other authors is the fact that he could command the attention of the modern book-buying public with Battlefield Earth *and the ten-volume* Mission Earth, *while also having been immensely popular with newsstand magazine readers in the 1930s and '40s.*

In other words, he knew something basic about attracting readers; something—or things—so fundamental that they were readily adaptable to any public, over half a century in which the world changed a great deal. And so powerful that he was not merely successful, he was recognized as being unusually successful. He had reached that point few authors ever reach, where his name on a story was more important than the title or what the story was about. And he first reached it in his twenties, and was still able to reach it in his seventies. He knew his craft as few have ever known it.

He knew what was important, *not just what was considered acceptable or what was popular at the moment. Knowing just those latter things will gain the plaudits of contemporary commentators and the attention of those who must read the fashionable. What L. Ron Hubbard knew about writing goes a good deal deeper than that. And, to an unusual degree, he has continually been eager to share it.*

WOTF has an invitational writing workshop program for its winners and published finalists. As texts, it uses articles on writing by L. Ron Hubbard; short, effective pieces of advice. At the first such workshop, in 1986, Jack Williamson was one of the instructors. Jack sold his first story in 1928, and has been a steady and respected practitioner ever since; he has won the Grand Master Award of the Science Fiction Writers of America. He was holding one of those articles in his hand, reading it. He looked up suddenly and said: "I just learned something!"

"Circulate," the piece we're bringing you here, is one of the group of articles in the WOTF course pack that has since been used at places as diverse as Sag Harbor, Long Island, and Moscow, Idaho; at Pepperdine University, Brigham Young University, and Harvard. It's from a 1935 issue of The Author and Journalist—*just one of the popular writers' magazines that vied for Hubbard articles when he was already a legend in a dozen different fields of fiction. He was 24.*

As Director of the workshops, I've seen it happen again and again. People look up and say: "I've just learned something! And it's so simple!"

Yes, it is. Fundamentally simple. And it doesn't matter what year it is, or what mode of writing you particularly favor, or where the career opportunities of the moment may lie. It works. The bottom line is: it works, it did work, it will always work. And here's one of the key pieces. . . .

Jack London possessed a secret
and he put it to a use which amounted to little
less than alchemy. He knew the magic formula
which permitted him to write about the things he knew best
—a bag of tricks in itself.

Like the rest of us, Jack had his ups and sub-zeros, but
unlike many of us he knew the correct way to combat them.
He knew that work was the only solution, and far more than
that, he knew how to get to work. He knew what to do when
his pockets sagged with emptiness. He knew that sitting
around bewailing a writer's lot was a poor method of creation.

Down on the San Francisco waterfront, there was a
bookshop which handled mildewed volumes and second-
hand pulps. It was close to the Embarcadero and the ships
and the saloons, and its proprietor was close to the heart of
Jack London. At those trying times when the checks were
few and small, Jack would drop around for the purpose of
borrowing half a dollar.

It was not that he was hungry. That fifty-cent piece was
much more necessary than that. For with it, Jack London
would head for the nearest saloon. Straight for the swinging
doors and the bar flies.

Sailors would be there. Sailors from Alaska and China,
and the South Seas. Sailors whose ships were lately on the
bottom or whose crews were lately serving time for muti-
ny. And from that crowd Jack London would select himself

a tough old salt who looked garrulous. And then the fifty-cent piece would diminish across the mahogany and the old salt would pour out his heart. Perhaps the things he said were lies, perhaps divine truth. But whatever they were, they stimulated.

With the half dollar gone, Jack would depart with a quick stride and end up at his writing desk. Seldom would he write what he had heard. It was enough that his mental wheels were revolving once more and that he could again taste salt spray and listen to the singing of the wind aloft.

That was his trade secret. By applying it, he was soon enabled to place a silver dollar in the cash drawer at the bookshop.

"But I only lent you fifty cents!" protested the proprietor.

"I know, but I'll be wanting it again. Take it while I've got the money."

Jack London never allowed his interest in men to lag. And because of that he grew to know men and could write about them, and what they did, and why.

Circulate was his motto, and circulate he did. Everyone on the Embarcadero knew him and liked him and brought stories to him.

Often our ears are filled with the advice, "Write about the things you know. The things close to you." And, in despair, we wail that there is nothing of interest in our surroundings or in the lives we lead. We say that and we believe it. And in despair, we pound out a bloody thunderer, using the other side of the world as our locale.

The reason we cannot write about the things at hand is apparent. If we *knew* our surroundings well enough we could put them on paper. Someone else comes around, looks us over and studies our environment for a brief period and then goes off to write a novel. Why, we moan, didn't we write that book? Surely we knew more about it than the lucky one.

But did we? To know a thing, we must first find it interesting. And it's certain that we can never see the hovel next door while we yearn for the picturesque scene hundreds of miles away.

People pass our houses to and from their work each day. We know their names and what they do, but we are not really interested in them. Even though each is a potential story, we pass them all up because, as with the postman, we never really see them.

Down on the corner is a drugstore. Occasionally we enter to buy copies of our prospective markets, but do we ever get to know the clerk? Or the loafers out front? Or the cop who parks his motorcycle at the curb? Or the fireman just off duty? Or the high-school seniors who suck up sodas in the booth? Or . . . ?

No; probably and sadly not. Even while we look at them we're probably thinking about the story we are going to write about the North Woods and the girl caught in the outlaw's cabin. The outsider comes in and looks our people over, goes off and writes about them, and then, quite reasonably, we get sore about his stealing our neighbors for material.

Jack London's environment was the sea. He knew it well. Too well, in fact. He knew he had to work hard to keep up his interest. As a boy he was an oyster pirate. Then a member of the fish patrol. Later he was a seaman on a sealing vessel. From there he went to the Klondike, to Japan, to Mexico, and finally around the world in the *Snark*. No wonder, you say, he wrote about the sea. It was fascinating. No wonder he dealt with wild animals. They had attacked him. His environment, you say, was intensely interesting.

Jack London, strangely enough, didn't think so. He had to work hard to whip up flagging interest in the things he knew so well. He aspired to be, and became, the best known American Socialist. His finest works, so he and the literati thought, were *The Iron Heel, The War of the Classes, Revolution, Martin Eden,* and *The People of the Abyss.*

But he made his money on adventure and sea stories, and to write them, he found that he must know them better than he did. He circulated among the men who were to become his characters. Long after he had given up the sea he still forced himself to study his subject. He too wanted to graze in greener fields. He said that he wrote his adventure novels solely for the money.

In other words, he did not revel in his environment any more than we do in ours. Yet he forced himself to study it thoroughly and write about it because it was his means of livelihood. He never allowed himself to go stale. He circulated constantly.

And now, how about our drugstore? The clerk knows all about the trouble Mrs. Smith is having with her back and why young Smith had to come home from college. The loafers out front have fought wars and excavated ditches. The fireman can tell why the mansion on the hill went up in smoke and just how that affected his little boy's school work. The cop leaning on his motorcycle played a big part in the late kidnapping. He knows the inside story and he'll tell it. He also knows a hundred rackets which are worked right under your nose. And those high-school seniors could fill a novel with their hidden adventures.

But most of us just walk up to the magazine rack and thumb the copies and wish to goodness we could think of something worthwhile to write about. We wish we could be in New York or Texas or Tahiti so that we could gather some real material.

The point of it is, we'll never be able—most of us—to shed our present environment unless we can make the well-known bucks. And if we can't sell, we can't earn. And if we can't think up stories, we therefore can't move on. In short, we're trapped.

It is not that our present locale is the best, but that it will have to do—emphatically. And the only real solution lies in circulating. In moving around and talking. In studying our neighbors and associates as closely as if we were about to transfer their likenesses to canvas.

If we don't *know* the average man, we can't write about him or for him, and our assets will shrink in direct ratio to the pile of cancelled stamps on the return envelope.

In other words: CIRCULATE!

Rachel's Wedding
by
Virginia Baker

About the Author

Virginia Baker has a B.S. degree from Brigham Young
University in Near Eastern studies, specializing in Arab/
Israeli relations, Near Eastern cultures, Hebrew, and terrorism. She also has a Master of Arts from BYU, for which her
graduate thesis was a book of poetry.

She was born in 1958, on Christmas Day, in Germany
while her father was in the U.S. Army. She's spent the last
ten years around Provo, Utah, lately working for a computer
networking company as a documentation editor, then in the
marketing department writing brochures, advertisements and
video scripts. Today she's the managing editor of a major computer trade publication.

Along with past WOTF First Prize winners Shayne Bell
and Dave Wolverton (from WOTF III), she's a member
of "Xenobia," the very productive SF writing group based
around BYU.

Lyrical, textured, and expert, here is her first published
story. . . .

Barshak's Log:

A compromise is a compromise.

I have been taught that all my life, in varying guises. To eat meat on a plate reserved for dairy products is a compromise. To cut the sidecurls that show your devotion to God, especially to go to a gentile school, is a compromise. To study science and technology instead of Talmud is a compromise, even if you also study Talmud every extra moment. "How many more hours could you have devoted to Talmud, had you gone to yeshiva instead of that goyim school? Barshak, you could have been a rabbi. What is science to God?"

I have studied this, and haven't found an answer yet to give them. And what could I tell them? If I could answer them, with a truth they could not understand, to them it simply would not exist. To study science is to compromise a nation. To make war with that nation is not. To them, this dichotomy makes sense—an irony as natural as man and woman in their differences, and about as equal to their minds.

I can look at the Rebbe Poul and tell you—he understands these things as flawless balance, absolute and inviolate. He still measures distance by the number of steps he takes, time by the rise and set of the sun. How can you tell a man like this—? That Shabbat can never come in space, if he looks for it by the first evening star? He would say every day is Shabbat, and not go mad in his logic.

He comes to Solomon's Row like a bridegroom who knows the bride is unwilling. He is Poul. After Syria, she is all but broken to his will. He will have her. She will submit to him because she is from his rib, and she knows it. If she resists him, he will prove to all the wedding guests who watch below—she is a harlot at heart. And he is sure that Solomon's Row, the estranged daughter of Israel—in orbit above the earth by nature and by science—will be shamed into accepting him.

But I am not so sure. By law, she cannot throw him out. And by her heart, she cannot take him in.

Light from the solars warmed the place, quivering the sheaves of wheat that clung to metal pipes. Three good miles of piping, stacked seven rods deep, stretched a maze of color—mostly green—like a jungle under the shuttered windows. Plants held to the pipes like seaweed, wandering with each movement around them, swaying in the low gravity.

At the east end of the garden, Jacob took hold of the shutter key. He steadied his balance, spinning slow, his feet leaving the floor—then he tucked, twisted, leveraged against the solid wall. The key turned. The shutters, one hundred feet above his head, more than a mile wide, rolled aside, rasping a slow, pneumatic wheeze.

Jacob looked up as they parted, saw the blue haze of Earth just off to port, the glow of Mars not far beyond. The asteroid was just beginning to turn its solars portside, the windows moving away from the Sun.

He said, "The soil is lousy here. You must be a Zionist to do so well, Dr. Rosen."

She turned to look at him, her dark hair floating around her face. She adjusted the hydration struts that were water

Illustrated by David Dorman

and roots to the greening plants. "It's not too different from South Lebanon. Even the thinnest soil can be made to grow green. If you pay the cost."

"The *fat* of our land grows diamonds. That will buy us a lot of things."

She moved lightly; it carried her above him, to the second row of wheat. "Eventually."

Jacob nodded, thumbed a stalk of the grain. "Eventually." He closed his hand around the plant's heart. "Sara—the supply shuttle is coming in today. They have Rabbi Meyer with them, leading a contingent for the yeshiva we discussed."

Sara stowed her worktools in a pocket. "I thought we had more to discuss on that. I don't remember any decisions being made—"

Jacob shrugged. The wheat moved in waves around him. "I suppose it was made for us, at the New York conference."

Sara picked at the older husks, pulling them away from the tender stalks. "Well, I'm not doing any extra work for them."

Jacob nodded. She let go of the dead sheaves and watched them rise in the vortex of gentle air. The mild breeze swept the area continually, sucking the light refuse into open grates. Looking at them, she said, "Maybe they can clean the mulch chutes."

"I don't know how we're going to work it," Jacob said. "We have to at least teach them how to survive here. Rabbi Meyer has agreed to have them work part time—"

"Work? They don't know the half of it. What will they do? Even scrubbing the toilets takes a degree in physical mechanics."

"You're exaggerating. They can learn co-op—watching the children, things like that. It would free us for the smelt."

"Don't count on any cheap labor, Jacob. How many

yeshiva boys do you know cook and clean even on Earth? They won't be any less work for us here—only more.''

"I never knew any yeshiva boys on Earth. But I do know that these people are at least bringing an MIT graduate with them. That's better than we had hoped.''

"MIT,'' Sara said. "So next they'll be using reflective tablets to read Torah and crystal chips to store the Tanach. That doesn't make them any more useful to us.''

She maneuvered a slow arc so she could bounce off the upper wall. Jacob passed her, but she didn't drop to the southern door. He climbed along the ceiling struts to sit beside her. From there, they could see the miles all around them.

"This is not a room,'' Sara said. "It's Eden. Our Eden. We had no god to make it. *We* did this—''

"What's bothering you?'' Jacob asked.

He watched her carefully. She looked toward the northern part of the spread, lost in thought and the mists that condensed around the garden pond half a mile away. At the pond, where the asteroid's pull made gravity, they had planted dark Haifa soil, fruit trees and a gathering of utterly useless, beautiful foliage.

She is right, he thought, *we made this place, with our own hands.* A place to go just after the solars were set low and the asteroid turned to the darkness of the stars; a place to swim bare in warm water, surrounded by lush plants and the simple joy of being alone.

"Sara—''

"It's nothing,'' she said. But a shimmer of light on the distant pond water made her skin prickle. "I was just wondering. What will they think of us, bathing nude here where not only a king but a whole community can see—and are welcome to look?''

He didn't answer, but took her hand and pulled her in down to the southern hallway.

• • •

Their first sight of him was Biblical. A scene etched from Old Testament parchment: clouds of water vaporizing, rolling billows along the floor; a figure, blackened by robes, barely visible in the hissing clouds, with upraised hands.

The water was from the shuttle, venting and condensing moisture from the sub-zero vacuum outside. The man— God only knew. Moses leading the children of Israel out of Egypt. The bay should have dwarfed him; somehow, it did not.

"That is not the purser, I think," Sara said to Jacob. A dozen members of the kibbutz stood with them. Other kibbutzniks—a growing group of them—clustered close on the other side of the bay, some with breathers hung limp at their necks, many with their arms crossed tight in front of them.

Marta Bunt, certainly the oldest woman of the kibbutz— one who had been born on the eve of the Six Day War and had seen six months of the Orthodox Civil Conflict before fleeing to Paris, to New York, to here—stood on her toes to whisper in Sara's ear. "Poul. This is the Rebbe Poul. Meyer does not lead them." For the fear in her voice, she might have said, "This is Satan, come to punish us for our sins."

Jacob turned to Moshe, a big red-haired kibbutznik who smiled behind his beard like a leprechaun. "What is he doing here?" Jacob asked.

Moshe shrugged, watching the mist die away to a lone figure—the old man with sullen eyes, and sidecurls that wound down his chest. "I don't know. Leading the yeshiva, maybe."

Jacob leaned against the wall and closed his eyes. Sweat beaded on his forehead, and was quickly evaporated by the soft hiss of coolant.

"What do we do?" Marta Bunt asked. "Jacob, you must do something."

"What's to do?" Moshe asked her. "Poul's a great man. Very respected. Like all the old prophets—not afraid to piss against the wall."

"He does that here, he could be surprised," Sara said.

Several women stepped down from the shuttle, their low heels clattering on the metal floor. One, a beautiful girl, and older, opened her eyes wide and looked around the bay.

"Rachel—"

An old woman poked her hard in the back. The girl looked quickly down at the floor and moved on. Sara leaned toward Jacob, whispering carefully, "There are your cooks." And when he glared at her, she shrugged and said, "What else does a Hasid yeshiva need women for?"

Jacob pushed gently through the newcomer Hasids, who stood passively in dark rows around the Rebbe, eyes cast down, like virgins facing a matchmaker.

A boy stood in the inner circle, stood at the Rebbe's right hand, much nearer than the Rabbi Meyer, and Jacob stopped and simply stared.

He was no more than seventeen, the boy. His people had been Ashkenazi, certainly—nothing else could account for the hair, so blond, and the Nordic lines of his face.

Jacob noticed he was staring when the boy smiled, when the joy in him exploded like a nova; when the boy threw his head back and laughed.

They smiled with him, all of them, even Poul, and Jacob thought of Proverbs, of Saul and David and the harp of the boy's laughter.

Jacob smiled with them also. But when he spoke, the smiles died, all but the boy's.

"Rebbe Poul," Jacob said. He saw the boy's eyes, that they were very blue, like most of the Ashkenazi boys he had known—but too intensely focused. Jacob turned back to

Poul. "Rebbe, I am Jacob Golani, commander at Solomon's Row. You and your people are welcome to any of the services this station can provide. If anyone is tired or ill from the pass—"

"No one," Poul said, "is ill here." His eyes dismissed Jacob—dismissed all concerns not his own—and turned to a man among the yeshivim. "Barshak—"

The man came when called and stood beside Poul and the boy, but Jacob saw that this Barshak, still in his twenties, wore his sidecurls short, his clothing modern. . . . And that he was Sephardic.

Jacob nodded at Barshak's jeans and jacket and his freshly ironed MIT T-shirt. "I thought the war had changed all that," Jacob said.

"Not in New York." Barshak glanced quickly between Jacob and the Rebbe. "And I never lived in Israel."

"Take us," Poul said, "to where the map says there is a synagogue."

Barshak hesitated. He looked toward the kibbutzniks; none of them spoke, though a few of them shrugged and broke into laughter. He turned pointedly back to Jacob, as if to extricate himself from an acutely embarrassing joke.

"Excuse me," he said. "I am Barshak Rabin. Doctor, MIT."

He extended his hand.

"Barshak." Poul intoned the name, the heavy whisper of a ghost. "Not here. It is not the time."

Poul held out his right arm and said, "Saul."

The Ashkenazi boy took Poul's sleeve and followed.

So it is Saul after all, Jacob thought, as Poul's people straggled after Barshak, the Rebbe and the Ashkenazi boy.

At the door of the kibbutz proper, Barshak turned back to Jacob and yelled, "*Later.*" The word echoed like a warcry over a battlefield. Barshak grinned at Jacob. Poul gripped the blond's arm, tight enough for the boy to wince.

They trailed out slowly, their robes brushing stiff whispers on the metal floor. As they passed, the girl, Rachel, glanced once at the kibbutzniks. Jacob smiled. She opened her eyes very wide and looked away, and Jacob realized she had no idea how beautiful they were.

The tambor pulsed a rhythm against her legs. It echoed in her body, in the sweat on her breasts and the honeycombs that fell at her feet.

Men and women danced the Hora around her, sang the songs of Solomon. She danced alone, her feet pounding with the tambor. Beneath her, a vat of grapes turned to wine. Fruit split with each step she took. The juice splashed against her thighs and tangled in her hair. Each drop turned to blood there, falling upon her lips. The taste of it was sweet. Shivering, aching with its touch, she pulled her skirts as high as they would go and drove her feet deep into the gathered fruit—

Rachel opened her eyes. She lay still, her heart beating against the small mattress. Sweat pearled around her eyes, on her cheeks.

She looked around the small room. Low, ruddy strips of light ran along the ceiling. The walls glistened, like glazed wings, warm and dusky and unbearably smooth. They should have had the smell of blood on them. Instead, they smelled like nothing she had ever known.

Rachel got up from the bunk. Women stirred around her and moaned against the walls. She walked past them, carefully. At the bathroom, she got in and closed the door behind her. The automatic lighting burst over her. She quickly shut her eyes, saw the mirror's outline etched against her eyelids—and in that bright ghost of shadows, the girl who had danced.

Rachel opened her eyes quickly. She turned on the tap and washed the sweat pooled between her breasts. In the mirror, she was just Rachel again.

Slowly, she looked down at her feet, lifted the soles to the light.

They were wet, but with sweat only.

She had dreamed of a winepress, of dancing with her shoulders bare and her hair a raven's wing around her face. An echo of the tambor pulsed in her ears, beating a rhythm so strong against her ribs, she could not breathe.

"*Rachel?* What are you doing?" The door shook with the old woman's pounding—a good part of it in Rachel's heart.

"Nothing, mother. Washing my feet."

The woman opened the door, stared down at her. "Your feet?"

Rachel looked down, not at her feet but at the dark gray floor. "My face. It was hot. I'm sweating all over."

"You moaned in your sleep."

Rachel's skin bloomed a mottle of pink and scarlet, though she could not remember any more of the dream than lifting her skirts at the winepress. Her mother nodded, the lines in her face tightening. "Dreams like that will make you crazy," she said. "Then you'll look like Leah with the weepy eyes. You're nearly past the age of usefulness to a man—soon you'll be too old to carry his children, to keep his house and warm his bed. The Rebbe will send you back then, with no husband and no children to give you honor—"

"Why did he even bring me here? I'm older than most of the students. Unless I could learn Torah with them."

Her mother slapped her wrist; Rachel quickly covered the stinging welt.

"Your father put such dreams into your head. Reading you Songs of Solomon and poetry a girl should never read."

"They were beautiful," Rachel whispered.

"And what does an old maid know of it? He put so

many ideas in your head, nice boys your age knew better than to marry you.''

The old woman turned back to her bunk, left her daughter alone in the cool gray light. Rachel nodded, though her mother had already gone. She turned off the light, then lifted her head. An image flashed behind her eyes: a dancer with red feet, with the stain of wine upon her thighs.

"Jacob, you cannot let them stay."

"I cannot send them out."

"Send them to the Arab Utopia." This from Sara, sitting at the back of the room. "The Moslems are also orthodox. They will surely know what to do with them."

Laughter ran through the room, sprung from the children of crueler times.

Moshe, smiling through it, said, "They're just here to make a yishuv."

"With Poul?" Beni Mott asked. "It would make more sense to establish Christianity with Judas Iscariot. Poul is no scholar."

"He *says* he is a scholar," Moshe said.

"After Syria, you trust what he says?"

Moshe said, "I know it's hard. But it's over, Beni, remember. These people were sent here to start a school—the first off-world yeshiva. If it works, it's an accomplishment. We can all be proud. It's a compromise with technology, no? If we make them go back on that, what will it make us?"

"Survivalists," Beni said.

Jacob stood. "Beni, we do have patrons back on Earth, people who expect us to face this situation—"

"*Yes, patrons!* People who financed an expedition of liberal Jews to create a world where, even among Jews, God forbid, state and church should exist separate and apart. You don't have that in Israel any more, Jacob, no matter how hard the Knesset tries to get it back."

"Poul can't touch that here," Moshe said.

"Like he couldn't touch it in Syria?" Beni asked. He threw back his head, gave them a hooded glare; standing against the wall, he looked very much like any street kid who'd fought in south Jerusalem—which, of course, he had.

Moshe stood too, against the opposite wall. "Syria was different. He couldn't *do* that here—he wouldn't know how. If he wanted that, why would he bring only one boy who knew anything about technology?"

"That boy was first in his class at MIT."

"In materials engineering. Even in Syria and Lebanon, the Rebbe's Sephardim knew how to use a shovel to work the ground."

Most of the kibbutzim stared at the table. A few opened their hands and slowly spread their fingers out over the smooth surface. Others pushed back in their chairs, propped their feet on the table, chuckling softly among themselves.

Sara smiled with them. "Apparently, nobody taught them how to shoot in Syria," she said.

Laughter, some backclapping. Beni shook his head, but he smiled with them.

Then, Rosa Stern stood from the back of the room. "Jacob, they've brought women here, to breed like cattle. They'll build a majority. Sooner or later it won't matter why they've come. They'll take over the vote and change the constitution."

"We don't know that, Rosa," Jacob said.

"What do you need?" Beni asked. "Poul has made a tradition of trouble. We haven't seen the end of it yet, Jacob. *He is going to take over here.*"

The outer door buzzed; they jumped to silence, like trained soldiers.

Outside the glass door, Poul stood. With him, stood Rabbi Meyer and the two younger men, Saul and Barshak. Jacob cancelled the lock.

Poul paused in the doorway, and smiled. "You are discussing our future. I would not think it unusual, then, that we should be here."

"Of course not," Jacob said. "But since you are not yet a part of the council, Rebbe, you cannot expect—"

"An invitation? Is this a dance, Jacob Golani? Not the Hora, certainly. Good Jews embrace during the Hora."

Jacob shot a warning glance at Beni, who sat still and watched the Rebbe in the way a hungry dog guards a bone from other hungry dogs.

Poul went directly to the head of the table. Rabbi Meyer followed. Saul followed also, but slowly, pausing to touch the com on the wall or stare into a molecular screen— behind Poul's back. And still his eyes were strange.

Barshak did not follow. He looked around the room, openly curious, studying the planes and angles surrounding them.

Poul sat. "So. What do we discuss at a Jewish utopia council meeting? I hear economics was the daily topic in the Knesset."

"It used to be," Jacob said. "Why do you ask, Rebbe?"

"I don't ask about the Knesset. I ask about you. You are not up here to be closer to God, are you Jacob? This is an *economic* proposition—diamonds. Coal into diamonds."

"Graphite, not coal—" Beni said. "And good Jews have been working diamonds for years."

"Cutting, yes," Poul said. "But not making them, or giving them minds of their own. You are breathing memories into your diamonds. And sometimes, even, putting them into the minds of men."

In the silence that followed Poul's words, the kibbutzniks each turned to stare at him. Jacob said, finally, "We do not allow our goods to be used for implant, Rebbe."

Poul made a noise. "Next you will be putting the Torah into these diamonds," Poul said.

And from the back, someone yelled, "We already have."

Poul looked around the table. "Diamonds from coal. Maybe you grow pigs here, too. Or do you call them zebras, like the kibbutzniks in Israel?"

"We are not, at least, raising children like cattle," Rosa said.

Poul did not acknowledge her voice, or her statement. "There are many empty fields here," he said, very softly. His words were not lost on any of them. Rosa turned her face stiffly away from the Rebbe, and Poul smiled. "We seem to have a problem. The WJO has instructed you to see to our problem, no?"

"Insofar as the problems relate to your people settling here, in establishing their yeshiva, yes," Jacob said. "What do you want, Rebbe?"

"Barshak has led us to the place you call the Commons Room. This is the room in which you say you worship?"

"Few of us find need of formal worship, Rebbe. It is usually something we do in private." Poul snorted. Jacob paused, looked at the Rebbe. "If you wish to use the Commons Room for worship and for shule," he said, "we can arrange an appropriate schedule to accommodate you."

Poul brought his hands up into the air, slapped them flat against the table top. "Worship? We are here to establish a holy place in this wilderness, and you are suggesting that we worship in a *bar?*"

Sara and the others began to titter. Poul stared until each of them fell silent—some of them sullen, others bewildered and amused. "You will build me a synagogue."

"You must be crazy."

The words were out before Jacob could recall them. The Hasids blinked, surprised, but no more than his own people and no more than Jacob himself. "We have things to do, Rebbe—"

"You will build me a synagogue or we will leave this place on the next shuttle. We will not stay unless you build it; we will not stay in a place that does not preserve the house of God."

"Our schedules are not niceties here, Rebbe. We keep them to survive."

Barshak stepped between Poul and Jacob. "*I* can build it," he said.

Poul recoiled; his sidecurls lurched on his chest. "No."

Barshak tilted his head, regarding the Rebbe as though he still stood at a safe distance. "Why not?" he asked.

"You are a student. You will study," Poul said.

"You need me to build a synagogue more, I think, than you need me to read. For that, you have Saul as first reader."

Poul looked to Saul, who said, simply, "It would be wonderful, to have a synagogue built by our own Barshak."

Our own. Poul narrowed his eyes and smiled. Saul smiled also. They all smiled. But when Poul turned to whisper with Rabbi Meyer, Jacob saw Saul's smile die quickly.

Sweat was covering Saul's face—not just his cheeks, but his neck and forehead also, beading down his chest.

Jacob said quietly to Barshak, "You get the specifications."

"Where are *you* going?" Barshak asked.

Jacob nodded toward Saul, who had cupped trembling fingers around the molecular screen and was peering as deeply into it as a feverish man to drink. Barshak withdrew from Jacob, a measurable inch, but a chasm of perceptible shifting opened between them.

"What's wrong?" Jacob asked.

"Saul is," Barshak shook his head, "not well."

"How so?"

"Ask him. He won't tell me, but I think I know. And I don't want to be right." Softer, but still with that distance that did not broach questions, Barshak said, "I'll ask Poul what he wants from the synagogue. I'll tell you later, what I know."

Jacob let Barshak go. Barshak sat, a young man with his elders, and asked Poul what he wanted out of this synagogue they would build. His voice held respect. But not reverence, Jacob noted.

And while Barshak sat with the Rebbe, discussing how big the synagogue should be and the requirements he had for it, Jacob moved to Saul and stood beside him. The heat of Saul's cheeks left steam on the molecular screen. Saul looked up and smiled his aching smile; his eyes saw and did not see Jacob.

"You need a doctor."

The smile wavered; the beauty did not. "No. I'm fine," Saul said.

"Serious illness generally means deportation. Our hospital is set up more for research than—"

"No. It's just a small infection, from recent surgery."

"What kind of surgery?"

"I can get by with suppressants," Saul said. He kept his voice low, for Jacob's benefit or because he couldn't speak clearly any other way. He held up his hand; it shook. The sweat began to smell on him. "*Please.*"

And Jacob knew, watching Saul half close his eyes and tremble against the monitor, that whatever spell he held over Poul, it was as innocent and unasked for as the beauty of David's harp—and as vulnerable to a king's wrath.

"We'll talk later," Jacob said. "I'll have you see Sara, our doctor."

Saul nodded, his hair wet against his forehead.

Across the room, an argument was starting.

Jacob left Saul at the screen and moved to Sara, who watched raptly as Barshak shook his head and the Rebbe grew more agitated with each of the young man's denials.

"What's this about?" Jacob asked.

"Where to put the synagogue," she said.

"So what's the problem?"

Sara smiled up at him. "Apparently, there's only one place big enough to put it. The Pit."

Barshak struggled against the wall of the freight elevator, pulling on magnetic boots. "I suggested coming down here to ease their fears," he said. "I hope it wasn't the wrong thing to do."

Jacob said nothing, only slowed the freight elevator to a stop. He drew out eight belts from the car's utility closet—like dog leashes, except for the caster magnet where the leash clips should be. Barshak took a leash, spun the rolling magnet with his finger. Behind them, Poul steadfastly refused to put on the boots.

"Don't worry about it," Jacob told Barshak. "Just make sure every one of them is secured. If you can't get Poul to wear the shoes, at least get him anchored to the railguide. I don't need him floating into the air compressors."

Barshak nodded, securing one end of the guide to his wrist. "Do you always use these? I mean, how do you work?"

"I wear boots," Jacob said. "And I know how to move in low G. If you know that, you're okay. If you don't, you get hurt. For you and your people, I don't want to open this door unless every one of you is secured with boots and leash."

Barshak tied the Hasids by their wrists and hung the magnetic ends to the walls. Poul yanked away, said something in Yiddish Jacob did not understand and didn't care to. He started up the car.

As they neared the Furnace, gravity gradually loosed its hold. Those with boots stood normally. Poul began to rise, unable to keep his feet on the floor of the car. Barshak and Rabbi Meyer grabbed and held on to him. Poul's knuckles whitened against the railguide. Jacob stopped the car.

"If you'll wear the boots, Rebbe, you won't have such a difficult time adjusting to the difference in gravity."

He gave Poul no time to answer, promptly starting the car again. Behind him, the Hasids quickly moved to help the Rebbe on with his shoes.

The door opened. Jacob helped the Hasids out of the car slowly. He thanked God they did not have to cross the Pit. But he knew they had to skirt it. And he knew what it was like, seeing the Pit for the first time.

At the elevator landing, the Hasids huddled in a tight group. Jacob secured their tethers to the far wall and gave each of them a breather.

Rabbi Meyer put the breather to his face without even looking at it. He tilted his head and looked at the domed ceiling that stretched half a mile above them; then, as he looked back down, into the Pit itself, his eyes widened.

"It is the Inferno," he said.

"You have read Dante?" Jacob asked.

"That was not the inferno he had in mind," Poul said, pressed against the far wall.

The Pit stretched half a mile below them. At the bottom, Jacob saw the lights crawling through the black haze— the taillights of the trawlers, his crews working with small, bright hardhat beacons. But the Hasids saw only the specks of a ghostly light, pinpoints of hellfire, and the black plumes of graphite that rose in the low gravity—skeins of dust that swirled slowly up toward the dust collectors at the ceiling; veils that snaked up from the belly of the Pit and danced gently around them before going on. The trawler beacons dipped and swayed, like capricious souls beneath them.

Rabbi Meyer quoted snatches of the Torah; his lips were white and barely moved. "What is this place?" he whispered.

"A graphite mine," Jacob said. And opened the door into the Furnace.

Light filled the walkway, crazed and darting colors that made a maze of straight lines. Jacob brought them all into the workroom complex.

The furnace was at full smelt.

Three encased conveyors pushed chunks of raw graphite, funneled them into laser pulse bulbs. The bulbs were transparent rotating spheres at the end of the conveyors. Beyond them, gravity-null globes, shaped like minarets, condensed liquid into hardened crystal eggs.

Jacob said, "One thousand atmospheres of pressure in the globes turns the pulp into liquid. Just like melting ore, or fashioning sheet metal. After this, we put the crystals in a gyre. Only the outer layer cools. The interior stays raw liquid. That's what we program—the liquid conductive properties of the crystal."

Most of them returned his explanation with glances to ward off the evil eye. In one of the globes, the implosion pulses entered a generation phase. The lasers began to strobe, striking an irregular pattern, thin and quick, like serpents' tongues against the globe. The graphite churned with each strike. Whole chunks of it popped, dissolving into pulp; the pulp writhed along the walls of the bulb and oozed in slow waves against strainers. It came out as liquid, crackling with clarity, that filled the null globes instantly.

Some of the molt flowed back into catch-troughs that ran along the windowed sides of the room. Saul moved to the troughs and stared down into the pools of sharply glittering liquid. Jacob touched his shoulder, and felt him shiver under the coolness of his hand.

The panels began to hum, a pitch that rose just slightly over the sound of the smelt. The panels shimmied and bucked against the initial jolts, then settled into a low drone and a fast, solid vibration. "We're facing the sun right now," Jacob said to Saul. "They're collecting energy."

Saul nodded, smiled, went back to gazing at the molt.

He bent down to the trough, brushing his hand lightly over the transparent tubes. Jacob took Barshak by the arm, he steered over to Saul. Saul didn't even look up. "Keep an eye on him," Jacob said.

In the midst of strobing lights, Poul stood against the solar console—too close to nearby panels. Jacob went to Poul, laid a hand on his arm. Poul jerked it free.

Jacob held up his arms and crooked a finger, motioning: *I will not touch you, but come away.*

Poul stared back at Jacob, angry, uncomprehending. A panel shivered its final cycle. Poul looked over his shoulder. Behind him, the other panels began to shudder under the transfer of energy.

Poul moved. He tripped over his boots; they clung to the floor; but he still moved, almost into Jacob's arms. Even so close, to be heard over the noise, Jacob had to shout.

"You have a sick man here, Rebbe. Saul. He needs help. We have a doctor—"

"A *woman*."

"She is qualified for the job," Jacob said.

"That's not the point," Poul said. "The only woman to see a man like that should be his wife. That is our law."

Jacob looked at Poul and shook his head. He said something, lost in the solars' hum. Poul said, quickly, "Argue about it another time. Not here."

Jacob's smile was dry and bitter. "Perhaps you would like a tour of the facility, Rebbe," he said.

Poul shook his head. "This is enough."

Jacob nodded. "I would imagine."

Poul glanced at him sharply, but said nothing.

"There is room," Jacob said, "at the far end, for a

small building. If you built the synagogue here, you would at least have ample illustration of the flames of hell."

"If you are suggesting such a thing—"

Jacob waved a hand; in the strobing light, his arm shot suddenly into the air, the flesh mottled and unreal. "I'm only joking."

He glanced over at Saul. Barshak had joined the younger man at the trough. The light of the lasers snaked a dozen colors between them. Saul knelt at one of the null globes. Barshak bent over to him, laying a hand on his shoulder.

Poul was saying, over the noise and the heat, "There is nothing about your jokes that is funny. We will not put our synagogue in any *room*. It must be large enough for a full yeshiva community."

"There are very few places that big left on this asteroid," Jacob said. "And we certainly don't have the tools to carve one out."

Barshak took Saul's arm, to drag him back, but Saul pulled away and leaned his head against the globe. His hands caressed the belly of it. Barshak stood, helplessly, beside him. Saul clung to the globe, burrowing himself against its bright, warm side.

"It must face east, or it cannot be a true synagogue," Poul said.

"There is no east in space," Jacob said absently, watching Saul and Barshak.

Poul snorted. "When God made the east, he made it for the whole universe—" Barshak swung around, pale, the lasers' light strobing on his face.

Saul fell.

Jacob took a step, wrenching his boots up off the floor, and pushed his body into a spin; he arced past Poul and through the room. As he landed, Jacob reached for Saul. Around him, his people dropped into emergency procedures: the watch captain contacted Sara in the clinic, the console operator shut down the smelt and the solar panels. In the silence, so abrupt it hurt, Poul shouted in Hebrew—words Jacob had forgotten years ago.

Jacob turned Saul, carefully. Saul's pupils dilated, widening until his irises were little more than slivered rims around the black.

The remote stretcher lowered to the floor.

"What happened?" Sara asked.

Jacob shook his head. He helped the orderly and Sara move Saul to the stretcher.

Poul cried out, finally seeing, after the overheads filled the room with hard, pale light and understanding. He stumbled to the stretcher. "What has happened to him?"

"If I knew, I would tell you," Jacob said.

"Where are you taking him?"

"To the clinic."

"I'm going with him."

"You can't."

The orderly secured the strap latch at Saul's chest. Poul howled and pushed the orderly aside. Barshak caught at Poul, too late. The orderly flailed in the low gravity, his boots torn from the floor. He catapulted up toward the solar panels, slammed hard against a pipe guard. Steam billowed around them. Circuits popped, sending up sparks like small fireworks. The orderly hung to the pipe, bewildered. Then he let go, dropping slowly to the floor.

Jacob and Sara exchanged a black look between them, and ran the stretcher out of the Furnace. Poul moved after them, stumbling in his boots, clinging to the rail like a cat over water. Jacob picked him up by the haunches and threw him into the elevator.

Sara pumped medicines into Saul's left arm, slapped a tracer to his heel.

Poul knelt at Saul's right. He moved to touch him, and pulled back as Saul smiled. Poul clenched the metal rails around the stretcher, wringing them as Saul tried to speak. Each word was cut from him, like a finger tracing fire at his lips.

"I have seen paradise," Saul said.

"You have seen hell," Poul whispered.

The stretcher tore from his hands. Jacob and Sara stood and ran into the hall, pulling air struts out from under the stretcher, taking Saul farther and farther from him. They disappeared before the elevator doors closed. Poul, still in his corner of the elevator, curled himself against the harshness of the light and shook against his knees.

"I should speak to the Rebbe about you. Nursing a boy like Saul, and you not even married."

Rachel stood against one of the clinic walls. Her mother said again, "Did you hear me? Saul is not a boy. And you are not a married woman."

Rachel shivered against the wall. *Not married, not married, not—* "I know First Aid," she said.

Sara, standing implacable at the other end of the clinic, raised an eyebrow and smiled oddly.

"Ha. You know too much," Rivka said. "Where did you learn such things?"

"In school, *imma.*"

"They taught you too much in that school. I don't like this."

Sara turned her back and began measuring biological inferences on a sonorhythm.

"I'll speak to the Rebbe," the old woman said. "If they make you nurse him, I'll speak—"

"Why don't you ask the girl what she wants to do?" Sara asked, swirling the matrix in three-dimensional pictures on the laser screen. Three thousand colors stared at the old woman, making one inhuman face after another.

Rachel felt the sharp edge of a counter at her back. She

put her hands against it, said to Sara, "I came to work."

Her mother said, "She won't nurse the boy. I won't have her nursing the boy."

"Who, Saul?" Sara laughed, more bitterly than Rachel or her mother could understand. "Don't worry. She won't touch him."

"Or see him?" Rivka asked.

Sara looked at the woman, at the wrinkles that made her old and the eyes that were ancient with centuries of moral imperatives. And though she knew what the old woman had meant, that this virgin daughter of hers should not look upon a man in his nakedness, Sara knew her own answer meant something very different. She nodded and said, "Or see him."

At the sono screen, error bells rang; the soft, piercing notes raised hair on Sara's arms. She turned back to the sonorhythm, shut off the alarm and brought a new program up on the screen.

Two women haggled in the kitchen—Mirim, Rabbi Meyer's daughter, had Rosa cornered at the sink.

Sara, coming into the kitchen with Rachel, almost laughed at the sight—Mirim in black broadcloth from neck to toe, raging against Rosa, who bent against the rush of words as though against a heavy wind. Seeing Rosa's face, any laughter left in Sara died. "What's the problem?" she asked.

Rosa left the room without answering.

Mirim, seeing Sara, rounded on her immediately. "These kitchens are not kosher. How can we eat food that is not kosher?"

Sara's eyes widened like black, angry seas. She folded her arms and with a stiff body stood more firmly on the floor, as though by having her foot on that spot she could have her foot on the necks of them all.

"This kitchen is not kosher because this community is not kosher. If you wish to build a kosher kitchen, you are welcome to do so. Otherwise, learn to eat every kind of food, the way the rest of us do."

Mirim thrust her bosom forward, though her breasts did not make the same impression for her as they did for Sara. "What kind of Jew are you, Sara Stern? We would starve before seething a kid in its mother's milk."

Sara narrowed her beautiful eyes. "I have seen starvation. I've seen people die of it. A bullet is faster. I've seen that too. You'll have to suffer with tight bellies a very long time before you can start another war up here."

Mirim clenched her fists, and Rachel thought she might strike Sara. Instead, Mirim turned quickly to the door. "I'm getting the Rebbe."

"Ohhh, she's getting the Rebbe!" Sara moaned and threw her arms up in the air.

Mirim ran.

Sara chuckled, a wicked thing justly pleased with itself. "Sara, you really should be *nicer*," she said. Rachel pretended not to hear, and Sara pretended that nothing had been said. She gave Rachel a bin to fill, and pointed to a large door. "There's fresh fruit in there. You make the choice."

While Rachel stood, still staring at the bin, Sara said, "Someday, you'll have to open your own doors," and touched the dark square at the door for her.

The big door slid aside, sucking the air from around them. Rachel clutched at the doorframe, pulled forward with the sudden suck of cool, musty wind. It eased with a sigh.

The pantry inside was bigger than her mother's house in New York. For a long minute, Rachel only stood outside and stared.

"Are you going in?" Sara asked.

Rachel nodded and walked deep into the pantry. Fans swirled the air, cooling it slowly. Goosebumps prickled her arms; her breasts hardened against the cool swirling breath and the old smell of apples. She crossed her arms. Outside, the kitchen door hissed open. Rachel looked behind her.

Poul. Poul had come to the kitchen.

He surveyed the place slowly, and where his gaze rested, Rachel thought the foreign metals must be burned forever.

Sara stopped her work to glance up. Poul crossed quickly to Sara. Rachel closed her eyes. Their voices exploded behind her, pounding at her shoulder blades.

As Sara threw Poul's comments coldly back to him, Rachel felt a rush of water at her eyes. Tears.

She looked at their trace on her hands, bewildered, as terrified by their clear drops as she had been at fourteen and the first stains of blood had soiled her child's underclothes. She wiped them from her cheeks, quickly.

The droplets splashed against the metal of the shelves. In moments, the suction fans had withered them to specks of salt, barely seen and easily overlooked.

Jacob walked into the clinic.

"There was a problem in the kitchen?" he asked.

Sara, alone, did not look up from the optiscope. "What else, with these people? Poul—he won't eat food from a non-kosher kitchen. I've told him I'm not the chef, but he doesn't seem to believe me."

"What about Saul?" Jacob asked.

Sara stopped rotating the optiscope, holding the gyre tight between her fingers. "I can't help him," she said. "Not here."

"What's wrong with him?"

"An implant. Badly done."

"What can we do?"

Sara laughed and shook her head. "Bury him. Jacob, you know what implantation means. The synapses can't integrate. Implants—they go insane and then they die."

"And there's nothing to do?" Jacob asked.

"You've looked through an infinity matrix before. What do *you* think? Five hundred grams of liquid crystal opens up and suddenly this kid can't stare into his own head and *think* anymore. If he didn't soon believe he was God, he wouldn't think at all. Just sit and stare. This one started to scream. I put him on ice."

"That should keep him alive until we think of something—"

"Jacob, no one can treat implants. Not here, not even Earthside."

"Procter was working on restoration techniques before we left Earth."

"That could take years."

"We have the time."

Sara rubbed her eyes. "That much, yes, I suppose."

"How did he even get into implants?"

"Sounds incredible, doesn't it? A nice Jewish boy like that. Not between the yeshiva and the synagogue, that much is certain." She paused. "I thought I would copy Saul's R.E.A.L. memory into the crystal itself, using the live tissue as peripheral."

"You're going to use him as a resource, Sara?"

Sara shrugged. "He won't feel a thing."

"You could kill him. The Hasids—"

"It's a place to start, Jacob. And as far as they are concerned, he is already dead. They don't believe in thermal sleep."

"There's nothing else you can do?"

"I won't do anything to *hurt* him, Jacob. Listen—I'll download the crystal's core drive to a modal first. The OS should tell us something. At least the version and the serial number.''

"Do it. It's a good idea, Sara."

"But ghoulish. Moshe would say I have no respect for the dead.''

"He isn't dead. Remember that.''

Barshak's Log:

Tell me. What is virtue?

I had a friend at MIT. She was thirty years old, and still a virgin. She was a good girl, her Rabbi would say. She wasn't so sure. Even she couldn't tell if her virginity was prompted by deep belief or was simply the result of not being tempted enough to fall.

Saul fell. Only one thing tempted him, and I suppose it says something, that he should succumb so blissfully to his first experience with the apple.

Crystal implantation is illegal. There are reasons for this. Though the diamond's liquid memory can achieve speeds of comprehension and calculation breathtaking in artificial frameworks, the human mind cannot keep up with it. The implant has a language of its own—a protocol of power and speed the brain cannot translate. Very few have accessed this power. Others, it has simply driven mad.

Legitimate labs would never touch implantation for anything but metal hosts. So, the really desperate brain jockeys go down to Mexico or sometimes the Hong Kong bazaars. But by the time they go in for AI implants, most of them are already whacked up by expansion drugs and simple transistors. They crave it—the speed, the program capabilities. Multitasking for human minds. Windows to fly through. Forget the logic of death and the fear of it. Juice is everything.

And it isn't the hit alone that makes this addiction so

powerful. It's the subculture. In Osaka, in Silicon Valley, the juicebunnies gather in concerts to take in that power etched in soundwaves, their bodies swaying as it hits them. At the foot of the Ngong hills, Kenya has come into primary economic status by making tech a national religion. Implants and meditation are standard practices for Beta monks. It could be the meditation technique they use; maybe it's the faith. They aren't telling. But they are among the few to survive the implant.

That perpetuates the myth.

Some physicians theorize that it is not the fever or infection that kills the victims. If they survive the implant, if they overcome the infection, if there are no other complications, they should come out of it alive.

But they don't.

They jump off bridges or out of windows; they run in front of cars or drink cleaning acid.

My grandmother once told me, when I would not eat or sleep because I had to read, as compelled to books and their words, to the rhythms of the words, as Giselle to the dance, she said to me one hot, sleepless morning in August, "To hold hands with God is to flirt with madness, however divine that madness might be."

Seeing AIs work, even in metal—and being a scholar, compelled to the clarity and perfection of liquid thought—I, too, could be tempted as Saul.

But I am not God's lover yet.

Barshak came to the mines faster than Jacob expected. "You didn't stay to finish shule."

Barshak, measuring each curve of the domed ceiling, did not answer.

"This isn't the place to get a good look," Jacob said. "I'll take you to the Rim."

Jacob led Barshak to the farthest edge of the Pit. It was little more than a shelf, only partially encased in plexiglass.

"Watch yourself," Jacob said. "There's some suction here, from the way the ventilation hits the mines. Move slow here."

Barshak leaned over the side of the clear rail. Diggers worked the ground far below them. As they backed, their yellow and red lights lit the cavern. The dust of each load trailed shrouds that floated toward them in the median gravity, then caught in the vent's suction and disappeared.

"It's a bit macabre," Jacob said, "what your Rebbe wants. It could be, as he said, the Inferno. But it's the only place that meets his requirements."

"There's no other place?" Barshak asked.

"Not unless you want the yeshiva students to go to shule in gravity units. I don't think the Rebbe would go for that."

"No, it is unlikely, though it would be very funny. He asks many questions, the Rebbe Poul."

"And wants no answers," Jacob said.

Barshak glanced at Jacob, then sat on his haunches to gaze into the Pit. "Has he asked about Saul yet?"

"Yes," Jacob said, curling his fingers around the rail.

"Have you told him about the AI?"

"You think I should?"

Barshak stood and looked out around the Rim. The domed ceiling was at least 500 feet above the far strip where they stood, the circumference of the Pit well over a mile. "The dust is pretty bad here," he said. "It obscures the view of the Pit—that's what makes it so spectral. There's nothing you can do for that?"

Jacob shook his head.

"I didn't think so. We had better plan on a containment of some kind."

"For Poul or the synagogue?" Jacob asked.

Barshak smiled. "The building. It would be easier, if he would let me build it into the wall. But to build on the outside? I could put it off to the side. Or suspend it in the middle, maybe—"

Barshak gazed up to the ceiling, letting go of the rail and craning his neck to see past the shadows to the top. The ceiling was smooth, like the vault of a cathedral. Venting units lined its sides.

"So that's what you do with the dust. I didn't think you could afford to let it float away. Those are reprocessing stations, aren't they?" Jacob nodded; Barshak made a circle in the air with his hand. "Something to filter the air and collect the residue of graphite. Then there is definitely access to the upper portions of this place?"

"Yes. But you couldn't get heavy machinery up there. We travel mostly by elevator to the top. Nothing big enough to build with would fit in them."

"No," Barshak said. "But it is possible, you know, to work with the low gravity instead of against it. I'll have to build a scaffolding first, but after that—"

"How did you know about the AI?" Jacob asked.

Barshak glanced back at Jacob, then looked up to the vents. "I know the signs," he said. "I had a professor once, at MIT, who implanted."

"What happened?" Jacob asked.

"He died."

After several moments, it was clear Barshak would say nothing more. He stared at the midpoint arc as though he could see angels fighting a silent war on the dome. Jacob followed Barshak's gaze, half thinking he could see that vision too. But Jacob saw only an immense metal dome, grayish-blue and bruised with the dust of raw graphite.

Rachel held a child in her arms. Around her, most of

the kibbutzim children slept. This one squirmed, casting about on her shoulder. He began to cry, his voice sharp in her ear. She held him tighter to her chest. He lifted his head, sniffling against her ear, but found nothing in the nipple of her lobe that he could want. He gave a sharp sigh and began to cry again.

"Shhh, hush. Please, be quiet—"

He looked up at her, pushing against her shoulder. His head wobbled, but his eyes followed her voice as though he could see it move. "What do you want?" Rachel asked, and he leaned against her chin. She stroked his back and closed her eyes. She hummed, a snatch of a song. The low sounds, though barely voiced, were loud in her ears. But the child put his head against her breast and listened to the sound vibrate in her chest. She opened her eyes suddenly and looked around the room, then shifted in the chair. It was a child's chair; she was too big for it.

But the babe had fallen to sleep at her breast, suckling softly against the fabric.

"*Rachel?* What are you doing here?"

Rachel closed her eyes, clutched the baby firmly for that one moment, while her back was still to the door and the child at her breast. Then she let him go, easing him onto her lap.

"Nothing, mother. Just putting a baby to bed."

Her mother came around the chair, bustling her skirts and apron. "And who was crazy enough to put *you* in a roomful of children? You so much as look at a baby, it cries—"

Rachel stood. "Be quiet, mother. He's asleep." She laid the boy in his crib, covering him with a comforter. His lips suckled against the blanket, and her nipples ached against the heavy fabric of her dress.

"They still should not have you working here," her mother said.

"I should not work here. I should not work in the clinic. Where would you have me, mother?"

"The kitchen, maybe, preparing for Passover."

"The kitchens are almost completely automated, mother."

Her mother folded her arms. She stood beside the crib, watching the baby sleep, frowning. "Well, not here."

"Why not?"

"Because it's cruel. There's no use making you want something you can't have."

"Can't have?" Rachel asked. "I'm not barren."

"How do you know? Let's not talk about it. Anyway, it doesn't matter. Give you another five years, alone, like you are now, it won't make a difference if you even bleed anymore."

Rachel sucked air into her lungs, tasting soft talc and salt. She opened her mouth, but her throat was tight, the words harder to bear than the singing. "Why do you say such things to me?"

Her mother toyed with the blanket, covering the baby's toes. "I don't want you to be disappointed."

"I'm not disappointed."

"Then you're not a woman," her mother said, and stroked the baby's arm, smiling.

Rachel moved away from the crib, shivering at the small wet blotch at her breast. "I am going to bed," she said.

Her mother didn't turn to say goodbye.

The thin cloth covered but did not hide. She lay down by a well. Above her, the night was a clear, black canopy. The water plunged into the well from an outer fall, spraying against her hair, laying a crown of droplets at her thighs. Beyond the darkness, there was light, the sound of laughter; the pulse of the tambor began. It peaked with the sharp cry of a prophet in the wilderness—

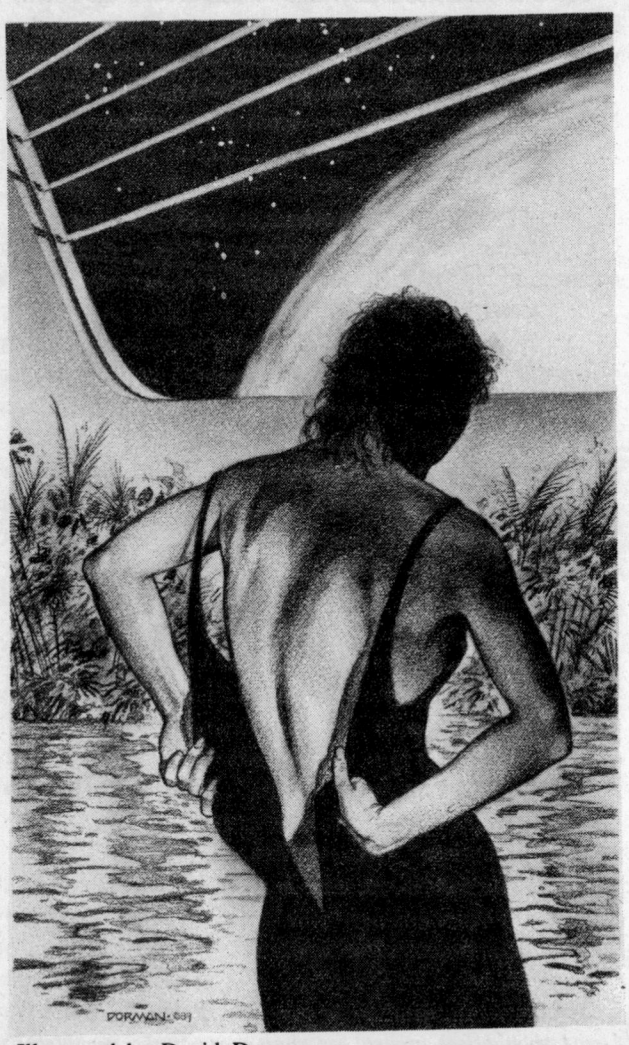

Illustrated by David Dorman

Rachel woke, suddenly. She looked around the room, down at herself. She wore her heavy nightshirt, and the women slept around her.

She lay back and tried to breathe regularly, to make her breathing match that of the women surrounding her. The air in the room was stale, the bodies too close.

She was sticky with the sweat of her dreams.

She lay with her head on the pillow, her eyes wide. Once again, she would wake with her bedclothes damp, her cheeks the color of apples, to face again the knowing looks of the women.

She pushed away her blankets. The bathroom was empty and dark, but it was small. The square at the door caught her eye; she stepped to the door, put her hand to the square.

The halls were dark. She wandered. In front of her, a door opened, spreading a wave of warm, moist air around her.

She saw a well, a small fountain that opened into a pool. A window above let in a thousand lights. All around, a jungle grew. The breath of honeysuckle, orchid and iris surrounded her, tugging in her hair. Amaranth, jasmine and rose: fresh and sweet, the whispered colors all around her.

"I am dreaming again," she said, softly. Her voice echoed against the sky and came back to her sadly. It held the lament of her surrender, bitter and sweet. And in her dream she stripped off the heavy nightshirt and stretched in the glittering light. The sweat on her body rippled, and she stepped into the water.

Barshak's Log:

Voyeur is the polite word for pervert.
I should feel arousal or shame or, at the very least,

judgement. But I see only beauty, and the exacting stroke of telling something just as it occurred.

Rachel, Rivka's daughter, came to the well last night. I was there. So, too, was Jacob Golani.

I sat unseen and read Talmud, taking notes among the leaves. I miss green, the cool green of leaves and trees and a good book that is read beneath them. He swam in the pool. I think it's the only time and place he is alone, when all this very small world is asleep and the only bed that is truly empty is the plot of land they have made here in the image of the Earth. So he swam and I read and she came into the room in a white nightgown. And took off that nightgown.

My father is right, perhaps. Maybe I have grown worldly. But while I did not avert my eyes, I saw in her only a beauty as ethereal and untouchable as the stars surrounding this place. My first experience with aesthetic distance. Stephen Daedalus taught me that. It was certainly not the Torah.

She went into the water with something like a sigh, and neither she nor Jacob saw the other until their bodies had touched and tangled in the water. I feared the worst.

But he only kissed her. Then swam away.

She stood in the water, naked and dripping; her eyes were wide with her vision of him, as though she were somehow dreaming.

Jacob very quietly left the room. I admit to a growing respect for him. He did a thing not many men could do—neither running away from his dream, nor possessing it fully.

I am sure he did not learn that in the Torah, either.

Sara laughed deep in her throat. Her voice was rich with milk and honey promises. She stretched, her breasts rising against the canvas work clothes. In the smelting room, the laser light drew her face in bizarre colors, painting and unpainting her lips and cheeks with cherry, azure, and pearl.

"Why did I never marry you?" Jacob asked, smiling.

Sara stowed the last of the small equipment and turned the laser off. The room wound down to silence; the main fans shut off, the small circular fans began to turn, and the low worklights threw warm gold light against both of them. "You still could. For tonight, at least."

Jacob smiled again, and shook his head.

Sara nodded, her lips mocking their own wisdom. "It must be love."

"Why do you say that?"

She took his face gently in her hands. They were covered with earth, with the soil that surrounded the pond, though she had worked kiln for over an hour. "It's not as though anyone has a secret in this place, you know."

Jacob looked down into her hands. They smelled of earth, sweet and brown. He could weep in that soil. Instead, he burrowed his cheeks into her palms, against the warmth of her skin and the warm, earthy sweat.

"Sara, what am I going to do?"

"What's to do? You're falling in love with an Orthodox girl. I don't have to tell you the trouble you're in."

He turned toward the inner windows. Outside, from the Pit, black dust formed spectral tendrils and dipped over the metal handrails—as though no power from the vents moved them, but they stirred from a malice dredged in from their souls.

Sara closed her hand on his, then slipped away.

The hum of the circular fans touched him with the faintest breath. He lifted his head and saw the fans, suspended on thin, silver lines, with the sweet shape of a woman's breast and the sound of a scimitar slicing through the air.

Rachel woke to her mother's weeping. She stretched

out her hand, brushing back the hair that had come down from the woman's knotted braid.

"Mother—"

"Look at yourself. *Cover* yourself."

Rachel looked down at the sheets. She was naked. The sheets were wet and smelled of springwater. Her mother's weeping shook in the small room, in her ears.

"I am talking to the Rebbe today. I will tell him," her mother said.

Weeping struck against Rachel's throat, echoed there. "I don't remember," she said against the sheet. "I didn't—"

"They used to stone girls like you," her mother hissed, and ran from the room.

"So Saul made the trip to Mexico City," Jacob said. He and Sara ate in the Commons Room. On the other side of the room, a dozen chairs were lined in neat rows; they faced a table. The table held a Torah so large it would take two men to carry it any distance. Jacob looked back to Sara. "So why Mexico?"

"Barshak says he went to visit a grandfather who supposedly has a synagogue there. I've looked into the boy's record. He hasn't got a grandfather. Both of them died when he was young. What does that suggest to you?"

"The *Loja* are South American," Jacob said, "But they're Brazi."

"And expanding every day. Mexico City has a lot of connections in that area. So do we."

"What do you mean?"

"You won't like it. I downloaded the serial number of the crystal."

"And?"

"It's one of ours."

"*Ours?* We don't ship to the Southern states—"

"Some of our stuff goes to the Silicon Valley complex,

for their industrial computers. It's not far from there, Jacob—Mexico City.''

"Our diamonds? Being smuggled for implants?" He pushed his plate away, ran his hands through his hair. "God, Sara. How do we sell industrial, knowing that?"

"Jacob, don't *do* this—"

"There are other uses for quality diamonds. They don't all have to store LCM. We can do other things with them."

"Like what? Are you planning to sell jewelry door to door these days?"

Jacob covered his face. From between his fingers, his voice words stretched thin and slow, like gravel on a hard dirt road. "No. I know."

"Jacob, Saul is not your problem."

"I *know*."

"But we will have to be more careful. A lot more careful."

"We *were* being careful."

"I mean here—it's not something to tell the Hasids."

"God, the Hasids. Have you tried your experiment on Saul?"

"Yes. It didn't work."

"Why not?"

"You were right—the transmission rate between the organic and inorganic is too different. The impulse is there, the synapses spark, there's just no communication. But even if I could dispose of the brain altogether, and just dump everything into the crystal, it still wouldn't work."

"How do you know?"

"I tried it."

A grin twisted Jacob's lips, perverse and not entirely welcome. "And?"

Sara twisted in her seat. "I can't access his *soul*, Jacob. I can put all the info in the crystal, but I can't put *him* there. Theoretically, it works. I can operate the whole thing from a console, make him breathe, lift his arm, even speak. But they aren't his words. I can type *dog* and he'll say dog—"

"But only if you enable it from the console?"

"Yes."

"Do you mind if I visit him?" Jacob asked.

"What's to visit?" Sara shook her head. "No, go on, if you have to. But you can't do anything for him, Jacob."

"No. But maybe, if I see him, I can sleep through the night, eh, Sara?"

She looked up at him, her eyes dry and hard. "What do *you* think?" she asked.

Rachel came to the clinic, looking for Sara, calling her name. She was not there. *I am alone,* Rachel thought, *utterly and truly alone. The Rebbe will come. I will be delivered of my mother like a babe with seven crosses burned upon its forehead.*

"Oh God, what have I done?"

Her knees shook beneath her. She opened the door into the supply room, to Sara's office. "Sara?" But the older woman was not in the outer clinic.

Rachel came to the inner clinic door—a door she had never gone beyond, though she had seen Sara go there. Rachel touched the green square; the door slid away.

"Sara?"

Rachel stepped inside the room.

Light crazed against metal and glass. The floor scattered patterns, a pebbled mosaic, and panels, like clear sarcophagi, lined the wall. Inside, a mummy smiled, baring his teeth, grinning like a wild monkey. His eyes stared, the blue of the irises calling her name—

Rachel closed her eyes. *No. I've opened the wrong door, opened it into sleep.*

But when she shook her head, her hair moved against

her arms. She stood still. Nothing changed, not even the glare against her eyelids. Slowly, she opened her eyes.

"*Saul—*"

He stared at her, his eyes open in their delirium, his skin whiter than her own. He stood upright, floating in a clear canister—just one open grave among the empty caskets that lined the wall.

A whine began around her, a sound like steam through a teapot. Nothing moved. But the sound rose to a high buzz in her ears. She ran; it followed her into the anteroom. Shaking, Rachel slammed her hand against the panel at the door. The door opened. The whining stopped.

Jacob stood in the doorframe.

He looked toward the canisters, where Saul hung quietly in his freezer. Rachel looked straight at his chest. Goosebumps pickled her skin, and when he took her hands, they were cold. He pulled her out of the clinic, step by step.

"Rachel, listen to me," he said.

But she said nothing to him. *Nothing, nothing, nothing—*

Jacob took Rachel to the garden, sat her beside the warm pool. Color blotched her cheeks; she no longer shivered, and he knew she was aware of him and of her surroundings. He wrapped a thin tarp around her shoulders. She let it fall.

"He isn't dead," Jacob said to her. "You understand? Just suspended, thermally. I can't tell you why—"

"*Why?*"

Staccato. The firing of a bullet.

He said nothing. She stared at the water, waiting.

"I didn't think you would understand," he said.

"What's wrong with Saul?"

"Did you know him?"

"Yes. If he isn't dead, what *is* wrong?"

"Nothing. He's just asleep," Jacob said. "Thermal is a state of sleep, really."

The generator rumbled to life; the droplets condensed on the plants around the pond suddenly shuddered off the leaves and dropped into the water. Her eyes caught the ripple. She reached out, grazing a fern by the well. At her touch, it spread a fine, spiderwebbed light throughout its veins. She dug her fingers into the soil beside it.

"You're lying." Then, "You don't like the Rebbe Poul, do you? Is that why you don't tell him about Saul?"

"I have reasons, Rachel. Good ones."

"Because of the war? Because he's Sephardic, and can't understand?"

Please not that, Jacob, please. Because I'm half Sephardic, too—

But Jacob only said, "No. It's because he wouldn't understand."

Wouldn't. Couldn't.

Rachel closed her eyes. "I can't—don't understand."

"But not because you can't," Jacob said. "Barshak knows, and *he* is Sephardic. It's not the war, Rachel. It's something else. Something Poul wants that I can't give."

Won't.

And Jacob said, "I could tell him that any Jew is a good Jew here, but he wouldn't see it, because he *will not* look at it."

"Won't see that a Jew is a Jew?" Rachel asked. "Even if he can't operate a computer or a diamond smelt?"

Jacob smiled, and dark laughter broke within him. "Right. You are right. Thank you. That hurt, you know."

But she didn't return his smile. Her muscles tightened; she leaned forward to balance on her knees, and looked into the pool as though it were a teacup she could read fortunes in. In the water, her image joined with his.

Jacob sat back and looked out, across the pond, to a

fine spray of mist. Beyond the spray, tubes spilled out recycled water, gurgling into the pond like any waterfall. He could count the chemicals and elements used in the process, recall the exact number he used to order them in quantity. He pushed it away. *Let it be a damned mist,* he thought.

"I've never seen you pray," she said, abruptly.

He looked at her. "I pray—"

"What do you say?"

"How did you learn to ask questions like this?"

She laughed, and the sound rippled through him as his image had moved through hers on the water. "Not from the Rebbe Poul."

She moved her hand over the plant, shivering, as though its life was something electric, that moved across the leaves to her blood. "My father sang his soul to God. And God heard him."

"And you think I should sing to God as well?"

She bent her head. He brushed her hair back in place. She looked up at him and he saw very clearly what ripples he had made in her eyes. "I think I should take you back to Sara."

"Have I said something wrong?" she asked.

"No, you said nothing wrong. But it's time to go."

He led her to the outer door, away from Sara's garden growing in its strange and fertile soil, from the dreams of a water that haunted him. Away from what this girl could do, that could leave him so easily desolate, though he knew that, in her barest touch, she had left him utterly destroyed.

At Passover, the Rebbe Poul sat at the head of Jacob's table. The dining area was cramped. Of the Hasids, most wore black and sober faces. Their women served, and when there was no more food to pass around, they sat behind the men in extra chairs and ate.

The room was hot. They had to speak loudly to one

another over the constant hum of the cooling system—when they spoke at all.

Poul allowed Rabbi Meyer to perform the rites. The bread was broken and eaten. The wine, they drank together.

Beni Mott whispered to Sara and Jacob. "Poul is in a mood. What canary has the fat old cat eaten?"

"Or what soul has he taken as reaper?" Sara asked.

The reaper stood—Poul, ensconced in black, spreading his arms like the wings of a large, black bird. His voice, like the light ferns in the garden, started as a rumble and spread a tremor through his audience.

"Rabbi Meyer has asked you why this night is special, revered above all other nights. And you have answered well, as you have been taught. But it is special for another reason, also. A reason that demands celebration."

The Hasids whispered among themselves. The kibbutzniks looked at one another, raising eyebrows.

"On this night," Poul said, "I have a great occasion to announce."

"Here we go," Sara said.

Poul put his hands together. "It is . . . a wedding."

A sigh broke out among the kibbutzniks. Around the room, the Hasid students appraised one another. Barshak, sitting with them, looked around the table uneasily.

"You do well to wonder who," Poul said. "But our young scholars can relax. They have only their studies to worry about for some time yet."

Some laughter, all around the room.

"Akiva, stand up here with me," Poul said.

Akiva, a man well into his old age, came from his chair next to Rabbi Meyer to stand beside the Rebbe Poul.

"Akiva has requested a wife," Poul said. "And I have given him one. After careful consideration, I have decided that this honor, the honor of being wife to our learned brother Akiva, should be conferred upon Rivka's daughter, Rachel."

Rachel bolted from her chair. Solomon's white roe was wounded. She stood, trembling, her eyes wide and dark. Quivering, she laid her hands on the table, gathering strength to her shanks—to leap, to run.

But the Rebbe looked at her, and the heat of her dreams burst between her loins. Her body turned to salt; rivers of it pouring beneath her arms, traced a squirming line down her belly.

Only three men noticed: Jacob, Barshak, and Poul. Poul, especially; he took in Rachel's gaze on Jacob, in the plea she held there for him.

The other Hasids congratulated old Akiva loudly; some began to sing.

"You can't do this," Jacob said to Poul, his voice barely topping the loud outbreak of singing voices.

Poul said, "You cannot stop me."

Sara touched Jacob's arm and held it firmly down on the table.

The old men at Akiva's table began to dance.

"Where, in God's name, did a rabbi learn to do what you have done?" Jacob asked. "What text has taught you to do this?"

"It is for her honor. I could have excommunicated her."

He could have excommunicated her? Jacob thought. *God, he's trying to be modern.*

"For working in the clinic?" Sara asked.

"For lying with a man."

Jacob leaned toward the Rebbe, placing his fists on the table. "What man?" he asked. "And be careful with your answer, Poul. You may yet teach me the profit of a cunning lie and gainful misunderstanding."

Poul swept his arm between them, scattering cups of wine from the table. "I do what I must to save my own."

He pointed to Rachel, who stood with her back to them, her head buried against the wall like a child in its mother's lap.

"She," Poul said, "was found naked in her bed. I have made this compromise—I have given her to a man who will have her thus. I cannot bend the law any more than that!"

"She was with *me*," Jacob said.

Poul, his tirade cut in two, his vindication both gained and lost, turned from Jacob, pale as a fury. Saying nothing, he stepped away from the table.

And Beni Mott said, "Finish it, Jacob. Tell him about Saul."

Poul stopped. "*Saul?*"

"He's in thermal," Beni said. "Half alive, half not—"

Sara said, "Beni, God—"

Poul jerked once, a spasm that racked his flesh and bones and quelled all natural movement in the man. "He is dead, then."

"He is not," Jacob said. "Let me explain."

"*He is dead.*"

"We can help him. It *can* be done, with time, research—"

"There is no resurrection for Jews, Golani."

"Let us help him!"

Poul's breath, taken like a cat sucks milk, became a swelling wind in his lungs, then a howl. "I will bury him, here, in this place that killed him. And when I am done with him, when he is in the ground with peace, I will come and clean this temple of its moneychangers and make it a place of learning. I will do that for him—*But I will bury him.*"

Jacob lunged at the Rebbe. The Rebbe fell against the wall, and Sara and Beni caught Jacob and held him back. Rachel, still against the wall, uncovered her ears and stared at Jacob.

Jacob, struggling against Sara and Beni, shouted, "Now you are Jesus Christ! If you love Saul so much, then *you* raise him from the dead! Or come to me, and beg me to do it for you."

Rabbi Meyer wailed. The Hasids gathered around the Rebbe while the women cried *"Shma, Yisrael!"* and helped him from the room. The women followed after, weeping, dragging Rachel wide-eyed behind them.

In the corner, Barshak covered his face with his hands and wept.

Early into that night's sleepshift, Barshak shook Jacob awake. "They have found Saul," he said, and as Jacob dressed, "They have taken him to the garden, to bury him there."

The Hasids gathered at the open grave. Rabbi Meyer shook dirt onto the canister, chanting words in Hebrew. Poul stood in the shadows behind him, shrunken into the ferns.

Rabbi Meyer spoke of the angel of death.

Jacob went past Meyer, to Poul. No longer angry, Jacob's words were tired and hard. "Stop it. And get your people out of here."

Poul said, "We do not leave the dead to rot in unclean liquids and metal. I will put him in the ground. That is *decent.*"

"Alive? That is *decent?* We could heal him."

"Not in your lifetime, Golani."

"Maybe tomorrow. *Listen* to me—"

"Never again."

The ferns behind Poul shivered; with the hiss of recycled water and his beard spreading fine webs around his shoulders, he looked as bent and sinister as any changeling.

"Nonetheless," Jacob said, "I am in command here,

and until I declare this boy legally dead, I will not allow you to bury him.''

The Hasid women began to weep, all but Rachel, who stood behind her mother—pale, but without tears.

Poul shot his hand in the air and took hold of the sleeve. Slowly, he tore the fabric down to the elbow. Many of the men followed suit; the tearing echoed like the hiss of adders.

Jacob turned away from Poul, setting his shoulders against the sound, against their leaving. He heard them go by the sound of weeping, that it was weaker and weaker until he could hear it no more. When he turned, he was not alone. His people were with him. Rachel stood at the well. And Rabbi Meyer stood still by the gravesite.

The old Rabbi stared into the rift of black soil, where Saul looked up at him from inside the canister with his wide blue eyes. Meyer brought his hand up to the lapel of his coat and pulled until Jacob thought it could not stand any more and would surely be torn like a limb from the old man's body. Instead, the Rabbi pulled the lapel over his eyes and stumbled from the room.

With a sigh, Jacob called for help with the disinterment.

Barshak's Log:

What is left behind, when the angel of death passes by?

The synagogue goes unfinished. It sits in the rafters of the mine, a skeleton enclosed in its fragile bubble. It has no flesh or soul. The gray steel seems charred, and the whole structure looks gutted, having never been given the flesh I had dreamed for it. I would take plastique to it, drop it into the bottom of the Pit. But I haven't the heart to see it fall. Let it be silent; let it stay a haunted place.

This has been a week of other silences, unbearable as bright light or sound. No one speaks, no one says anything.

Only the Orthodox women are happy. They have a wedding to prepare. A wedding is a beginning. You'd think they'd be sick of beginnings, and maybe they are. But this beginning brings them back. To themselves, their origins. They are happy as vindictive larks.

The men are beginning to catch on to it. They read Torah for vindication, while the women prepare to marry an unwilling daughter to an old man she will never love.

My God, oh my God, how misery loves its company.

Rachel shook. Her skin prickled at a breeze; the door opened, the door to the room where they held their worship and the books she could not read. Her mother nudged her from behind. Two other women, smiling, took her arms and passed her over the threshold.

Here, the old men had sat in their black robes and talked discourses. They had never even looked at her before, in this room. Now, they all looked at her. The women no longer touched her. But her left foot took a step, and her right foot followed. And they continued to stare, to smile, while her foot took another step.

The candles made the small room glaze with heat and wavering air. There was no solid light in the room, not a single flame to focus on. *Would the lasers in the station look like this?* she thought, *or would they be bright, and filled with color—?*

Her mother pulled on her arm. Rachel stopped. She lifted her head. They had come down the aisle, past the bar and rows of men sitting in their robes. They faced the Torah—the scrolled book half her size.

Rebbe Poul smiled down at Rachel. A shudder jumped in her bowels. He took her hand and patted it, and did not notice how cold it was.

"Rachel," he said, and smiled, though his hand held hers tight. "Today you will be espoused to your old friend Akiva. Remember when he held you on his knee? Of course not. You were only five. But you are not so young any more, hmm?" Poul smiled again, like the women had smiled. "It is time to become the rib of this man, to bear fruit to him and to our community. What do you say to this, Rachel?"

She said nothing. She only stared at him.

Poul looked past her, to her mother. Then he turned his black eyes back to her. "Rachel, do you accept Akiva?"

And she found words, a whole well of them, though not the words he wanted.

"Why do you ask me? You never asked before, what I wanted or did not."

Poul crooked his finger. Akiva came forward. He stood beside the Rebbe, very close to Rachel, his black robe almost touching her breasts. He smelled of ointments and stale powders. Rachel stepped back, one step. Her nipples tingled with the warmth of the men standing so close to her—but it was not these men she remembered.

She had been swimming. And she had risen from a well and come to know a man.

"Jacob," she whispered.

"Do you accept Akiva, Rachel?" Poul's question echoed, as though spoken far off in a dream, rippling on the water of her well until it shimmered so bright it burst behind her eyes.

She looked up at Akiva, at his old face and his hands that smelled of powders. He held out his hand, took a step closer to her.

Rachel turned.

Men stood behind her, men she had known all her life. They looked down without knowing her, knowing her, and the women did not stop them.

She cried out, pushing. The men came in waves, heavy and dark. She struggled against the currents, holding her breath under the rough, black water and searching for the opening of the well. A man pushed with her, slammed against the dark square at the door. It slid aside, opening into the light of the hall.

Without a look back, Rachel pushed past the men she had known all her life, and ran through the open door.

She walked into the open hall, into the dimmed lights of sleepshift. The voices that murmured behind held the anger of startled adders. She quickened her pace, but she would not run. Goosebumps prickled along her arms. She rubbed them as she walked.

She came to a door. They looked so much alike, these doors. But this one had a green gloss over it, like one she had seen before, where there was—

Water. A room with water and the scent of mimosa. A place to swim bare in warm water. Under the dark of the stars and the joy of being alone. The simple joy of—

The fans threw a cool splash of air against her as she opened the door. The sweat on her breasts cooled, nippling her skin, drawing out the dark points sharply. She drew in her breath, astonished at the delight of it.

But there were neither well nor stars here; the chill of the fans was suddenly cold.

She looked around the room, her eyes adjusting to the light of the dim tracers. One shape was long and low, like the bunk she slept in, close to the wall. Breathing brushed softly through the room. The place was quiet, with no noise from the outside.

Next to the wall, there were lights; nightlights. She turned them on, and the tracers threw faint, orange light through the room.

Jacob slept on the long, low bed by the wall.

Rachel covered her mouth, biting her fist to keep laughter—giddy, crazy laughter—from rushing out into the silence. She went to the closet and drew down some blankets. She undressed, shedding her sweat-drenched clothes and the sick chill with them, and wrapped herself in the fresh blankets. Then she sat by the couch, leaning her head against his knee.

The touch of her skin awakened him. He stared at her, uncomprehending. And extended his hand and met the warm, soft reality of her flesh.

"What are you doing here?" he asked.

She said nothing, but bent her head to hide her face between the mattress and his knees. He touched her hair and stroked her head. Then he unlatched the clasp at the nape of her neck. Her hair spilled over the sides of the couch.

"Rachel," Jacob said. "What are you doing here? What's wrong?"

She raised her head. Her lips were still wet.

"What's happened?" he asked.

She said, "I can't go back. I have refused them and I can't go back."

He gave her a chance to say no? Jacob thought. But he *said,* "Who have you refused?" And held his breath.

"Akiva. The Rebbe asked if I would have him."

"What did you say?"

She lifted her face to the ceiling, closing her eyes tight. For a moment, he didn't think she would answer him at all. Then she began to rock. All the muscles in her body labored, and she drew a rasping breath through the tightness of her throat. "I ran. I just ran—"

"Why?"

She spun around. Her hair swung at her face. "I don't know. I was their *sacrifice! His!* But I didn't *want* to go. He had no right to it, no right to ask it—"

Startled, she sat upright. She looked up at him, from where she crouched on the floor at his bed. Suddenly, she held his gaze as fiercely as she held herself.

Rachel stood, walked to the door—her eyes never leaving his face. At the threshold, she looked out once, then back at him.

"Please, don't go."

"You are telling me to stay?" she asked.

"I'm asking."

She looked out the door. "I think I will not stay tonight."

"Then have the sweetest dreams, wherever you rest," he said, fumbling with the words, their poetry a surprise that frightened him even more than she now did.

She stared into the hall, not really seeing it. Once again, he found himself holding his breath.

"I will come to you in the morning," she said. "Like Ruth, I have lain at your feet. I have lain at your feet and I will make you mine."

"If they let you," Jacob said.

But she was gone, as though she had been more shadow and dream than flesh and blood. Jacob lay back in his bed. The circular fans began to whir, their soft *hew, hew, hew* hovering like hummingbirds at a window. He closed his eyes to the shape of them, round and slowly moving in the shadows.

Barshak's Log:

My eternal soul may be in some jeopardy.

I helped Rachel escape the Commons Room the night she ran from her engagement. I helped her part the sea of bodies; I opened the door as she wept against it, pounding. She does not remember this, I'm sure.

But Poul remembers. And has said nothing, yet.

I have not seen her, though I have been with Jacob often enough. When I ask, he says only that Poul has barricaded her behind the wall of her mother's breasts. He does not seem worried, and this worries me.

He prays in the garden, by the pond. What do you say to a man who stands in a world he has made with his own hands, naked, with only a tallit spread across his shoulders? His words are not written. They are not even spoken.

But he believes he will be heard. And so, I think, he will.

The synagogue progresses. Jacob's people help me with it. They don't believe that he will give Rachel up against her will, and neither do I.

But the Rebbe's people believe it.

They believe it enough to come to me, to take into their hands tools they never would have touched before. They willingly help the kibbutzniks put up the walls and the roof, and walk out onto a bubble of glasure—a transparent womb hung over a pit they have more than once called hell.

They will stand over that pit, even smile and laugh into it. And as long as they stand together, they will somehow feel they are safe.

"Don't look so enthusiastic," Sara said. "Here, have some coffee."

Barshak took the cup, pulled the pumpstraw between his teeth and suckled.

Sara held on to the scaffolding ropes and sat down beside him. In the low gravity, her hair floated from her body and her clothing gaped and spread itself thin around her curves. Barshak looked into the eye of the Bell meter he held.

"What are you doing?"

"Checking weight states," he told her.

She raised an eyebrow. He shifted on the scaffolding. "Heavy plating needs a fairly normal thrust ratio to raise it to the roof. The lighter plates need very little thrust. I don't think I can teach the Hasids how to move that gently. Even tethered, they could hit the roof, maybe hurt themselves. Your people had better take care of it."

"We took care of the large plating, also," Sara said.

Barshak shrugged. "So, all right—the Hasids can do the canopy."

"The *Hasids?*" she asked. "Are you trying to tell me something?"

"Nothing I want to talk about."

She nodded, perhaps even sadly. "It's not something easily discussed. Does this mean I don't need to ask who you are betting on for tomorrow?"

"No one. Anything could happen."

"It could." She shifted on the scaffold. "Barshak, Procter has made a breakthrough on the implant. It's not tested—"

Barshak looked down into the pit. The veils of dust wavered, slid along the base of the bubble. "You'll kill him," he said.

She narrowed her eyes. "He can't get any more dead than dead and buried. It would give him a chance."

"And Poul could excommunicate us both."

"So?"

"Sara, excommunication is—"

"What? Death?" she asked.

"Yes," he whispered.

"So somehow it's worse to be kicked out than to just leave on your own?" Sara pulled on the ropes, slid closer to him. "Listen. When I was in Jerusalem, during the debates for disbanding the Mossad, we used to bait the Hasid kids with quotes. We went at them like Baptists—quoting from the New Testament. We'd say things that sounded like the commentaries, and the Hasids would get confused. They felt like they should know these quotes, but of course they didn't."

Barshak smiled. "So what happened?"

"When their rabbi found out, he gathered together a bunch of rocks. Next time we came by, the Hasid kids picked up the stones and chased us off the block. I got a broken rib out of that one, but the uproar sent a howl throughout the city. When the city is Jerusalem, that means something. The debates were stalled. The Mossad stayed in operation, conducting intelligence raids on the Syrian militia. For a little while, anyway."

Barshak smiled. "Are you suggesting that I place piles of AI crystals in front of the canopy and let us all have at one another?"

"No," Sara said. "Not that it wouldn't be a good fight. God, it would be funny—the Hasid women floating in the air and Poul hanging on to the handrails and screaming at us all."

They sat together, laughing, then fell silent.

"We could beat him," she said softly.

Barshak reached for her hand. "Maybe. If Procter's solution works. But one month and nine pregnant women don't make a baby. What can we do here that they couldn't do?"

Sara took his hand. "We can raise the dead. Come down to the lab."

In the clinic, Sara turned the laser probe to a focused point at Saul's skull. Out of the thermal, he was pale, the skin thin around his bones.

"He looks like Methuselah," Barshak said.

"As long as he doesn't smell like him, we're in business." Sara adjusted the probe; the steady stream of light widened at Saul's head. Barshak looked away from it. She enabled the digiCam's CRT, and the screen relayed the picture caught within that light.

A knot no bigger than a thumbnail focused in the dark area of the screen. "It's digitized," Barshak said.

"Has to be," Sara murmured. "No lights in the brain. No lights, no camera."

"The radioscope would give you holos—"

"Not this deep. It's too delicate."

Barshak looked at the screen, at the winding conduits that coiled around the AI, and realized with a sickened, hollow thud in his loins and his stomach that these twisted, pale wires were Saul's. Brain mass.

"You're not going to do surgery?" Barshak asked.

She didn't shake her head, barely let out her breath, but Barshak knew from the set of her shoulders what her answer was. Instead of taking up her instruments, Sara turned to her computer. Coordinates appeared over the screen, holo printouts of baud rates, block addresses, interactive ports, versions of operating systems and interactive programs—a matrix of the AI's internal logic.

Sara searched the records, punching the marker for each critical element. They began to form a packet. She named the packet "Version 2.0a." Barshak looked into the coordinates window and read the implant's serial number and version—686ZDF425, Version 2.0. Sara covered the coordinates window; the 2.0 barely showed, a faded etching on the screen. From this new window, Sara called up another file—"Procter." The icon was engraved with the Procter logo. She took from it a frame and bundled it into the 2.0a packet.

And brought up the worm.

Barshak almost grabbed her arm. He stopped himself— her hands were working the keyboard fast—but shouted, "What are you doing? You could erase the stem."

"You're thinking of a virus." She said it tight, a warning in her words and in the way she pounded the keys and clutched the optical. She pointed, clicked the optical and dragged the 2.0a packet—with the AI coordinates and the Procter frame—to the worm program. On the screen, it disappeared within the worm, as though the worm, like some soft-bellied leech, had sucked the file's raw juice and had digested it.

Barshak watched the byte count rise. When it stopped, Sara punched the baud rate and address blocks into the modem and selected wireless transport to the crystal's resonance carrier.

"The signal—" Barshak said. "You're *programming* him! Sara!"

She barely shook her head. "Not him. The AI."

"*Shma, Yisrael!*—"

She struck the Enable key.

Barshak stood, watched the worm disappear from the screen. He half expected it to pop up inside the digitized shape of the AI onto the holograph readout of brain and fluid and the foreign shape of the crystal. It did not. In fact, nothing in the room—or Saul—seemed to change.

Sara loosened her grip on the keyboard, flexed her fingers.

"What now?" Barshak asked.

"We wait. The matrix will regenerate, will form the bridge I've programmed in the worm."

Barshak took a breath, the big one he needed to speak, to ask the question. By the time he forced it into his lungs, she had stretched her muscles brutally, had walked over to Saul to check his sentience levels. Barshak asked, "What kind of bridge?"

"A protocol," she said. "An interface between the AI's operating system and the brain."

"*Sara—*" He tried again. "Sara, that wasn't Procter's solution."

She bent over Saul; her hand was quiet at his throat, the pulse beating a feathery count on her skin. "No. Not all of it," she whispered, and adjusted the airflow of the catheter in his lungs.

The next morning, three hours before the wedding, Barshak dressed in his finest black linen. The robes were stiff to him, the wide-brimmed hat heavy. The touch of his sidecurls surprised him. He had not slept.

In the Commons Room, he waited for the procession to begin.

Jacob sat on the synagogue steps. In groups, his people joined him. Moshe jostled Beni, almost set him flying against the bubble but showed at the last second that he had his hand tight around Beni's wrist. Beni shook Moshe's hand off. Pale and ready, they waited.

Jacob asked, "Where's Sara?"

Sara waited in the clinic. In a regular recovery bed, Saul was breathing on his own.

In her room, Rachel let her mother dress her in white. Her mother said nothing to her. Her lips were tight, her skin drawn hard against her cheekbones. She touched her daughter with brusque, competent gestures, buttoning the buttons at her back, fastening the clasps at her wrists. As she bent to smooth the hem of the wedding skirt, Rachel touched her head.

The old woman stopped moving, her back rigid; abruptly, she stood and walked to the table. She gathered the veil and shook it out. Her wrists were brisk; the white net fell quickly into place.

She came to Rachel, placed the veil on her head. She held the wide, delicate front piece in her hands, and fanned it over Rachel's face. Before she brought down, and closed, the fragile web, she looked hard into her daughter's face. Then she lowered the veil between them very gently.

Rachel closed her eyes tight.

"Don't cry," her mother said. "You have chosen what you have chosen. If you don't look behind you, you may be happy. Keep your eyes open. Keep them dry."

Rachel bit her lip and nodded. When she opened her eyes, she held her mother's hand.

Sara came to the synagogue by way of the venting halls. Her pace was slow. She half carried Saul, half floated him. But he made each step himself.

In the bubble, across from the synagogue, the elevator door opened. The Hasids came down the narrow access bridge, one by one taking hold of the monowalk rails to ride smoothly to the synagogue proper. They could not help but try to walk in cadence with their prayers.

Rachel was in white. She walked slowly, but held her body straight, as she had at Jacob's door eight nights before.

The Rebbe walked in front of her, with Akiva.

At the synagogue proper, the Hasids and the kibbutzniks met on the artificial grass surrounding the synagogue steps.

Barshak looked at the kibbutznik group, at its size and the low murmur of hard voices in it. He did not see Sara.

Poul took his place at the canopy. Akiva stepped beneath it. Rachel did not. Poul began the ceremony's prayer.

Barshak said, "A moment, Rebbe."

Poul lowered his hands. "What do you have to say, Barshak?"

"This woman cannot marry Akiva."

"You have a reason for this?" he asked.

"She is a harlot."

A sudden wind passed through the crowd, the breath of outraged whispers.

"That is a grave accusation, Barshak," Rabbi Meyer said.

Barshak apologized, in Hebrew. "*Harlot* is too harsh. But still, she cannot marry Akiva."

"Explain yourself," Poul rumbled, his hands twisting the text he held.

"She has lain with Jacob Golani," Barshak explained. "According to the law, as exemplified in the Book of Ruth."

Rabbi Meyer turned to Rachel. "You have offered yourself to him, then?"

"That isn't plain enough?" Barshak asked.

"I am asking Rachel."

Rachel nodded. "I have chosen him."

"That is not the law," Poul said.

"It is written," Meyer said.

At the canopy, Sara joined Jacob, stepping down from the synagogue steps. He took her hand. "I didn't see you come in."

She only smiled. "I came by way of the venting halls," she said. "I brought someone with me."

"I know what is written," Poul said, "and I say it has no bearing on this situation. She will marry Akiva."

"She will not go to him," Jacob said politely.

"Take care, Golani," Poul said. "It is also written that women caught in harlotry must be stoned."

"But she is a virgin," Barshak said.

"She is a harlot," Poul said. "In her soul if not her body. She has given her heart to this goyim Jew if she has not given her flesh to him." He turned to Jacob. "You

are behind this interference. It will not work. Stall for
years, but I will wed her today, to Akiva or *any* other
man I choose. It is a punishment fit for the both of you.''

Jacob stood, came closer to the Rebbe. "Do you think
she and I will honor it?"

Poul struck Jacob hard in the face, and pulled Rachel
out from the crowd and under the canopy. He bent her arm,
until she fell to her knees with an enraged cry. ''Take your
harlot in adultery! Take her any night and any time you
wish. But you will not have her by the law. And if you will
not live by the law, you will surely die by the law, night by
night as you lay together and by every day she is not yours."

"You would sanction adultery?"

The voice was calm, the only calm voice in the room.
Sotto voce, except that it was tired, very tired.

"She is only a harlot," it said, from the shadows of the
synagogue steps, ''if she has given herself before marriage.
And only an adulteress if she does not marry the man she
has given herself to."

Poul did not turn. He set himself in his bones. The
blood went out of him. His skin became like parchment,
with black runes written beneath his stricken eyes. He
turned to Jacob, but not toward the synagogue steps. ''You
haunt me. You have taken his mind in your crystals and captured his voice. *You know how I loved him—*"

But Jacob stared himself into the doorway of the synagogue. Poul reeled around. His feet, clothed in the magnetic boots, came up from the floor. He held to the canopy
pillars, backed himself against them as he looked wild and
blind into the darkness shrouding the synagogue doors.

At the steps of the synagogue, pale and thin, Saul held
himself still, without the flush of fever or madness. To Jacob
and Sara, he gave a ghost of a smile. But as he turned to
Poul, that smile wavered.

Barshak's Log:

As with all things that survive disaster, we have each found some beauty uncovered that we did not see before. There is a cleaner smell about the place. Jacob governs the council, and Rabbi Meyer holds service and shule at the synagogue. He is building quite the reputation for us with his scholars.

He married Jacob and Rachel by the garden well three weeks ago.

Saul is recovering. He has suffered some damage, though not as much as we had feared. Most of all, he has purged at least some of his desire to flirt with madness. Though he can access the AI easily, he has chosen to use its capacities for storage only. That is for the best, perhaps. Even with the interface to translate, it is still easy to get lost in the matrix. His own mind has become a foreign, frightening place for him, and he is exploring it more cautiously this time. Certainly, he is no longer the moth seeking to outdo the flame.

I have cut my sidecurls. I no longer go to the synagogue to sit with the men and add my voice to the commentaries.

But I am building here, things with my hands that I am proud of. I have built a kosher kitchen next to the old one. This, Rabbi Meyer received gratefully. And I enlarged the library section of the Commons Room to hold a little alcove. It's quiet there, and many come to worship. I saw Sara there yesterday, sitting on the floor before two lit candles. She was bent above them, whispering a prayer. The Rebbe calls it the kibbutz chapel, and talks of buying us a cross. But I am glad to see people come who would not have come at all before.

For the most part, Poul's voice has dwindled to mutterings in the darker corners of the synagogue. Saul says he is showing symptoms of space sickness. Yesterday, they found him huddled in a vent, murmuring songs and snatches from *the scribes. When the next shuttle comes, I think he will go with it.*

We have expanded the garden. The water in the well is clear, and I cannot help but make a wish on it.

That some day, as I sit here, sharing my thoughts with the empty pages of this book, I too will find my Rachel rising out of Jacob's well.

The Wallet and Maudie

by
Dan'l Danehy-Oakes
& Alan Wexelblat

About the Authors

As has happened once before (see WOTF II), a collaborative team has won a Contest prize. It is in fact a First Prize, for a story which was written electronically by passing it back and forth between California and Texas via modem. The authors had met only on a computer network and had never seen each other face-to-face until the story was nearly completed. That has never happened before. We are, indeed, living in the future.

Dan'l Danehy-Oakes is married to Sheila Danehy-Oakes and lives in Alameda with her, a housemate, and a boy and a girl. He has a degree in computer science and writes training manuals for Pacific Bell's marketing employees.

Alan Wexelblat works in the software field in Austin, Texas. His wife, Jennie Faries, is in theater, and his mother is a professional copy editor. He writes technical papers.

And the next time someone tells you technology has dehumanizing results, show them this. . . .

Illustrated by Todd Hamilton

Maudie woke up with someone standing by her—a Solid Citizen, who wanted to use the money machine. She grabbed her bags and pulled them out of his way. The paper was warm from the hot air that blew all night from the bank's ventilation system.

Maudie sat up in the kiosk, watching the Solid Citizen stand there, waiting for the machine to give him his money. He was looking at her with little furtive glances from the corners of his eyes. She couldn't tell if he was afraid of her or sorry for her or just repulsed by her. She wanted to grab him, to yell, *Don't look at me like that! This isn't me!*

He went on his way with a hurried, harassed air, leaving Maudie staring at the patch of condensation her breath made on the kiosk glass and at the morning traffic beyond. She gathered up the scraps she used for blankets and stuffed them into the Wanamaker's shopping bag. Then she pushed out into the cold morning and started up the street toward nowhere.

There had been a big melt yesterday. The icy slush got in everything, from the kiosk to her clothes. She still wasn't dry, and the thaw had ended overnight. The cold Philly winds cut deeper than usual; her socks felt like they were trying to gnaw her ankles off.

Every street citizen has a mantra; they are the liturgy of the streets, and you can hear them every day. Maudie's mantra was simple. "Never even had a chance," she muttered as she slogged along. There were jobs available; she knew that. But she saw herself reflected in the windows she passed and knew there were none for her.

She was thirty (almost, almost; don't accept it a minute sooner than you have to), and looked much older. The street creases and grays flesh in ways most Americans don't know and wouldn't believe. Clothing hung from her in layers— sweaters, shirts, scarves and skirts piled on thick to ward off the cold. Her bags hung from her hands, an extension of her arms.

She was about to cross Market Street when she saw the wallet.

It lay on the sidewalk, no one near it: bright green fake leather with red trim. Undoubtedly the ugliest wallet she had ever seen. People walked past it quickly, holding collars and hats against the wind, oblivious to its existence, but it shone like a beacon to Maudie.

She waded through the jostling stream of people, hating the bumping and not-quite-shoving. She looked down at the wallet for a moment, then put down one of her bags and picked it up. It was light, thin; couldn't contain much. Still, there might be a reward.

She pried at the Velcro with numb fingers. When it fell open, she almost dropped the wallet: inside was a driver's license, embossed with the official seal of the Commonwealth of Pennsylvania. Looking at the picture on that license, she knew nobody was going to pay a reward for this wallet. The name on the license was Maud Grierson. The face in the picture was hers, only a little cleaner, a little less wrinkled.

She slumped against a trash basket and sank slowly to a huddled, sitting position. Arms on knees, she buried her head in her arms, and sobbed. The face in the picture was smiling and so, so pretty. "Never had a chance," she murmured. Around her, the traffic of morning flowed, oblivious.

She wiped away her tears with the arm of a sweater. A

little corner of green stuck out of the billfold—the damned thing had some money in it after all.

She sat upright, pulled the billfold open. Or tried to: the wallet was soft and flexible, but somehow the billfold resisted Maudie's attempts to open it. She didn't try too hard; the plastic seemed so cheap.

She grabbed the corner of the bill and pulled, gently, careful not to tear it. It came out smoothly and easily, and she found herself staring at the stern face of Andrew Jackson. Another corner protruded from the billfold where the first had been. She eased out another bill and looked at the two of them.

Both bills were crisp and new, smelling like they'd just come from the mint. In fact, they had consecutive serial numbers. Her first thought was that the owner had just been to the money machine—but that was crazy, because the damn thing had no owner, and Maudie'd never had a card for a money machine in her life. Her bank hadn't got one yet when the restaurant closed, and the only bank in her life now was the one she slept against.

Another corner stuck out of the billfold.

Maudie thought about things for a while. She hadn't eaten last night; no handouts, and it was too cold to grub in the restaurant bins. She thought about the juice. She'd taken a bottle or two when the pain got to be too bad. But right now her stomach growled, her body demanded food. She needed to clear her head, get her blood moving. Then she'd know what to do.

Maudie knew a coffee shop two blocks up Market. At this hour they might be too harassed to turn her away. She folded the twenties gingerly, afraid they might pop like soap bubbles, and placed them in the pocket of her outermost blouse; the wallet went several layers in. Those kids weren't out yet. But they knew her. They might come after her again.

Wallet tucked safely away, she heaved herself to her feet

once more, picked up her bags, and went slushing up the
street, wobbling only slightly as an older man hurried out
of Market Street Station past her.

The tables were mostly full and the waitress was in a
hurry. She acted like Maudie was a regular customer. Maudie took a tiny booth in the back corner, and ordered coffee
and hotcakes with scrapple. While the caffeine and sugar
started working through her bloodstream, she let her mind
wander around the problem of the weird wallet.

She had never owned a wallet remotely like this one. Of
that much, at least, she was absolutely certain.

She was sure, too, that she had no current driver's
license. Even before *L'agneu Ivre* had gone out of business,
she'd never owned a car, and drove one perhaps twice a
year. You had to be crazy or rich to have a car in her part
of the city. She had kept a license for cashing checks more
than anything else.

Once last year she'd thought about having the license
renewed. The Solid Citizens had been unusually generous,
her belly was full, and she thought she could afford the fees.
She'd gone to the Bureau with her money and her tattered
old license and asked for the renewal form.

The lady behind the desk wore horrid, pointy glasses;
they made her look at Maudie the way a praying mantis
looks at a grasshopper. She asked to see Maudie's old
license. "This expires next week," she said, "so what we
do is give you a little form that makes it good for 90 days
or until your new license arrives. Now, is this your current
address?

Maudie glanced left, right. There was a line of people
behind her, shifting impatiently. They were staring at her.
"Uh . . . No."

The insect lady made *kt-kt* sounds. "You're supposed to
report an address change to us within six weeks. Now, what
is your current address?"

Tears welled up in Maudie's eyes, and she fled from the insect lady, from the building, from one more tie with her old life. She realized, after she left, that she'd forgotten to take her old license with her. But she never went back.

Yet here was a new one. For a brief moment she considered the possibility that there was another Maud Grierson in Philadelphia, or that someone was using her name. But the picture on the license was unquestionably hers, and much more recent than the one she'd left at the Bureau.

The waitress brought Maudie's food. "Would you like some more coffee?"

Maudie nodded without thinking; she was missing something. The Bureau lady wouldn't leave her mind, her voice kept ringing in Maudie's ears: "Now, what *is* your current address?"

In the middle of buttering her hotcakes, she jumped. The knife crashed to the table. There had to be an address on the driver's license! She craned her head back and forth, wondering who was watching: nobody. Of course. The coffee shop was full of Solid Citizens wolfing down a quick bite before heading off for their Good Jobs.

She reached slowly inside the layers that covered her inner pocket and drew out the wallet. The third corner was still sticking out of it. She pulled it out, a little less gently than before; another twenty. Briefly she considered the possibility that she might be dreaming, but she hadn't dreamt in months, and when she dreamed, the dreams were all full of overdue bills, pink slips, and demanding landlords.

The corner of another bill stuck out of the wallet. A pattern was beginning to develop here, but Maudie wasn't going to investigate it now. Even this booth was too visible, too public. If what she believed was true, she wasn't going to risk losing this baby.

She inspected the driver's license again. There was

indeed an address on it, way south, off Delaware Avenue. This, she decided, bore investigating. She had a plan.

Harry trudged up Chestnut Street, stamping through the slush. All around him, people bumped and tripped over each other, but Harry kept his space clear. A bag lady came out of the Chestnut Cafe in far too much of a hurry, and Harry had to swerve to avoid knocking her over. That was the second one today. For the umpteenth time, Harry wondered what idiot had let all these people out of the mental hospitals. In his day, vagrancy was still a *real* crime.

Another lousy Monday morning, and he was going to be late to work again. After seventeen years of shift work, he couldn't seem to get used to working 7 to 3:30. He turned up the alley to the service entrance. Several of his people waited by the door, leaning against the dumpster, shivering in the thin wind.

" 'Morning, Harry."

" 'Morning, Bryan—Gail—Steve."

He fumbled his key ring out of his overcoat pocket, but he had to take off his glove to separate out the right key. The cold made his callused fingers clumsier than usual; eventually, he managed to get the key in and the door open. He held it open so his people could go inside.

There was a clang behind him. He turned around and came face-to-alcohol-scented-face with a vent man. Before Harry could say anything, the man's eyes swelled up and he began to heave.

After ten years of working behind a precinct desk Harry knew this scene by heart . . . if that was the correct organ. He grabbed the man's collar, spun him around, and held him leaning over the dumpster while he puked his guts out.

"Good move, boss," some wiseass opined.

When the wino finished, Harry started to ask if he was all right. But the man squirmed.

"Lemme GO!"

Harry released his hold and the drunk staggered off, cursing, into the street. Harry shook his head—typical of this lousy city, he thought. Then he retrieved his keys and went into the employees' washroom.

Cleaned up, he walked out onto the sales floor. The store's morning bustle was pleasantly chaotic. Display lights accented the winter sun. The perfumes and specialty food shops laid their mixtures on the air like patches in a quilt. There was an indecipherable hum of conversation as counters were unlocked and inventory was laid out. It made Harry smile.

His people were already spread out through the store, ready to become part of the crowds. The uniformed guard sitting on his stool by the door waved to Harry. Harry waved back.

Harry was always much happier in the store than outside. Outside, the city was grey and hostile to old men. Inside, he had friends and duties. Considering how well he'd handled the Christmas rush, he was beginning to think his bosses might even be pleased with him. The rule of the world was that there weren't many good jobs for ex-cops, but Harry Duggan, John Wanamaker's Head of Store Security, was going to be the exception to the rule.

She got off the K bus and walked the remaining block and a half to the address on the license. It was an old neighborhood, and not very well kept up. It seemed to be hanging between gentrification and senility. Still, Maudie didn't feel the sense of danger she felt in center city. She smiled and waved at the old folk standing on a stoop. She didn't even mind when they stared and didn't wave back.

It was a tall old brick hotel, the kind that had been converted to monthly rentals when the new hotels had opened downtown. The placard set in the wall beside the door read "Skinners Arms Lodge: Philadelphia's Finest Historical Hotel."

Maudie raised a dubious eyebrow, climbed the dozen icy steps to the door, and went in. The lobby met all her expectations: small, dimly lit, smelling of disinfectant. On the left side of the lobby stood two ancient elevators; on the right side was a dully shining registration desk.

The man behind the desk looked like he'd been there since the Skinners Arms Lodge had been built. He was staring into a crossword puzzle magazine, without a pencil in his hand, and didn't look up until Maudie was leaning on the desk over him.

"C'n I help you, ma'am?" His voice said: I doubt it.

Maudie shook her head. "Can you tell me which is Miss Grierson's room?"

"Yes, but she hasn't arrived yet. Are those packages for her?" His eyes kept darting back to his puzzle.

Maudie thought about the question for a minute. It seemed terribly important to answer it correctly. "Well, yes. Sort of. I mean, they're mine." She shook them a bit to demonstrate possession.

He tossed his crossword magazine onto the desk, stood, turned to face Maudie. The front of his shirt was blotched with ink. "You're Miss Grierson?"

She fidgeted helplessly.

"Well, are you?" The clerk's face wore a hungry look, though in a pleasant way: he wanted her to say yes? "They said you'd be arriving today. I told them that you'd have to have proper identification to claim a prepaid room, so I hope you brought your driver's license or passport or something . . .?"

He thought she was Miss Grierson. Why did he think that? And what did he mean prepaid?

"Uh . . . Oh. Yeah." She dug the wallet out again. The clerk gave the license a perfunctory glance and pulled out a large key. "Room 334, take the elevator and turn left; it'll be on your right. Please sign here. . . ."

He held out a worn registration book that had probably been in use when Franklin Slept Here or whatever made the Skinners Arms historic. He pointed to a line that said "Rec'd: $1200 fr 3 mos." Maudie stared at it. "Right here," he said, and pointed a pen at the blank next to the "mos." Maudie thought of asking who the clerk had rec'd $1200 from, but decided she had enough to deal with for now. She signed, and the clerk handed her the key.

Room 334 turned out to be small, comfortable, and clean, which was more than Maudie could say for herself. Most of all, it was *warm*, something Maudie knew she'd felt before but couldn't remember. She threw herself across the (soft!) gray bedspread, bounced a few times to feel the bed, then shuffled through the pile of the carpet to the bathroom.

When she touched the doorknob, she jumped and stifled a little scream: the discharge hurt, a little, but the shock was more joy and recognition. How could she have forgotten? And there the spark was, like an old friend, welcoming her back to metal doorknobs in carpeted rooms.

Maudie suppressed an impulse to go shuffling around the room, zapping the lamps, the radiator, the hot plate; instead, she went into the bathroom. It was bigger than she'd expected, with a full-sized tub, sink, and white porcelain and white tile and white ceiling and white everywhere so that it was almost like being back out in the snow, only *warm*. She turned on the hot water in the sink: it knocked twice, and began steaming almost immediately.

She rubbed some on her face (trickling warm, so warm down her skin) and looked for the soap: of course, there was none; it was a residence hotel, not a transient place. She'd have to buy some.

Which brought her mind back to the most important unanswered question of the day: how much was *in* that damn wallet, anyway?

Back in the main room she sat on the bed, worked her hands in through all the layers and found the precious bit of plastic. Another Andy was sticking out of the billfold, and when she pulled it out there was another. She pulled that, laid it on the first: another. And another and another and . . .

. . . several hundred dollars later, she was brought up short by a strange feeling in her ears. She puzzled over it for several minutes before she realized what it was: they didn't hurt. For the first time since winter had really started, her ears didn't hurt.

She suddenly noticed that the pile of money was several times thicker than the wallet, which hadn't grown noticeably thinner. "A money machine," she whispered, overcome by a strange elation. "Oh, God, I got my chance."

Plans formed in her mind, fluttered away as quickly as they came.

There had to be some limit—best to plan for the future. Or was this the future; could it go on forever? She wondered whether she was dead and this heaven, but that couldn't be true because she still hurt in places.

Some kind of magic justice, then, somebody maybe rewarding her for not stealing when she'd had the chance— though that was pride more than any virtue. How much— how long?

She had to know.

She had no way to know.

"Get a job," she said. "Get cleaned up and get a job, so if it runs out you ain't back on the street." But a job required clothes, Solid Citizen clothes. And good shoes. And a real handbag, not a paper sack. And a zillion other details that made an employer want to give you a regular pay-check for regular work. All these things needed to be bought, but where to go?

Since she had been a girl, there was the Dream, one lots of kids had: turn me loose in Wanamaker's with a credit card. Well, this wasn't a credit card, but it was close enough, and before this day was through Maudie Grierson would be somebody an employer would look twice at!

In the mirror her face, months of grime streaked from the hot water, streaking again from suddenly released tears, mouthed the words. She ran back to the bathroom, scrubbed her face, her hands, did everything she could without soap. At least there was toilet paper; she used that to scrub and dry. Then she ran her fingers through her hair to simulate some kind of order. She had to be neat.

There was a cheap alarm clock on the bureau. No way of knowing it if was set right: 9:30 seemed early for a day when so much had happened. But it was still pretty early in the morning, she knew. She wouldn't make it to the store by opening, but not long after . . .

Harry walked the escalators from floor to floor. His concession to exercise—walk some, ride some, keep the paunch in line. On each floor, he checked. Sales people, floor managers, and security all got a careful once-over before he moved on. Even though most of it wasn't his direct responsibility, he still liked to be sure things were ready before he opened the store. And yes, he admitted to himself, there was a certain amount of ego-gratification in it. A sense of responsibility and feeling important that came with having a job. Mandatory retirement indeed! What did city regulations know about the worth of a man?

He took the elevator back down and made a final circuit of the main floor, quietly enjoying the sun-lit openness. Oriental images stuck with him as he made his final round.

The theme this month was Japanese and the store's decorators had added a number of displays and subtle touches designed to get the customer in the right buying mood.

By the makeup counter, the Clinique ladies were setting up to offer free facials. He made a mental note to have Gail watch the area; last time they did this promotion some lady almost lost her handbag to one of the street punks. He shook his head, wishing he could keep the evil elements of the city out, knowing it was impossible.

Harry threaded his way toward the large marble stairs that led up to the balcony where his office was. He stopped at the top of the well-worn staircase as usual, and leaned on the broad railing. He smiled, thinking of other kings surveying their demesnes from balconies. Here and now, he was king of Wanamaker's for an instant. Already the first shoppers were waiting between the two sets of glass doors, out of the kingdom of the street but not yet in his world.

Exactly as the main clock ticked over the 9:00 a.m., he nodded to Leon, the uniformed guard by the doors. Leon moved to unlock the doors and let the shoppers in, and Harry turned to unlock his office and start on the day's paperwork.

The first thing, she had decided, was to get her hair done out. However, the receptionist at the Wanamaker's salon seemed to believe that Maudie was some lower form of life. She succeeded in not noticing Maudie until Maudie leaned over the front of her desk, grabbed a pen, and used it to point at the open slot in the appointment book at 1:45.

"There," she said. "Put me there. Maud Grierson. Shampoo, cut, and style." She offered the pen back to the receptionist, whose pert little preppie nose wrinkled, making her look like a mutant snow rabbit.

"Will you be paying for that with your Wanamaker's

card?'' she sniffed. Clearly, her nail filing was more important than Maudie's appointment.

Maudie curled her lip. ''Wanamaker's card?''

''In cash, then. Since you aren't a regular customer—'' Maudie let out a raucous guffaw, which the receptionist did her best to ignore ''—we have to ask that you pay in advance . . .'' She trailed off, obviously hoping that this would scare Maudie away. Maudie knew it was a lie, but decided it wasn't worth challenging her. Maudie had a *much* better comeback.

Maudie pulled out the magic wallet and smiled a sweet, bitchy, dirty smile. ''How much?'' she asked and handed over three bills.

The receptionist's expression made Maudie's heart dance. She pocketed her change and walked happily back to the main sales floor.

What next?

Maudie spent about ten minutes just riding up and down the escalators looking around at all the *stuff;* stuff she used to have, stuff she'd always wanted, stuff she'd never even heard of. She remembered they were just starting to sell phones in stores when she got kicked out on the streets— now they had gazillions of them, from little plastic things that looked like they'd fall apart if you looked at them wrong to a big electronic thing that dialed for you when you said a name to it. She liked that one, but there was a phone in the hotel room and she thought that would do her just fine for now at least.

Then there were the televisions. They had great big ones like in bars, and teeny little ones you could put in your purse. Maudie thought seriously about one of those, but she had to get some clothing so she could get a job. That was what she came here for.

She'd almost forgotten.

At the top of the escalators, she shook herself, twice,

hard, and walked around to the elevator. When it came, she climbed in and pushed for the second floor. A man got in, too, but didn't push any buttons.

When the doors shut, her eyes went wide, her breath got caught in her chest. How could she have forgotten that elevators were so *small?*

"You all right, ma'am?"

The man who'd got in with her was holding her arm, steadying her. He was a nice-looking fellow, about twenty-five, with powerful shoulders and big, big hands. Maybe a bit overweight, but not fat. Something about him bothered her—something about the way he was dressed—but that was silly; it was just a little conservative, black slacks and a dark gray sport jacket, shirt and tie. But still . . .

She looked again. Jacket, yes, but surely that wasn't all? In this weather?

"Ma'am?"

Maudie shook her head to clear it. "Yeah, I'm fine. Just the heat, I guess. Bundle up for the weather and you can't go anywhere inside."

He nodded. "I know what you mean."

"So did you lose your coat, or would you rather freeze than fry?"

The stranger did a double take. He looked like he was about to say something, but the elevator stopped at two and he got off. She did too, and watched him turn the opposite direction.

She saw him again ten minutes later as she was picking out sweaters. He was holding something gray and cashmere; it looked very expensive.

And again in Lingerie, where he was fingering indifferently through the bargain-priced brassieres. She didn't say anything, but made her choices rather hurriedly and almost forgot to take her change when she hurried away from the register, her arms bulging with packages.

"Ma'am?" the woman said, "don't you want . . . ?"

She spun and dropped a sweater. "Damn." She dropped the rest of the parcels on the counter, took the change, stuffed it in a blouse pocket.

"You're buying so much, why don't you take a couple of these?" The clerk rummaged under the counter for a moment and produced a pair of shopping bags, obviously left over from Christmas. Red and green and with WANA-MAKER'S in white script letters.

"Shopping bags." Maudie half-smiled, sad, amused. "Wanamaker's shopping bags." Her head turned itself slowly, ten degrees left, ten right, as she slipped out of time, into the eternal now of the street.

Then the moment passed and she smiled all the way. "Thank you, miss." The clerk handed her the bags and helped her pack them.

She saw the coatless stranger again in Ladies' Shoes. Twice might be coincidence; three times was a conspiracy. Or something. She thought about confronting him.

Did he have something to do with the wallet? Or the hotel room? Maybe he was a psychiatrist. She remembered hearing about them putting strange wallets on the street and seeing what people did with them. They were trying to see if people were honest or what?

Or what. That didn't make sense; the wallet was there for her, not whoever picked it up. It had her picture in it.

Then was he going to take it away?

She didn't know, and asking him seemed like a very bad idea. So she just stared at him while he looked at the pumps with great interest.

Finally, he couldn't ignore her staring and came to her. "Ma'am?"

"Yeah?"

He looked nervous. "I couldn't help notice you watching me—in the other departments and here. Why?"

Confusion: did he think she was following him?

No. Too obvious. He wanted her to think he thought that. Unless he really thought that, in which case someone else—

But that just made her brain hurt. He was following her, had to be. Why?

So she had no choice but confrontation. "Because I think *you're* watching *me*. Following me. And I wanted to make sure. And I want to know why. Your turn."

He pursed his lips, and nodded, once quickly, then twice slowly. "All right. You've got me. My name's Bryan Kinnison, Wanamaker's store security." He reached into the pocket of his jacket and offered her his I.D. It looked real enough. "And yes, I've been watching you." He stopped talking. Apparently he thought that he'd explained himself.

"And?" She looked him in the eyes. They looked like he hadn't been sleeping well lately; the lids drooped slightly and there were the faintest dark circles under them.

"And? What do you mean, 'and'?"

This wasn't getting anywhere.

"And *why* have you been following me?"

"Oh." He smiled. "Because Harry told me to."

"Harry. . . ?"

"Harry Duggan. He's my boss. I guess he thought you looked suspicious or something. Don't ask me, lady, I just do what they tell me."

She remembered hearing that argument before, and let her face show what she thought of it.

"No, really, lady. Look, I'm really a nice guy, I'm just working my way through school. I'm sure it's a misunderstanding or something. Really. How about I'll take you up to meet Harry and he can tell you what's going on, because I sure can't."

He went to one of the store phones on the support columns and began dialing. "Just stay there, okay? We'll get this straightened out ... Hi, Harry? Bryan ... Yeah, she's right here. No, she made me ... No ... No ... Yeah. Look, do you want to talk to her? I'll bring her on up, okay? Okay. Great.'' He replaced the receiver and looked at her.

''He wants to talk to you, okay? Nobody thinks you're stealing or anything, he just wants to *talk* to you.'' He turned and headed for the stairs.

Maudie thought about not going with him. What business did they have following her around the store and watching her?

But if she didn't get this straightened out right away, they'd just be more careful not to let her see them. So she went.

Harry watched Bryan escort the lady up the stairs, trying to guess what he could about her from her looks. She was young middle-aged, probably about forty. Short. Probably thin, though who could tell under all that clothing. Stringy hair, no makeup. She was carrying a couple of left-over Christmas bags, full of her purchases.

Something about those bags bothered Harry. They gave her a funny walk, sort of leaning from side to side. With a start Harry realized she was a bag lady. In fact, he'd almost bumped into her on the street this very morning. What the heck was one of *them* doing in *his* store?

Harry was glad his cop instincts had told him to have her watched, even if Bryan had managed to screw it up. Stupid college kids, but what can you do when McDonald's is paying six bucks an hour for people to flip hamburgers? Anyway, there was definitely something wrong with a bag lady coming in and suddenly making lots of expensive purchases. And paying cash, too!

Have to get rid of her quietly, thought Harry. Can't have that sort of person bothering the *real* customers. He sat down behind his desk.

Bryan knocked on the door. "Come in," Harry called out. The door opened and the bag lady walked in. Up close Harry was sure it was the same one that had almost barged into him that morning. Harry motioned to the empty seat and waited until she sat.

She stared at him, but he ignored it and turned to Bryan instead. "Anything more to tell me?"

"No, boss."

"All right. Get back out on the floor. I'll call you if I need you."

Bryan left, closing the door softly behind him; she was still staring at Harry. He returned the stare as frankly as he could without being excessively offensive. After a few moments, it became clear she wasn't going to say anything. Harry decided on a neutral opening:

"Can I get you some coffee, Miss . . ."

"Grierson, Maud Grierson. And no, thank you. I don't want anything to drink."

Harry waited for her to add something nasty like, "from you." These sorts always blamed Harry for their problems, even though he was just trying to do his job here. But she didn't say anything more. He got up and poured himself a mugful.

"You see, Miss Grierson, we like to run a nice quiet store here. And we . . ."

" . . . And you don't want any nasty dirty street people coming in your store and upsetting the regular customers is that it?" She said it all in a rush without stopping to inhale. She looked at Harry with something like contempt in her eyes.

Harry closed his mouth and looked at her. This wasn't going the way he expected. Weren't these bag ladies all retarded or something? This one talked like she had some education. He decided to try a different tack.

• • •

Maudie stared at the flabby rent-a-cop. This old wreck was the security boss? She found it hard to believe.

And then it was easy. She still had some pride, she'd never descended to stealing, even to eat. And here she was accused of stealing when she was actually *buying* things.

He scratched his head. It was a weird gesture; it looked like he was pushing something that wasn't there out of the way first. Then he said, "Actually, ma'am, we were just wondering where you had found so much cash."

Now what the hell kind of question was that? "My chance," she muttered.

"Beg pardon?"

"I got my Chance," she repeated, louder.

"I'm afraid I don't understand," said Harry.

No. Of course he wouldn't. He was just a rent-a-cop. She relaxed a bit, sat a little less straight in the chair. How could she explain the Chance? She gazed off past the wall. That helped, sometimes, when she was trying to find words.

This time it worked. Still gazing, almost feeling like she was reading the words from somewhere outside herself, she said, "Do you know how thin the line is between your world and mine? It's as thin as the paper your paycheck is written on."

Out of the corner of her eye, she saw the rent-a-cop jump, just a little. She liked that.

"Imagine that one day you're working at a nice job. A job where you can take home $400 in tips on a good Saturday night. Then the economy starts to sour and business falls off and suddenly you're lucky to take home $40. And you discover you can't live on $1.78 per hour. That's what waitresses make, you know.

"And then it all comes crashing in: your credit cards stop working; the supermarket stops taking your checks;

your landlord gets angry, then grateful when the court order comes through and he can get rid of another deadbeat."

Suprisingly, there were tears forming in her eyes. She couldn't remember how long it had been since she'd let herself cry, and this was—what? The second time today? The third? All the self-control she'd learned on the street was slipping.

She shivered and looked straight at Harry: "I never even had a chance. But that was then. Now I got one."

The bag lady dropped something on his desk. It was, without a doubt, the ugliest wallet Harry had ever seen. Red trim bordering fake green leather—the sort of thing you expected to see cheap pimps carrying. Harry picked it up and opened it. A corner of a bill stuck up prominently from the billfold, and there was a driver's license of one Maud Grierson, age such-and-such, hair and eye color so-and-so, no driving restrictions. The license was current. He handed the wallet back to its owner, who was eyeing him apprehensively.

"I'm sorry to hear what happened to you, Miss Grierson, but I'm afraid I don't see what this . . . wallet . . . has to do with anything." He raised his eyebrows. "I still don't understand where you got all this money."

"You don't?!" Suddenly she was shouting at Harry. "Well, I'll show you!" And she pulled a bill out of the wallet and slapped it down on his desk. Then another and another and another and another. She glared at him, challenging him in some weird way.

Carefully, he picked up the bills and looked at them. They were twenties, crisp as the ones he got at the bank on paycheck-cashing day. They also had consecutive serial numbers; forgeries almost always had the same serial number. So here he was holding $100 that couldn't possibly belong to this street person, but had clearly come from her wallet. And if Bryan's report was right, she had spent nearly a thousand other dollars already. So she was clearly a paying customer. But she was also a street person. Harry sat down; he needed to think about this.

"Look," she said. "It's almost time for my haircut appointment. Can I go now?" She put the money away in one of her pockets and gathered up her bags.

"Yes, of course. I'm sorry to have kept you." Harry got up and opened the door for her. As she walked down the stairs in that funny walk of hers, Harry stood in the open doorway of his office, sipping his lukewarm coffee, and wondering about the people in his world.

The hairdresser did a decent job, but not thirty-five dollars' worth. When she came out, Maudie was still steamed, not just at the rent-a-cop, but at the hairdresser, and the whole store. How dare they treat her like dirt?

She stopped by the escalator and breathed heavily for a few moments. She couldn't see anyone who might be following her, now. But perhaps they were just more careful than before?

She had to do something. To show them she wasn't what they thought. But what?

Harry stood staring down at his desk. The weekend's accumulation of paperwork stared back at him, still mostly untouched. It had been almost an hour, but he couldn't get the bag lady out of his mind. She was too much of an anomaly. That ugly wallet. Those crisp new bills.

Suddenly the office was stifling. He had to get out and move around. There wasn't anything wrong with that, was there? She had said something about getting a haircut . . .

There was a big display of Japanese TVs over by the

electronics department, where she'd seen the phones. Maudie strolled through the aisles and examined half a dozen.
They always put the most expensive ones out front where
they'd catch your eye. There were some that did amazing
things—they'd let you put one channel up in the corner
while you watched another, or hook them up to a computer
and make nice pictures—but none of them really caught her
fancy. She had never watched that much TV even when she
had had a job.

No, she had to pick something that she'd *use*. The
phones still fascinated her, but she didn't think they'd be
any better than a regular phone. And why did she need self-
dialing until she had someone she called a lot?

Then there were the stereos. Sometimes, when her
stomach was full and the present didn't hurt too much,
Maudie would dream about the past. Never the future; she
used to imagine her future, and it had betrayed her. Instead,
she would sit and recall how it used to be when sleeping was
in beds, and a friend wasn't just anyone who didn't look like
they'd spit on her.

But most of all, when she daydreamed, it was about
dancing. Maudie had loved to dance. More Saturdays than
not she'd spend getting ready for Saturday night and a dance
club. Had they dried up when the restaurants did? Maudie
didn't know.

But the stereos looked better all the time. She walked
through the row of stereos and stared at the little portable
compact disc players. She'd seen kids skating down the
street with them last summer. She listened to the one they
had opened for the display. It sounded good; real good.

She priced them out, and started counting bills in her
hands. Enough for a nice portable model with detachable
speakers and a built-in AM/FM receiver. Not that AM
radio had been worth much since Don Rose quit WFIL.

She started to pick the heavy box off the shelf and realized she couldn't carry it and her bags.

"Can I help you with that?"

She turned around and there was the rent-a-cop—Durham? Some name like that—coming up behind her. Maudie was about to spit out something to the effect that she'd take help from him when the damned went skiing, but bit it off. There was something in the blue of his eyes that, she didn't know why, she trusted. Almost apologetic.

"Yeah. Thanks." He picked up the stereo box and walked beside her to the sales counter. "How you going to get all this stuff home? You gonna buy a Mercedes to carry it all?"

Maudie stood, mouth open, another sarcastic reply cut off at the larynx. His tone wasn't mocking at all. He really wanted to know.

She shrugged. "Guess I hadn't thought that much ahead. I can't take this on the bus, can I?"

The sales clerk, a pretty black woman Maudie's age, finished with another customer. "Hi, Harry," she said. "Lady a friend of yours?"

The cop shook his head. "No. Just a customer. I made a mistake earlier and I'm trying to make it up to her."

The clerk turned to Maudie. "Cash or charge?"

Maudie handed her the bills.

"Cash it is." She started to ring up the stereo, but the cop touched her elbow.

"Loris," he said. "Do me a favor."

She looked up from the register. "Yeah?"

"Write up for comp delivery to, uh . . ." He looked at Maudie. "Where you want it sent?"

Maudie stared for a moment. "I, haa, uh, just a minute." What was the address again? She reached into her pocket and felt lots of money, the laminated surface of the operator's license—and no wallet.

• • •

Harry knew that look; knew it in his bones. You learned it fast walking a beat in Atlantic City. The nice tourist comes back to his towel from a swim in the ocean and his wallet or his keys are gone. A pain something like regret touched his ribs as he watched the lady's face crumble. As she searched pocket after pocket and her new handbag for something they both knew was gone.

He started to say something empty and consoling, but the moment had passed. She straightened up from the inside, and pulled out the driver's license. She handed it to Delores and said, "Send it here."

Harry watched in silent wonder. What was this woman? She wasn't a bag lady any more.

When the slip was written, and the license returned, he extended his arm to her, crooked at the elbow. "Mind if I walk out with you?"

She looked at him as if seeing him for the first time. Then, pragmatically, she handed him one of her overflowing bags. "I'd like that," she said.

They walked to the elevator, and stood in silence as it carried them down to the first floor. A couple of times Harry opened his mouth to say something. But he couldn't for the life of him decide what to say that wouldn't sound banal or patronizing or rude. Finally, when he was holding the door for her and she was hefting her bags before stepping outside, he said: "Thanks for shopping here. Please come again."

She considered him for a moment, then said, "Thanks. Maybe I will." Then she left.

Maudie felt like she should be wondering what had happened, but she knew. She knew she knew.

It had to be the stereo. She knew she was getting too greedy, but she couldn't have stopped herself by then if she'd wanted to. It was her damn pride: the same pride that kept her from stealing when she was poor had screwed her up when she was rich. Could it be that only the poor could afford to be proud?

She didn't know and it didn't matter. She had a place to stay for a few months. She had—how much money? Enough, anyway. She could eat. She had clothes. The Chance wasn't gone. Just the free ride.

The bus came. Maudie climbed aboard with her bags and slid her fare into the box.

Viola Lee stepped out of her shack into the Mississippi sun, a heavy load of laundry balanced on her hip. She set the wicker basket down on a rock, careful not to get any mud on this load of whites. Last time, Mrs. Wilson had almost had a coronary and refused to pay, all because of one fleck of brown. Viola couldn't afford to have that happen any more. Inside the wood box she called home, little Kim was crying again because Viola hadn't had money to buy her formula.

Picking up a fistful of clothespins, she set about hanging the wash to dry. As she threw the last sheet over the line, a flash of green caught her eye. In the bottom of the basket was undoubtedly the ugliest wallet she had ever seen: bright green fake leather with red trim. Sticking out of the billfold was the green-and-white corner of a crisp new bill.

Dear Mom

by
Stephen C. Fisher

About the Author

Stephen C. Fisher is one of four people in this volume with some close variation of that first name. (No one knows how these things happen.) He is also a musicologist in the Philadelphia area, and has now become acquainted with WOTF writer Lucy Carroll, (Vols. I and III), a Philadelphia-area musicologist. His faculty advisor was Gene Wolf, no relation to Gene Wolfe. He was named in part, he says, for writer Steve Fisher, no relation, who was one of his father's favorites at about the time our Steve Fisher was born.

He has been published in Mitteilungen der Internationalen Stiftung Mozarteum, The Haydn Yearbook, *and* Marion Zimmer Bradley's Fantasy Magazine.

None of the above information has prepared you for the tone and events in this quietly compelling story. But, then, it's not events that make a person; it's what the person makes of the events. . . .

892-5549 La Paz
April 28, 2193

Dear Mom,
   I'm glad you enjoyed the video of Nicholas's birthday party.
He loves the shirt you sent him and wears
it all the time. It'll be worn out soon, but
he's growing so rapidly that it's really a
race to see if it lasts until it's too small.
   Everything is quiet here. I had heard
about the problem with the bandersnatch-
es that was in the news, but that was in
West Martinia, 500 km from here and
across the Thorne River. We haven't had
any trouble around here. It's about like
hearing that something's gone wrong in
Illinois—I don't worry that it's going to
bother you in Kansas City. La Paz, after
all, has more land area than Earth.
   Nicholas is looking forward to having a little sister. Three months to go, and
in this climate I can't wait to get them
over with!

   I stopped dictating and looked at the display. I wasn't
satisfied, but I wasn't sure what else to say. How do you
explain life on a frontier planet—even one that approximates

Earth to within a few percent on most counts—to a city dweller back on Mother Terra who is only dimly aware that we're not in the same solar system? Our pioneer ancestors four centuries ago would have understood La Paz a lot better than most modern Terrestrials. Video transmissions help a bit, but they're too expensive to send every week, and we had splurged to give Mom a ten-minute glimpse of her grandson's third birthday (Earth reckoning—on a planet without distinguishable seasons, we don't pay much attention to the local year). The next one would have to wait until the new baby arrived. Meanwhile, I tried to find variations on nothing-ever-happens-here to use in letters. If anything ever did happen here, it would be either impossible to explain or so worrisome-sounding that it would be best left unmentioned—if not both. I wondered if Eve's daughters, writing back to her after they left home, had the same problem. ("Seth and I are fine. Lots of rain this week, but the roof is holding.") Probably.

I stretched. Maybe I should take a nap. It was (local) Sunday—a gorgeous afternoon—and I was taking it easy (La Paz has a twenty-hour day, so the local day rarely coincides with Earth time). Nicholas and I were alone in the house. Nicholas was indeed wearing Mom's shirt; I had not exaggerated the boy's fondness for the thing. (It was bright red with stripes of something glittery—garish is too mild a word. The enthusiasm with which Nicholas wore it almost justified the outlandish amount it must have cost Mom to send it from Earth.) Sam was down at the village playing soccer. All week he works the farm and complains bitterly about the heat; on his day off he walks five kilometers each way so he can spend hours running around in the same heat kicking a ball for recreation. So do most of the other men around here. They're all crazy. I guess Eve and her daughters could have told each other that.

Then Brutus let out a whoop. Brutus is our stud lagardo.

Illustrated by Alan Gutierrez

Lagardos, in Earthly terms, are somewhat like lizards and somewhat like ground-dwelling birds, though of course they don't really have anything to do with Terrestrial categories. They stand erect on their two legs, nearly a meter tall; the ancestral forelimbs have vanished over the course of evolution, though if you know where to look when you cut one up you can still find the vestiges of the bones. They have short, stout tails for balance. More importantly, they have big, sharp beaks and big, omnivorous appetites. They are covered with iridescent scales. They weigh as much as twenty kilos full grown. In the wild they run in flocks consisting of a dominant male with his harem and their offspring. The males without harems occasionally try to oust the dominant males; the combat is savage, using beaks and the three big claws on the feet. The winner takes all; the loser is frequently killed.

For the dominant males like Brutus it's a marvelously adolescent existence. If something doesn't move, Brutus will probably try to eat it. If it does move, his first impulse is to fuck it. If that doesn't work, he tries to kill it. If he succeeds, then he may revert to the earlier mode of behavior and try to eat it. It is a matter of some debate whether one may say that Brutus's three concerns in life are eating, sex, and violence or whether he recognizes any distinction among them. Add to this the blood-red tinge of his eyes and scales (the local equivalent of hemoglobin uses iron and is red in color, though the details of the structure are different from the Terrestrial protein), the huge wattles like an Indian's war bonnet that stick up from his head when he gets excited, his loud and uncouth screams, and the fact that he stinks to high Heaven, and you can understand why Sam and I aren't entirely fond of the beast.

"Bootus sounds angry," said Nicholas. My son, of course, is devoted to the creature with the passionate intensity of which only a three-year-old is capable, even though he cannot pronounce his name and is not allowed under any circumstances to go near his pen—if he reached in a hand to pet Brutus, chances are he'd never get it back.

"So he does," I replied. Of course, Brutus always sounds angry—it's part of his philosophy of life. If there is another part to his philosophy, I haven't figured it out.

Then Ralph began to bark. Ralph is the only critter of Terrestrial ancestry on the farm other than us and Ellie the milk goat. He's a purebred La Paz varmint hound. Purebred means that all his grandparents were dogs. One of them might have been a German shepherd. Ralph is a much more philosophical sort than Brutus (so, for that matter, was Genghis Khan) and generally does not kick up a fuss unless something actually merits it. Dogs had been allowed on the planet in part because it was obvious early in the day that there was no feasible way of keeping varmints out of the crops without them; conceivably some local species might eventually be domesticated sufficiently to do the same job, but we didn't want to wait a few hundred years to find out.

Now the whole chorus began. Ellie was bleating and Brutus's harem and descendants were raising a racket that could be heard for several kilometers each way. I thought I could hear other farms up and down the valley joining in. Any self-respecting varmint would have fled to save its hearing. Unfortunately, some varmints have no self-respect, and I was beginning to think that our visitor was one of that sort. I could either stay in the house and wait it out, or I could go see for myself what the problem was. Well, they tested us for self-reliance when they were picking colonists to ship here from Earth. I logged off the computer, stood up on a chair and took my varmint gun off the rack near the ceiling (it was placed in what, we hoped, was a part of the house Nicholas could not reach; there weren't many of them). I checked it out and loaded it; I stuffed a handful of extra ammunition into my pants pocket.

"What's the matter, Mommy?" Nicholas inquired.

"I don't know, Nicholas, but I'm going to find out. Now you and Greenie stay here and keep the door shut tight until I get back, okay?" Greenie, who is a kind of six-legged lizard who likes to crawl around on the walls of our house looking for bugs to eat, looked at me with his (her? how can you tell?) usual lack of interest in anything that wasn't a bug. Nicholas wasn't much more enthusiastic about the idea, but did give me a reluctant nod. That would have to do. There was no way to keep Nicholas in the house if he really wanted to get out. A high-tech optical computer/communications console is a necessity here, even in a log cabin such as ours, no matter how incongruous it looked to me before I'd been here a while. A door with a lock, on the other hand, is generally a luxury; I hadn't seen one since last I went to the bank. Just for once I thought of all the security systems I had left behind on Earth with longing rather than disgust. The best lock in the world is no substitute for neighbors you can trust, but once in a while one would be handy.

I closed the door as securely as I could and started off across the fields. The disturbance was taking place at the far end of the farm, down by the lagardo pens. (We had put them as far from the house as possible to provide some isolation from the noise and the smell, though when the wind is from the wrong direction it doesn't help that much.) I moved cautiously down the path through the middle of the fields, which are laid out in a carefully rotated patchwork of different crops in different stages of growth: Wu's milo, greencorn, tangleweed, kews, pturnips. As I went along I started a couple of small, four-legged dragons that flew off on membranous wings, illustrating the general principle that any large critter on La Paz has one pair of limbs less than you would expect while any small one has one pair more. The crops serve mainly to feed us and the livestock; we're

too far from a town to have a market for vegetables. Our
cash crop is lagardos—live ones, hides, and eggs. Brutus
does his job well; he keeps thirty breeding females happy
and laying eggs. We take some of the eggs to eat or sell (a
ticklish job, best done at night) and let the others hatch. We
raise the young in a separate pen. By neutering the half-
grown males we keep them docile and also keep them edi-
ble. (The flesh of an adult male lagardo tastes almost
as bad as its owner smells—the same hormones are responsible—but the younger females and neutered males provide
remarkably good eating. Not that there aren't times when I
have a desperate craving for an honest-to-goodness hamburger, mind you—no cattle on La Paz—but we could do a
lot worse.) Periodically we send a batch of them to Rio
Morado or Vineville; some of the meat is shipped to Earth
as a delicacy, and there's a Terrestrial market for the hides,
too. (I know it sounds absurd to send meat and hides across
all those light-years for the luxury trade, but the alternative
would be to send the ships back empty, so the freight charges
are much lower on the Earthbound run.)

I was about halfway across the fields when I saw the
cause of the trouble, and for a moment I thought about going
back to the house and calling for help on the communicator.
It was a woodwoose. Woodwooses aren't exactly varmints;
they're too big. For that matter, as it reared up on its legs
to stare at me, I could see that it was too beautiful as well.
It looked like the deluxe, aristocratic version of Brutus: as
tall as an adult man, scales a dazzling blue-black in the sunlight. (A bandersnatch is a yet larger version of the same
thing, about the size of an Allosaurus. You fight them with
military hardware. I was glad the ones that had made the
news on Earth were five hundred kilometers away.) It stood
there for a moment, nodding its head back and forth to give
both its right and left eyes a view of the scene in front of
it. (The taxonomic group that includes most of the larger

land animals on this continent had never evolved true binocular vision.) I had seen woodwooses before, but never while still alive and free. Supposedly they weren't found in this area any more, but there was still plenty of forest for them to hide in if they so chose. They are fierce, bloodthirsty predators; the accepted wisdom had it that if one got into your livestock, that was the end of it. Between the woodwoose and our flock of young lagardos was a single fence.

The woodwoose decided to ignore me. It gave a high, keening wail and crashed into the fence with both feet, breaking off two of the wooden fenceposts at ground level; the fact that the supertough plastic webbing still held was meaningless now that there was nothing to keep it upright. The young lagardos were crowded squawking at the back of their pen, easy meat for the woodwoose. In the other pen Brutus was yelling out a challenge at the top of his not inconsiderable lungs (his harem had prudently run to the far end), but the woodwoose clearly had its mind on the business at hand.

In the same instant, as I was hesitating between attack and retreat, dear old Ralph jumped into the fray. That did it; on top of seeing six years' work being destroyed I wasn't going to let Ralph face that thing alone. The rifle I had wasn't going to be of much use against the woodwoose except at short range, so I charged.

There was a flurry of motion and the woodwoose raised its head. Ralph's head was protruding from its beak. The rest of Ralph was nowhere to be seen, making it look as if the creature had swallowed poor Ralph tailfirst, though I realized that it had simply bitten through the poor dog's neck. The scene registered intellectually, but my emotions hadn't caught up with it yet. I planted my feet, raised my rifle, and fired from maybe twenty meters away as the thing started to come at me.

I am not a bad shot, and I can show you a few varmint hides to prove it. Had I had a bigger gun I could have settled things easily enough. As it was, I swear that one bullet actually ricocheted off the thing's beak and a couple of others could have bounced off the hide around the base of the neck (does a creature with no arms have shoulders?). Then I got it in the right eye. By reflex it turned the left eye toward me and I got that, too, with my last shot. It was still charging. I thought I had wounded it mortally, and it certainly wasn't in much shape to continue the fight, but it looked ready to rampage a bit before it accepted the inevitable, so I took off in what looked like a safe direction, toward the far end of the farm.

I had chosen wrong. The thing was coming toward me, still covering ground rapidly with its huge strides, though it was growing noticeably less coordinated. This was not good for me; if the thing had been moving in a straight line, I could have dodged easily enough, but it was going in the woodwoosean equivalent of a drunkard's walk. I altered my course in the direction of a row of fruit trees we were trying to grow (downapple, mostly), but the thing was too close and I felt one huge claw scrape me in the rear end as it lurched past.

Just as I was beginning to think it could see me after all, even without eyes, it crashed into a tangle of bushes at the edge of the woods, fell over, and lay thrashing aimlessly. It was to all intents and purposes dead; I had killed it. Ralph had died too quickly to have felt any pain. I had a flesh wound. We had lost a few fenceposts and some of the crops had been trampled. The flock, however, was safe. Furthermore, I had some idea of the price of a good woodwoose hide, and it was considerable. I just hoped the creature wouldn't damage itself too badly while it finished dying. As I took some deep breaths, I began to grin with triumph.

Now that the excitement was over, my unborn daughter was getting into the act. She was a lively kid. I had already told Sam I thought this one was going to make a good soccer player. He liked the idea. Some little brat should dance on *his* bladder for five or six months sometime.

The exertion was catching up with me. I should go back to the house and put my feet up for a while. I started rehearsing what I'd say to Sam when he got home. Should I be nonchalant? Not with Ralph dead; he'd really been Sam's dog, and a good one. I started back toward the house. The wound was bothering me a bit; I should get some antiseptic on it.

Then Brutus, who had calmed down a bit, started screaming again. "What now?" I asked him, and turned in the direction of his pen. There I saw the last thing I wanted to see at that moment. The woodwoose was back, standing at the edge of the forest, undamaged and glaring in my direction alternately out of two quite penetrating eyes. No, I realized, it was not the woodwoose I had just killed. It was another woodwoose, a bigger one, with a reddish tinge to the black scales. I recalled that they did sometimes come in pairs.

Well, Janie, I thought, it's time for Ole Betsy again. I was still holding the gun, of course, though I had used up the load. I reached into my pants pocket to get more ammunition.

My pants pocket wasn't there any more. It had gone when the first woodwoose had goosed me. (How big a moose would a loose woodwoose goose—never mind.) The shells I wanted were scattered in a patch of tangleweed. I supposed if I wanted to spend an hour at it, I could find them again, or some of them, but I didn't think this was the time to hunt for them. There was more ammunition back in the house; could I get there before the woodwoose got me? I looked in the direction of the house and saw the other last thing I wanted to see just now, even less than the wood-woose—a flash of iridescence of yet another hue. Nicholas was ambling down the path in our direction.

"Nicholas!" I shouted, hoping to carry over the din of the lagardos and Ellie. "Go back to the house right now!"

"Mommy, what's happening?" Nicholas asked cheerfully, hastening in my direction.

The woodwoose was moving slowly, cautiously, out of the woods.

Jane Wilson, I thought, you have fucked unspeakably up. That thing is going to kill you, and Nicholas, and the little girl who's not even due to be born for three months yet. Then it will murder all the livestock, and if it doesn't kill Sam when he comes home alone, unarmed and unsuspecting, Sam will be as good as dead when he sees that his whole life has just been wiped out. If you had just stayed in the house—if you had gone back in and called for help instead of letting Ralph's stupid sacrifice draw you into the fight—

I shook myself out of the mood. There had to be something I could do. Hadn't there? Maybe there wasn't. Maybe if I charged the woodwoose, Ralph-style, it would be distracted from Nicholas. If I could somehow free Ellie, maybe she would occupy the creature's attention for long enough for us to get away—or—

Brutus! Of course! That stupid foul-smelling lizard was spoiling for a fight. That pea-brain stood outside in thunderstorms, dripping wet, yelling challenges at Zeus to come down and duke it out. A mere woodwoose four or five times his size would hardly seem like a good sparring partner to him. I could let him out of the cage and leave him and his new friend to fight, and by the time the woodwoose had finished him off, Nicholas and I could be safely barricaded in the house with a loaded gun. Then I could call for help—no more heroics! Send for the artillery! Call in the Patrol to nuke the beast!

What with all the commotion, the woodwoose seemed to be taking his time deciding whom to kill first. Good. I worked my way to the end of the row of trees. I was now behind the monster. I took a deep breath, propped my useless gun against the last tree (Sam's was still in the house; I could use it to hold the fort), and ran across the field to Brutus's pen.

My leg didn't like the trip, but it held me up. I ran around behind the pen, confusing the woodwoose, which stood still for a minute trying to decide on which side to chase me. I made it to the gate. The woodwoose was coming around the other way, which was just fine with me; I undogged the latch and swung the gate wide open, getting behind it so the gate was between me and the woodwoose. The gate was hardly designed to keep something like a woodwoose away, but it gave me a feeling of security that I needed rather badly just then.

Brutus came out, slowly, shifting his face from side to side just like his opponent. The woodwoose stopped and the two creatures stood there, glaring at each other with every possible combination of eyes: left-left, right-left, left-right, right-right. When you discounted Brutus's crest, which was fully erect, the woodwoose was twice as tall. Brutus was more stoutly built, but the woodwoose still outweighed him some hundred kilos to twenty. Brutus continued to scream, but the woodwoose gave a wail that was even more penetrating than Brutus's cries.

I started to back away from the tableau, hoping the woodwoose was momentarily occupied. It wasn't; it swung its head to look at me. Then Brutus struck. Suddenly Brutus was hanging from the larger creature's neck, his beak digging deep into the woodwoose's throat. The woodwoose went down, writhing in an effort to dislodge Brutus; it rolled over and kicked him again and again with its huge clawed feet, looking like a lagardo scratching itself. I hurried around the pen, going around the long way to avoid the fight. Nicholas had made it all the way down by now. I reached the corner where he was standing and then looked at the scene of the fight again. It was over. The woodwoose was writhing on the ground, its head half severed, and Brutus was standing there facing us. He shook himself to knock off some of the dirt and gore on his hide and gave a shriek—of triumph, perhaps. It was a new one to me, and I had heard plenty of uncouth noises out of him over the years.

I stood there with Nicholas, wondering what to do now. Brutus in his own way was as dangerous as the woodwoose, and I would not have put it past him to finish both of us off just for fun, but he wasn't acting hostile, at least for the moment. It seemed uncharacteristic. On the other hand, he had just killed that thing, and saved his home and family and probably mine as well—and for the first time ever, I think I was feeling some sympathy for him. I wondered if his kind fought off predators this way in the wild—I was certain they did.

"You did it, Bootus! You killed the nasty thing!" Nicholas enthused.

Brutus was eyeing Nicholas as if fascinated at seeing him close up without a fence between. I decided on a slow retreat, no sudden moves. Maybe we could get to the house and I could get the dart gun and knock him unconscious long enough to put him back in the pen. He was too violent and unpredictable to be let loose; anyone who shot him wandering around would be justified in doing so.

I took a step backward, but Nicholas broke away and ran to the lagardo. "I like you, Bootus," he said, hugging him. Brutus stood there, swinging his head from side to side as always. There was still blood from the woodwoose on his beak. He still smelled terrible.

"Nicholas, let's put Brutus back in his home, okay?"
I suggested. "Just lead him in here. Now, come along!" I
grabbed Nicholas and swooped him out of the pen as
I swung the gate shut. I fastened the latch, leaving Brutus
inside. Brutus gave a squawk, but it was too late.

We went back to the house, carefully avoiding the scene
of Ralph's death. I made a couple of calls and a half-hour
later Doctor Liu's stub-winged VTOL plane set down in the
yard with Sam and the good doctor aboard. The Doc looked
over my wound and suggested I take it a little easier until
the baby comes. I gave Nicholas a good bath (insufficient,
alas, to remove the smell of Brutus) and put him to bed
while Sam said his good-bye to Ralph.

Over dinner, the three of us discussed the affair, particularly the reasons for Nicholas's friendly reception from
Brutus. Maybe it was just the shirt; Brutus might be wired
to treat that color pattern as friendly. Maybe Brutus had
momentarily had his fill of fighting after killing the woodwoose. (Hah!) Maybe it was that Nicholas was confident
and unafraid in his approach. Maybe it was Nicholas's small
size. Maybe Brutus recognized that Nicholas was friendly.
Maybe it was a lot of things. It took thousands of years to
domesticate the dog; maybe if we keep at it as long with
lagardos we can create a strain that can serve us as something more than a meat animal. Humans have been on La
Paz for less than a century; we're still finding out how we
can fit in here. It was dark by the time the Doc decided that
I needed no further observation or that he had eaten enough
and took off.

We'll split the price we get for the woodwoose hides
and use it for nest eggs for Nicholas and his sister; they
should find a good use for it some day. Oh, and Sam scored
three goals in the soccer game. That gave me some news I
could put into the letter to Mom.

A Little Womanly Advice

by
Marta Randall

About the Author

Born in Mexico City, Marta Randall is petite, demure, the mother of two, and watch out. While two-term president of the Science Fiction Writers of America, she brought a major publishing company and a leading literary agency to their knees when they tried to set up an arrangement Marta disapproved of. The agency swiftly put out a news release saying it had never happened, and the publishing company's upper-level executive resigned to pursue other plans. When her tenure was over, Marta went back to being an expert paralegal, a planner of special-education programs for the state of California, and the author of unique SF novels such as Islands *and* The Sword of Winter.

Her work is marked by carefully worked-out speculations on social issues and cultural taboos. Tough-minded, meticulous, and, above all, decent, these are compellingly told stories set in vividly real times and places not like ours. They are persuasive, rather than militant. Marta Randall would never appear militant. . . .

I've been asked to address women who want to write, or are just beginning to write, in the field of speculative fiction. What advice would I pass on to them? What warnings should I issue? If I were me, starting my writing career now, what kind of advice from my own hard-earned experience would I think it important to pass on to me, in order to further my budding career in my field?

Okay. I can do this. You be me, and I'll talk to myself like a Dutch Aunt for a while. But, I should warn us, the route we're about to take involves a few detours, some time travel, a bit of philosophical speculation, and a black hole or two. Ready? Great.

"This isn't a story about a woman," a male writer said sternly to me, back in 1972. He was talking about my first published story.

I looked up at him, rather surprised, since the protagonist of the story was most certainly and unambiguously a woman. Perhaps, I thought, he meant the story's setting.

"Well, I suppose you could say it's about the society," I ventured.

"That is not what I meant," the male writer intoned. "Your character is just a—a *man* disguised as a woman. Not a real woman at all." And with that pronouncement, he turned and marched off, leaving me in a state of considerable astonishment. Not a real woman? What in the world did he mean?

What he meant, of course, was fairly obvious. During

the 1960s, when I did much of my early reading in science
fiction, it was not difficult to find stories of the far future,
complete with decanted babies, robotized child-care, com-
puterized futures, global government, and wives in aprons
who stayed demurely at home and (presumably) spent their
time dusting the household computer. Alternatively, other
stories featured women who were there either to (a) be
rescued by the protagonist; (b) threaten the protagonist; or
(c) sleep with the protagonist. Except for the (b) type, most
of them were astonishingly passive and, despite any advertisements to the contrary, generally inept.

My heroine, on the other hand, did not fit easily into
(a), (b), or (c). She had adventures and took risks and faced
a decision made difficult in a number of ways, some of them
emotional, and made her choice and lived with it. This, I
suspect, was what put my male writer friend in such a quan-
dary. This fictional invention of mine, to him, was neither
fish nor fowl—she didn't fit his conception of what a proper
female character should be like, and she was most emphatically not passive: hence she was really a male character in
disguise.

I would have forgotten this incident, or relegated it to
the silly-memory file, save that a few years later I was,
briefly, part of a writers' group that met occasionally for
lunch and gossip, and during one meeting a male writer
of detective stories spent the entire meal trying to make
me give him some magic formula to help him create "believable" female characters. Our conversation went roughly
as follows:

HIM: What do women want?

ME: Food. Shelter. Love. Security. Good work. Respect. Not necessarily in that order.

HIM: No, that's not what I mean. How do they get
what they want?

ME: Think about it. Work for it. Ask for it. Take it, if they have to.

HIM: No, that's still not right. Why do women want what they want?

ME (getting annoyed): Why do men want what they want?

HIM: No. I mean, what do I have to do to create a believable woman character?

ME (in some exasperation): Look, a real character acts for her or his own reasons, not only to advance the plot, right? So, a believable woman character also acts for her own reasons, from her own motivations, not just to get rescued in Chapter 6 or *schtup* the hero in Chapter 7.

HIM: That's not what I mean! Women! You can't get a straight answer from them!

I didn't empty the pitcher of beer over his head, despite great temptation.

There seemed, I thought, to be something going on here, more than one writer's insistence that a woman character had to be passive and another's insistence that women are so different from men that their motivations and emotions are opaque to the male writer. It was, I decided, simply a problem of unenlightenment, and this problem would be overcome after the feminist revolution.

Well, the revolution came, and stayed, and waxed and waned, and a few years ago, as I sat on a panel with other writers, an interviewer asked me why I write fantasy. I don't. Of my twenty-three published pieces of fiction (six novels, the rest short stuff), two qualify as fantasy and another two as horror. I thought perhaps the interviewer simply hadn't read my fiction. But I discovered he assumed that all the men on the panel wrote science fiction, and all the women wrote fantasy. Advised that all the women on the panel wrote science fiction, he then assumed that we all wrote "soft" science fiction—you know, mushy stuff about psychology or sociology or stuff like that.

I've watched the definition of science fiction narrow in the past two decades, as more women write the stuff. It used to be that genetics was a "hard" enough science, except that I've since heard Vonda McIntyre's fiction described as "soft." I sometimes think that, as women successfully write more and "harder" science fiction, the (male) purists are going to narrow the field so much that eventually only stories written in equations will qualify. And when that bastion falls, they'll have to invent some new club that the girls won't be allowed to join.

There has been, for quite a few years, a raging discussion over whether or not fantasy is ruining the field of science fiction; that is to say, whether or not fantasy novels and stories are taking the publishing slots that rightfully belong to science fiction and, more particularly, hard science fiction. Mind you, no one to my knowledge has yet come up with a definition of "science fiction" that satisfies everyone; further, it is my personal belief that *all* fiction, mainstream, detective, fantasy, speculative, or otherwise, is a form of fantasy.

So this fantasy vs. science fiction argument is not one I pay much heed to—except for my sneaking suspicion that this is simply another form of sexism rearing its head. After all, it is just uncool for male writers, critics, and readers to claim that women, per se, are ruining the field (it would take colossal chutzpa to declare that the work of Ursula LeGuin, for example, is a detriment), or that they are unfit to write the stuff. There *has* been a feminist revolution, after all. So, the subtext to the argument becomes that fantasy is, for the most part, written by women; fantasy is ruining the field, ergo women are ruining the field.

I should mention that I intensely dislike endless fantasy series novels. I also intensely dislike endless science fiction series novels, it being my personal and old-fashioned opinion that a good novel wraps itself around a discernible progression from problem through conflict to resolution, and that most series novels resolve nothing, simply leave the reader with an unpalatable tangle of unsolved plot lines which are meant only to lure the reader into the purchase of the next volume. If there is any sort of writing that is in the process of "ruining" the field of science fiction, it is anything that smacks of the shoddy, the ill- or un- thought-out, or the venal, whether it be populated by elves and dwarves, survivalists, geneticists, sociobiologists, or physicists.

So, despite the feminist (quasi) revolution, as a woman writing in speculative fiction you can still expect that some folk will automatically typify your writing not by what you write, but by who you are. That is, I think, one of the worst insults someone can offer a writer—the thing must be judged *of itself,* regardless of who wrote it or who published it or what the cover looks like. More often than not, these typifiers will be the people who don't really feel the need to read the stuff, or, worse, those who, reading the stuff, will assume that either your speculations/facts are wrong, or that someone else came up with them in your behalf. My best advice to you is: Ignore these people. The only thing worse than being a fool is arguing with one.

Do women make as much for their novels as men do? Good question. And the answer is: there is really no way of knowing. Writers tend to be fairly close-mouthed about what they make from fiction, and trying to pry information like this out of a publisher is akin to extracting teeth from a wide-awake shark. With short fiction, the answer is yes, as a woman you will make as much, per word, as men do, because almost all fiction markets pay by the word for what they publish.

Does a woman writer stand a greater or lesser chance of

being published than a man? Again, there really is no way of knowing. The roster of the Science Fiction Writers of America shows more male than female members, but that is not really indicative. My feeling is that very few editors, if any, influence their decisions based on the sex of the writer (although I do have to admit that I know of one male-female editing team, years in the past, where the man threatened to remove his name from the publication if the contents page listed only female contributors. Presumably, he would not have felt so moved if only men had filled the pages.)

Do publishers spend less money on publicity for women's books than they do for men's books? This is the shark-tooth problem again.

Do readers buy books by women as often, or enthusiastically, as they buy books by men? It's hard to tell, although I have heard professional opinions to the effect that while women will buy books regardless of the gender of the author, men shy away from books with female names on the title page (under the assumption, I guess, that they may be forced to read about Horrible Women Stuff—babies? nursing? cooking? God only knows).

It is said that in order for a woman to succeed in any field, she has to be twice as good as a man—and further said that, luckily, this is not hard. Take this very much to heart.

You're starting a career writing speculative fiction. Good for you. Don't pay too much attention to awards, or advances, or the current popularity of red-headed sword-carrying physicist-spaceship captains. Don't pay attention to what you are *supposed* to write, by virtue of your gender or your age or your race or your religion or anything else. It will be difficult, but as your career progresses, don't pay attention to how much money Ichabod T. Hack got from Flybynight Publishers for *The Hell Dragons of Centauri*, or whether it won any awards.

Do pay attention to your characters, and your pacing.

Pay attention to your facts, and get your research right. Pay attention to the style of your story; pay attention to the story's logic, whether in terms of its setting, its background, or its emotions.

Write what you want to write, and write it from the heart, with every scrap of talent and attention you possess. Write honestly, and write because the story needs to be told, not because the extra dollars would be nice, or because stories about futuristic wizards' apprentices seem to be popular, or because novels about colonies threatened by supernovas have won awards. Write what *you* want to write, and resist writing what other people think you ought to write (unless, after deep cogitation, you decide that they are not entirely crazy). Write each piece as if that piece of fiction, and that alone, will be what you are judged on 100 years hence. No self-respecting storyteller can do less. If you have done your job well enough, there will always be a market for it, and an audience.

Sure, there's sexism in the field of science fiction, to the same degree as it exists in the rest of the culture. Sure, it's sometimes tough to be taken seriously and discouragement is usually close by. And sure, in order to make it, a woman needs more strength and perseverance and self-confidence than most men do.

Luckily, this is not hard.

Prosthetic Lady

by
Paula May

About the Author

Paula May won a Contest prize with this story. Earlier, as a Finalist, she appeared in WOTF III with "Resonance Ritual," as fine a short story as any SF reader could want. It was a great pleasure to discover, with "Prosthetic Lady," that she is clearly on the path to a significant career in this field.

Her father was a department chairman at Bowling Green University in Ohio, and in the course of growing up she won prizes in poetry, ensemble singing, and drawing. She also competed at the state level in English and plane geometry, and entered a series of science fairs. She went to college as a National Merit Scholar.

And—she met her husband, David, a landscapist, while in southern England, and worked for seven years as an administrator at the Open University in London. She and David live in Sandusky, Ohio with their two daughters; not, apparently, in the sort of situation with which the following story opens. . . .

Illustrated by Dell Harris

They'd laid down smoke with the barrage, so she heard the enemy long before she saw them. She sat in the servocar at the center of the line, feeling the subsonic rumble of their approach with her electronics, yet couldn't really believe the supertanks were there until their massive cannon thrust out of the haze, great snouts tasting the air for blood. Then there was time for nothing beyond the fighting.

The enemy machines rolled forward, impervious to gunfire or rocket, melting the permafrost with their weight, squashing Jeeps, soldiers and armored cars alike into the tundra. When one of the behemoths slowed to shell retreating infantry, she sent her sappers in to set charges beside the splayed arctic treads, but the driver saw them. She watched Jacobson go down under the huge treads and Inure (or was it Loo? She'd been with them so short a time that she didn't even have the names straight yet) and then the tank turned toward her. She scuttled the servocar backward like a beetle, right into a bog.

She fought the wires that wedded her to the car, got her good leg pulled up to her chest, but the injured leg was slow, was caught up in the servoleads, wouldn't do as she willed. The metal of the car screamed before she did under the treads and screamed and screamed.

Jen thrashed awake, the dreamscream a tight whimper in her throat. Her sheets were sodden. She needed to get to water to wash the fear away but the bad leg quaked with echoes of agony and she knew better than to try to stand on it. She twisted in the bed to look at the clock. Almost ten. She remembered checking the clock at five, holding sleep at bay until then. It had come for her in the end and the nightmares with it.

Jen pushed the covers back and dragged her legs over the side of the bed. Cautiously, she shifted her weight to her feet, standing slowly. She flexed her toes, bent her knees and straightened. The electronics were sluggish, but at least the prosthesis was holding her up. She limped into the bathroom.

She turned on the sink faucet. Nothing happened. She tried the shower with no better luck. Either the water system was down again or her hall was on essential-only rotation. Jen tried to count back to her last essential-only day, but she couldn't remember the days well enough to tell them apart.

She went to the kitchen, set a bowl in the sink and tried the faucet. The water came, sluggish with the low pressure of rationing. Jen filled the bowl halfway and turned off the tap. She had only three gallons for the day. She palmed a little of the tepid water into her mouth, then washed as best she could with the rest. Drying herself with her only dishtowel, Jen thought she ought to mark off the day on her calendar so she would know when to expect the next rationed day.

Jen stepped around to the side of the kitchen cabinet, but as soon as she saw the well-marked calendar hanging there, she remembered that it was a year out of date. Several lines of five-bar gates were scratched in pencil on the wall beside the calendar. She knew the tally marks were hers but she didn't remember making them.

The public messaging system built into Jen's mailsafe chimed for attention and played the annoyingly cheerful little jingle that announced the borough market open for business. Jen looked at the five-bar gates again, wondering whether she had been keeping track of rationing or market day. She went around to the front of the cabinet and pulled open the doors. The shelves were empty. She opened the tiny refrigerator nestled under the cabinet, to find it also barren.

Jen felt sweat sheen her face, and shuddered as the little twitches started in her forearms. She had to have food. She had to go to market.

Jen picked up the two empty string bags and her credit chip from the kitchen counter. She rolled the bags up under her arm and stuck the chip in her jeans pocket. She limped across the tiny living/dining room to the entryroom and pulled open the inner door of her apartment. Then the trembling muscles balked; Jen's arms hung useless at her sides, leaving her staring stupidly at the blast barrier that held the press of strangers at bay.

She could already smell the stale, human taint of the air that circulated endlessly through the subterranean halls the government had hollowed to replace the shattered spires of Manhattan. Jen had been demobbed from the military hospital in NewWashington and it had smelled the same. Warrens, the demob Psych had called the NewCities. Warrens they might be, overcrowded, underpowered, inconvenient in a thousand ways, but the NewCities were relatively bomb-proof. The constant chafing of her prosthesis's strap kept Jen aware of the importance of living bomb-proof.

Jen forced herself to close the inner door, then turn the knob on the outer door. When the anti-terror lock clicked open, she shoved sharply on the door. It swung open violently, crashing heavily against the wall of the dim hallway beyond.

As Jen stepped through the doorway, she caught a flash of movement from the corner of her eye. She half-pivoted to face the threat, sinking into a defensive crouch. The complex motion miscued the electronics in the prosthesis and the artificial leg collapsed. Jen sprawled into the hallway, her bags flying.

The neighbor whose opening door had startled Jen dropped the garbage she had been taking to the hallway trash dumbwaiter and scurried back into her room. Jen pulled herself into a sitting position. The prosthesis trembled with bioelectronic overload, so Jen could do nothing but sit there on the floor, panting, waiting out the attack. She reached down to rub at the chafing strap.

"Are you all right?"

The words were whispered, but Jen jumped as though they'd been shouted. The neighbor was coming out again, nervously glancing up and down the passage as though expecting trouble. The neighbor was crossing the hall, was stretching out her hand. The woman meant to touch her. Jen felt the strain which already warped her face extend deep into her chest. She closed her eyes, thinking that perhaps an unseen touch would be inoffensive.

"Maybe if you stand on it." The woman took hold of Jen's arm.

Jen's whole body stiffened at the contact. Occasional touching, like brushing against someone in a crowd, was bad enough, but deliberate touching was shocking. Jen had avoided touching people for as long as she had lived in the NewCity. She couldn't quite remember why she hated being touched so, but she had long since learned not to probe the blank places too deeply: Whether the Psychs had blanked it for her or she'd done it herself, the blanks were blank for a reason.

"Ready? Now try to stand."

The neighbor woman heaved, Jen pushed, and managed to get up on her good leg, prosthesis dangling awkwardly. Cautiously, Jen set the plastic foot flat on the floor, shifting her weight onto it gradually. The leg trembled slightly, but it held.

The neighbor was still watching the hallway. Abruptly, she dropped Jen's arm, scooped up her garbage and hurried back into her own apartment with the bundle. She pulled at her outer door, her bright, dark eyes darting anxiously to and fro. Just before the door swung to, she looked back at Jen, offering a tentative smile.

Jen felt an answering grin, a slobbery, puppy-falling-over-itself sort of grin, and she shuddered. She heard the deadbolt go in, heard the clicking and scraping of other locks engaging, then heard the pressure valve hiss as the inner door closed. Jen forced the mindless rictus off her face. She turned, secured her own door deliberately and retrieved her shopping bags. Limping heavily, Jen moved down the low-ceilinged passage toward the Anti-Terror doors defending the residence hall entrance from the larger space of the market hall.

Jen stepped on the pressure plate before the inner AT doors and they slid apart. She limped onto the middle plate and the doors slid shut behind her. She waited while the security cameras took her picture in several wavelengths, then backed up against the inner doors when the All-Clear chimed, watching the lock indicator for the outer doors. When the indicator's Disengaged sign lit up, Jen launched herself at the heavy, reinforced outer door, taking the shock on her forearms. The door swung outward and she came down on her good leg in the doorway. When the electronics in her prosthesis had settled back into normal mode, she stepped through into the market hall.

Jen had moved a few steps when the door alarm went off. Looking back, she saw that the self-closing mechanism had failed to operate, and so the door stood wide open. Not securing an AT closure was still a felony, and with all those security cameras, the conviction rate was nearly 100 per cent. Jen went back and started pushing on the door. Momentum was an acceptable substitute for the strength of two good legs when opening an AT door, but useless when closing a balky one. Jen grunted and shoved awkwardly at the massive slab.

"Allow me, Ma'am."

Jen's head whipped around. She stared into the bewhiskered face of the burly vendor whose stall stood opposite the residence hall doorway. Jen's body threatened flight, but she suppressed the reaction savagely, stepping back out of the man's way. He shut the door easily with his right hand.

"The terrorism died out years ago. We ought to leave 'em all open."

"Certainly make life easier for me." Jen tried to sound friendly.

The merchant chuckled and clapped her lightly on the shoulder. Jen flinched. The man didn't seem to notice. He sauntered back to his stall. Jen limped off toward the food booths, trying to keep the friendly vendor's face in sight. She wanted to see if his smile faded to pity as soon as he thought she wasn't watching, as strangers' smiles often did. The merchant met her eyes and waved. Flushing with embarrassment, Jen smiled tightly at him and hurried away.

The greengrocers had fresh fruit and no limit, so Jen endured the long lines to pay more than she could really spare from her pension for wizened, spotty apples which would have gone straight into the trash bin in her mother's kitchen. She thrust aside the thought of her mother and bit sharply into an apple as she walked away from the stall. The fruit smelled of fresh air, tasted of sunlit earth. Jen hadn't seen the sun since just after her discharge.

"Join the Marines and see the sun." She spoke aloud without thinking, was instantly mortified by the curious looks the remark earned her from passersby. The pressure of strangers' eyes squeezed Jen's throat tight, drove the air out of her lungs. She stumbled, was jostled from the back and she struck out instinctively at the danger. One went down, then another, as she fought her way clear. There was shouting and confusion, then she was out, leaning against the side of a booth, struggling to master her adrenal surge.

"Almost out of control," she muttered, muffling the words with clenched teeth. Keeping her back to the crowds, she stared over the wall of the booth at unintelligible little yellow cubes arrayed neatly on narrow shelves. Little by little the pain in her chest lessened. Her heart slowed. She realized that the cubes were butter. Packages of butter sized to put on one piece of bread. There had been a dairy in the Before Time, a place shiny with stainless steel, warm with the breath of cows. And great, pale thick wings of butter forming on the churn paddles. Her gaze moved down to the lower shelves, which held small chunks of cheese. *Bait-size,* she thought. *Well, not really. A little larger than that.*

The darting eyes of her neighbor came to mind.

A mouse, a terrified little mouse. This time the thoughts did not reach her lips. *Maybe we're all out of control, each a casualty in his own way.*

Then she remembered the touch. After she had come back from the Wars and the mine and Nome and the hospital, she had gone to the rambling house in the country her folks had bought for their retirement and been forced to move into when the cities became uninhabitable. There'd been no bombing in the quiet country town. The house was big and sturdy, the perfect image of home, haven, safety.

There her parents had stood on the porch, up all those damnable steps, and she'd dragged that hunk of plastic dead weight up one riser after another, staggered across the uneven planking, reached out for her mother and felt her mother's body recoil ever so slightly as they embraced. Her father had stood to one side, silent and solemn.

Mother had cooked a huge dinner. God knew how many weeks' worth of pension went to pay for the food, all foods intended to build up Jen's strength, mostly foods Jen

happened to dislike. Mother talked over dinner, talked over
the dishes afterward, talked over the TV when the government news hour came, her voice shrilling with fatigue. Dad
never said a word. That night bombs had shrieked down
into the distant city, shattering the quiet of Mother's town
as they passed over. They sounded like Mother. The next
morning, Jen had left the house before her parents awoke
and gone to live in the bombproof NewCity beneath the
ruins of the old city. In her tiny utility apartment, she had
been safely untouchable. Until the Mouselady.

Jen watched her hands pass her credit chip to the dairy
vendor with mild surprise. She hated cheese.

The Mouselady wouldn't open her door. Jen had tried
the call button. Now she was attempting to shout her way
into the room. Flashing lights up and down the hall told her
that her raised voice was registering in half the apartments
in the block.

"I'm from across the hall. I brought you some things
from the market. Your mailsafe won't accept them. I only
want to give them to you. I won't even come in."

Doors opened here and there, strangers' faces peered
out at Jen; this one curious, that one angry, all of them frightened. Jen felt her throat constrict. She turned to flee to the
safety of her own space, but paused at the sound of a bolt
being withdrawn behind her.

Hinges creaked. Jen forced herself to turn back to face
the darting eyes peering through the safety chains festoon-
ing the space between door and jamb.

Jen held up two apples and a twist of paper, sour with
the smell of cheese. "I only wanted to give you these."

The Mouselady's pale lips rounded at the sight of the
food, then twisted into a frown. Her gaze flicked continuously from one end of the hall to the other. "Why would you
want to give me that?"

"I thought maybe you were going shopping when I came barging out. I didn't want you to be hungry. You helped me."

The dark eyes ceased their crazed dance to regard Jen for a heartbeat. "Wait."

The door closed. Jen waited, feeling foolish. Finally, the chains rasped free one by one, the door opened and a trembling hand thrust from the doorway a neat paper parcel on its upturned palm. Jen took the parcel, replaced it with the fruit and cheese. The hand snatched its burden into the room. The door slammed soundly.

Jen looked around. The other doors had closed, too. She limped across to her own apartment and let herself through outer and inner doors. She settled gratefully into her only chair and carefully unwrapped the little package. She crowed with delight at the three teabags it held.

Market day was twice a week, but Jen was able to provision herself for a week in one trip, even with rationing, so she didn't go out the next market day. The vids came on only sporadically, usually to broadcast government war news, most of which was reprocessed recordings of battles from the opening years of the Wars. The NewCity's computer net was primitive at best, and often down, but it was possible to access the library delivery system. Jen was catching up on all the children's stories she had missed in youth. She kept to herself through the next week, reading and napping now and then during the day hours so she could stay awake most of the night. She'd learned that it was harder for the nightmares to get a good hold during the day. She used one of the teabags.

A week rolled around and it was market day again. Jen threw wide her outer apartment door and froze at the sight of a battered cardboard box on the floor. A bomb-sized cardboard box. She dove and rolled, coming up on her feet beside her easy chair. She put the chair between herself and the squat threat on her doorstep. As she reached for the chair cushions, a flashback struck, sharp images of flame mingling with the stink of plastique and burning flesh and searing pain. Her shattered leg spasmed and she went down heavily onto the injured knee, clutching at her head to protect her ears.

Silence stretched. Flashback faded. Jen lowered her arms and peered around the chair at the carton. A flicker of movement beyond caught her attention, and she squinted at the door across the hall. It was ajar. She thought she could make out quick, dark eyes peeping between the chains.

This was a simpler gift than death. Understanding brought momentary ennervation. Jen dropped her chin to her chest, waited out the giddiness, then rose awkwardly. She walked through the doorway, stooped and picked up the box. It was light, its contents rattling with an empty, slightly metallic jingle. Jen straightened, and smiled at the Mouselady's door.

"I'm going to market soon. If there's anything I can get for you, drop a note in my mailsafe."

Jen carried the box through her inner apartment door to her crowded little table. As she set the carton down, a strange odor teased her memory, familiar, but elusive. Gently, she opened out the tucked top flaps.

Within the box was an array of small white plastic rectangles, some quite dusty. Jen fingered one of the rectangles, discovered that it was not connected to its fellows, and gingerly lifted it from the carton. The plastic proved to be the lid of a small metal box, and as she stared at it, her eyes widened with recognition. These were spice tins! She found another layer of tins beneath the first. She began popping open little tabs on the lids, sniffing each one, carefully reclosing it before going on to the next. Each tin held something different. Some were full, others had been partially emptied, yet the emptiest of them was easily worth more than Jen's weekly pension. Together, they were worth a fortune.

When she had tested every one, Jen slowly repacked the box, considering the problem of hiding her treasure. The sterile environment of the NewCity suddenly teemed with threats to perishable wealth: rats, roaches, human thieves. Jen got up, clutching the carton, paced the measure of her spartan home, paced it again, heart picking up speed. Finally, she stopped in the kitchenette and thrust the box into her oven, engaging the cleaning lock after she closed the door. The odor of the Mouselady's gift lingered in the air.

The mailsafe chimed. Jen went over to the readout panel and found the receipt display listed a single item, passed as clean by the bomb screen. Jen keyed in the unlocking code for each of the four blast-proof locks and the chute swung smoothly inward. She reached in and drew out a delicately patterned envelope, the sort of thing she recalled from her mother's bureau.

Jen thought of the bureau, the pigeonholes neatly stacked with envelopes, glue, a stapler, the compartmented drawer filled with pens, pencils, clips, rubberbands, the vague floral scent rising from the stack of stationery sheets tucked beneath the pigeonholes. She broke the hold of the memory by tearing savagely into the envelope. Within was a sheet of matching stationery, bearing a neatly printed grocery list, folded around two hundred-dollar bills.

Jen stared at the money, unable to remember when she had last seen cash. None of the merchants were equipped to handle money, so Jen added a banking station visit to her errands. Tucking stationery and greenbacks into her pocket, she went to her doors. Cold panic raced up her spine, but she forced herself to stride out into the press of strangers.

Without the bearded vendor's help, Jen never would

have made it through the AT doors on her return. She limped heavily under the burden of three bags filled with food. She dropped one bag on the floor in front of her own door and walked unsteadily over to the Mouselady's door with the other two.

The little woman answered the buzzer promptly. Her eyebrows flicked upward, then puckered into a frown as Jen proffered the two bags.

"There is more than two hundred dollars' worth here." She staggered as the bags were shifted into her arms.

"I bought larger quantities, to thank you for the herbs and spices."

"You didn't need to do that." Brown eyes darted back and forth, to check the hallway in both directions, then returned to Jen's flushed face. "You shouldn't have carried so much."

"Was good for me. I need more exercise." Jen turned away, pressing the place where the strap rubbed.

The Mouselady's voice trembled. "Would you . . . may I make you a cup of tea?"

Jen's heart leapt into her throat. She forced herself to turn back, steeled herself to meet the little woman's eye, to refuse in a civil manner. When she met that eye, it was even more terrified than her own. She secured her groceries and went, all unwilling, to tea.

At first the time was filled with the preparations of the tea and its accompaniments, but the moment came when the women regarded each other across steaming cups and little sandwiches, wordless. Jen sipped the aromatic brew, savored its bitter edge. She ate one of the (delicate) sandwiches, then another, and another.

"You're hungry. I'll make you something more substantial." The Mouselady pushed her chair back from the table.

"I don't want any more." Jen flinched at her own words. "I mean, the sandwiches are very good, but I'm not that hungry. I'm . . . I guess I'm too used to my own company. Jumpy," she finished breathlessly.

The little woman settled back, smiling wanly. "Yes. Too much solitude makes for bad nerves. I find it very hard without my family."

"Bombed out?"

The Mouselady looked away momentarily. "No. I just can't be with them right now. What about you? Have you no family?"

"I have family, or did have last I knew. They just don't feel comfortable with me around."

"Because of your injury or the way you got it?"

Jen squirmed. "Well, both, I guess. Dad never said anything. At first, all Mother could say was that she'd told me not to go. Then all she could say was that I still had my pretty face. Over and over. Like it mattered." She could hear the voice again, uttering the same inanity without end. She squeezed her eyes shut against the memory, covered them with trembling hands.

The little woman sat quietly for some time. Then, in a soft, soothing voice she said, "You must have volunteered. I have two daughters, one fourteen, the other seventeen. The elder will be eligible for the draft soon, if this madness doesn't stop."

Jen dropped her hands. "Stop? Half the world is on the move. How can it stop?"

"It will stop when people can feed themselves."

"That sounds like the start of a sermon."

"Does it? I didn't mean it to. I'm in no position to preach to anyone."

Jen groaned inwardly. "I'm not trying to be hurtful. It just happens. I can't seem to talk to anybody without. . . . Can't seem to remember how to interact without pain." She stood abruptly.

The Mouselady rose, too. "You're not hurtful. You're hurting. I hope you're not offended. I'd like you to come again."

Jen stared at the timid little woman. "You couldn't offend me."

Bitterness twitched the older woman's lips. "You might be surprised. I'll let you out."

Jen waited as the Mouselady undid the various chains and bolts. "I forgot. My name is Jen Baker."

"Happy to meet you, Jen. My name is . . ." The Mouselady paused, considering. "I suppose it's all right. My name is Margaret Werner."

"Well, Mrs. Werner, I wouldn't mind if you wanted to come to the market with me next week."

The little woman froze with her hand on the doorknob. "Oh, no, it's really not safe, not safe at all."

Annoyance sharpened Jen's tone. "Look, if the Coalition gets this far, which I doubt, there'll be plenty of warning."

"Coalition?" Mrs. Werner pused the door open, peered up and down the hall several times before stepping aside to let Jen pass. "Comrades are the least of my worries."

Jen went out, turned to face the woman. "It's not the Coms you're afraid of?"

"No. Some time ago, I . . ." The trembling voice faltered. Mrs. Werner stared down at the floor. "I did something I shouldn't have. They'll be looking for me, to punish me."

Jen tried to look into the panic-pale face. "What kind of something?"

The little woman wouldn't meet her eyes. "Something bad," she whispered. She shut the door.

Something bad. The words echoed in Jen's head. She

stood motionless before the closed door, locked into memories of a gore-splattered bivouac, of a mission gone slightly awry. She and her partner had been decorated for the error. She shuddered, shook off the memory before it got a good hold. As she limped across to her own door, she wondered what the Mouselady meant by bad.

Jen took to shopping for two. Toting the extra groceries back from the market was very hard for her, but she accepted the pain as the price of tea and company. The banking station enquired after the source of the cash that Jen brought regularly to be changed, but Jen's tale of an elderly neighbor who distrusted banks satisfied the clerk and his computer.

Whenever Jen came to the AT doors, the bearded merchant materialized at her elbow, unfailingly cheerful, oblivious to her embarrassment. After a time, Jen found herself actually looking forward to the man's banter, although she was still not able to accept his gallantry as freely as he rendered it. She'd done nothing to deserve his kindness. Worse, something about him made her uneasy. She began to feel obligated to the man.

Returning with her purchases one market day, Jen marched up to the vendor's stall, resolved to repay his friendliness. He was processing a customer's credit chip, but acknowledged Jen's presence with an exaggerated wink. The sale completed, he turned his attention to Jen.

"I'll carry those to the doors for you," he volunteered, reaching for her groceries.

"No!" Jen snapped, wincing at her sharpness. "There's . . . I thought I'd buy something."

The merchant's joviality vanished. He shook his head. "You don't have to do that."

Jen looked at the display. Her eyebrows rose. "Linens. You sell linens." She looked up at him quizzically.

He smiled at her reaction. He laid his large, blunt-fingered hand lightly on a stack of lace tablemats. "Not your idea of a lace merchant, am I? I like linens. My mother's pride and joy was her fine collection of linens. Besides, most of my customers are ladies." He winked again.

Jen dropped her gaze quickly to the merchandise. She looked from one stack of goods to the next, desperately seeking something she could use. She felt her face flush. Her artificial leg began to shake.

"It's all pretty expensive, isn't it?" the merchant said. "Between shortages of raw materials and transportation disruptions, even the locally made stuff is sky high. Now that you know what I have, you'll know where to come next time you need household linens."

Jen's unsteady hand reached out for a dishtowel she didn't need, but came back with a small, handwoven tablecloth. The pastel shades of the delicate pattern were very like the colors glazing the fragile teacups in which the Mouselady served tea. Jen firmly resisted the urge to look at the price tag.

"This, please." As he took the cloth from her, the pressure in her chest eased.

"I'd never have guessed lilac to be your color." He took the credit chip she offered and inserted it into the reader.

"It's for my neighbor. I shop for her and she feeds me when I come in from shopping."

"Why doesn't she shop for herself?"

"She . . . hides. I don't know what from. She's scared to come out."

"People need to get out once in a while, even scared people." He handed back the credit chip and carefully wrapped the folded cloth in recycled paper. "And here all this time I thought you were toting grub home to a husband."

Jen looked up sharply from her wallet. "I've . . . n-never been m-married."

"Neither have I," the vendor replied cheerfully, handing her the wrapped cloth. "Pretty face like yours attracts lots of boyfriends, though, I bet."

Pretty face. . . . The strangeness of her mother's words in the merchant's mouth shortcircuited the flashback-suppression loops the Psychs had built in Jen's mind. She stared and saw Mark, the roguish grin as he turned to share a joke with her, the expression of surprise that washed over his face just before the blast threw them apart. Her leg took a big piece of shrapnel and she fell forward. She tried desperately to close her eyes before the next images got in but they got in anyway. His dear face registered confusion and pain, then horror as he saw her hand raise the pistol to his forehead. After that there was nothing left but blood.

Jen found herself on hands and knees in the middle of the concrete thoroughfare. She scrambled to her feet, peering anxiously about. There was no staring crowd. The vendor was balancing both of Jen's bags against one thigh while he carefully tucked her tablecloth down into one bag. He took a bag in each arm, turned his sunny smile on her.

"Ready? I'll carry these to the doors for you. Let you work that kink out of your leg. Long walk down to the food stalls, even longer back if you're carrying much. Hard."

He excused his way through the streams of people to the AT doors of Jen's residence hall. He shifted both bags into the embrace of one burly arm, cranked open the outer door with his free hand, blocked it open with his foot until he could get his right shoulder against it.

Jen stepped through the doorway, turned to hold the door with her strong hip, reaching for her groceries.

The merchant's grin relaxed into a gentler expression. "I'll be glad to carry these to your door for you."

Jen shook her head. "I'm much better now, thanks."

He held out one bag to her. "Whatever you say, Miss Baker."

Jen's fingers turned to ice. She nearly dropped the groceries. She stared up into the man's face, seeking a place for it in the Before memories or the Combat memories.

His grin flashed anew. "Credit chips have names on them, you know." He handed her the second bag. "Stop by my stall before you shop next week. I'll rig something to help you carry. Best get these doors closed or the alarm will go off. 'Bye now." He let go of the door.

She threw her good hip against the door, holding it open. "What's your name?" Anxiety raised her voice to a shout.

The merchant shouted back, "McKay, Ma'am," and grinned.

Jen winced, managed a sheepish smile. "Thank you, Mr. McKay."

"Any time, Miss Baker." The smile gentled again.

Jen's smile died. She spoke softly. "I had a boyfriend once, Mr. McKay."

He nodded. "And will have again, Miss Baker. When you're ready."

Ready? Jen stepped back from the door, let it swing shut between them. She limped through the inner doors and down the hall, examining the idea of a lover who was not Mark. She couldn't make any sense of it.

Over tea, Jen shyly handed the Mouselady her gift. Mrs. Werner unwrapped the cloth ceremoniously, then insisted upon taking up the tea things and re-laying the table with the new cloth.

As she settled back to finish her tea, Mrs. Werner sighed. "I used to love shopping. I wish it weren't so dangerous for me."

"He said you should go out."

"Who said?"

"McKay. The man I bought the tablecloth from, the man who helps me with the doors whether I want him to or not. He said even scared people need to go out sometimes."

Mrs. Werner looked confused, so Jen added "I've been saying . . . When I need to account for your cash, the extra shopping, I've said you were old and frightened of banks and of going out. I didn't think you'd want me telling much."

"I never stopped to consider that you would need to explain the money. I'm sorry."

Jen did not respond. She stared at her hands, focussing on the new blank place, trying to remember. She must have dropped the groceries, fallen; McKay must have picked the food up, yet none of that was stored in her head. All she remembered was the flashback.

Then Mrs. Werner spoke her name gently and the shame came tumbling out of Jen's mouth. "I fell down. He sounded like my mother and I thought he was Mark and I ended up falling down right in the middle of the market."

"Did you hurt yourself?"

"What?" Jen stared at the woman, couldn't understand.

"When you fell, did you hurt yourself?"

"Oh. No. When the prosthesis collapses, I usually go down on the plastic knee first. Doesn't hurt much."

Mrs. Werner nodded sympathetically. Hesitantly, she ventured, "I'm afraid I don't know who Mark is."

"Was. Who Mark was. First, he was my instructor. Then my, my friend. Then my buddy. When the Wars finally spread to Europe, we signed up as a special ops team. We were both national champions in our respective classes, see, so they took us as a team, trained us up. Bravo-Charlie team, they called us. We were good. Real good. But then he . . . got careless for a second and he died." She frowned. "No. Not quite."

She looked into the distance, puzzled by the way the details slipped away except in flashback. "The thing was, he kept trying to get up, but there wasn't anything to get up. He'd stepped right on the mine. There was nothing from the waist down. He kept saying, 'I can't get up. Help me get up, Bravo.' How could I do that? He wouldn't have liked being that kind of legless, so I shot him before he realized. Had to. The Code. Never leave your buddy alive in enemy territory.''

''Bravo? That was you?'' Mrs. Werner sounded a little hoarse.

''They started calling me Bravo Baker after my first title match, before the combat. Every time I scored a point, Mark called out, 'Bravo, Baker.' His last name was Charles, so we ended up Bravo-Charlie.''

''You were some sort of commando, operating behind the lines.''

''Behind enemy lines, such as they were.'' Images of the bivouac flashed. ''We were good, but intelligence wasn't. We were among the first to go into disputed European territory. We were the first to make contact with the enemy there.''

Intelligence had assured them that the bivouac was abandoned. They'd walked right into a nest of slumbering Russians. The soldiers had scrambled for their obsolescent M16's, but the armored commandos had blown them apart with their new, top-of-the-line concussion weapons. The soldiers hadn't had a chance. Neither did the families they had brought with them. Bravo-Charlie team had sped back to Command with the news that there was no invading army, only scattered bands of starving migrants. Command had replied by decorating the commandos and had continued to fight all over the world. Until Nome.

Jen realized that the room was silent. Mrs. Werner was busy examining one of her fingernails.

''I'm sorry. The Wars were different from what I expected.''

''That's because they aren't wars, not really.''

Jen frowned. ''That's what the papers call them.''

"I don't believe much of what I read in the papers, Dear. I worked for the Department of Agriculture, you see. Inside information."

Suspicion pinched Jen's throat. "You never said you were a Fed."

The older woman smiled. "I wasn't, really. I was a secretary. I started there long before the Wars, back when Agriculture was a poor relation, before food became all-important. The Food Wars made us into Feds, with security clearances, secret offices, Marines outside the doors."

"So how did you have access to information?"

"Before the Wars, we had an excellent system in place to monitor agricultural produce and supplies of all kinds, everything from seed corn to water shortages. When the fighting started, they expanded our capacity to include everything, even military materiel. We had data on stockpiles and supply routing. It wasn't hard to figure out what was really happening."

Jen considered the Mouselady against the backdrop of government. "What are you doing here?"

"I quit my job. I wasn't cut out for high-level government work like that."

"You just quit?"

"Well, when you're a secretary, nobody pays much attention to you. I doubt they even missed me." She busied herself with the cups and saucers, avoiding Jen's eye.

Jen found herself wondering exactly why it was that Mrs. Werner couldn't be with her family.

As soon as Jen came through the AT doors the next market day, McKay waved cheerily and beckoned to her. As she made her way through the crowds that thronged the wide hall, the man ducked behind his stall. He emerged a moment later, pushing an odd, wheeled contraption made of heavy wire. He maneuvered the thing toward Jen, leaning heavily on a padded rail that ran across the back edge of the wire enclosure, between upcurved twin handles.

"If it can take my weight without tipping, it'll take yours, no problem. Hope I guessed right on the height so you don't have to bend over to put your groceries in." He swung the vehicle around, backed out from between the handles and motioned Jen to try it out.

Jen tossed her empty bags into the cart. As she leaned on the rail, Jen realized that the basic parts of a supermarket cart had been reworked into the higher, shorter, sturdier vehicle before her. She stepped back.

"Did you weld it yourself?"

McKay nodded. "You rotate the handles up like that if you want to put your weight on the rail, but if you just want to push it, you turn the handles down, drop this metal latch over the two pins and you have a reliable single handlebar."

"I haven't seen a shopping cart for years."

"Lots of broken ones lying around up top if you know where to look."

Jen stared at him. "You go outside?"

"Couple times a month. Can't stand being shut up down here all the time."

"Isn't it dangerous?" Jen's heart-rate climbed.

"Not really. The dogs and cats are pretty wild, but they keep the rats and such in check, so I don't mind them. I have to keep an eye out for weakened buildings, but other than that it's pretty safe. No muggers anymore. Not enough people go up to make it worth their while. Of course, you can't drink the water." He chuckled.

"What about the bombs?" Perspiration slicked her forehead.

"I guess there are still thousands of solar-powered ones up there, riding the high currents on breakaway wings, but they rarely bring them down anymore. As far as I can tell, it's been nearly eighteen months since one hit here. The

Send in this card and receive a FREE GIFT!

Send in this card and you'll receive a free MISSION
EARTH POSTER while supplies last. No order required
for this Special Offer! Mail your card today!

☐ Please send me a FREE Mission Earth Poster
☐ Please send me information about other books by
   L. Ron Hubbard.

ORDERS SHIPPED WITHIN 24 HRS OF RECEIPT!

PLEASE SEND ME THE FOLLOWING:

___ Writers of The Future Volume I	$3.95	_____
___ Writers of The Future Volume II	$3.95	_____
___ Writers of The Future Volume III	$4.50	_____
___ Writers of The Future Volume IV	$4.95	_____
___ Writers of The Future Volume V	$4.95	_____
___ Writers of The Future Volumes I-V	$20.00	_____
___ MISSION EARTH hardback volumes		
(specify #s:_____)	$18.95	_____
___ MISSION EARTH set (10 vols.)	$99.95	_____
___ MISSION EARTH Vol 1 paperback	$4.95	_____
___ MISSION EARTH Vol 2 paperback	$4.95	_____
___ MISSION EARTH Vol 3 paperback	$4.95	_____
___ MISSION EARTH Vol 4 paperback	$4.95	_____
___ Battlefield Earth paperback	$4.95	_____
___ Final Blackout hardcover	$16.95	_____

CHECK AS APPLICABLE: SHIPPING*: _____

o Check/Money Order enclosed   TAX**: _____
  (Use an envelope please).

o American Express o VISA o MasterCard   **TOTAL:** _____

Card #: _____

Exp. Date: _____ Signature: _____

NAME: _____

ADDRESS: _____

CITY: _____ STATE: ____ ZIP: _____

PHONE#: _____

Call Us Now at 1-800-722-1733 (1-800-843-7389 in CA)

Copyright © 1989 Bridge Publications, Inc. All rights reserved. 3005881071

* Add $1.00 per book for shipping and handling. ** California residents add 6.5% sales tax.

shaft sirens are still operational, so if I stay within a few minutes of a NewCity shaft, I've got plenty of time between the warning and impact to get my head down. The things pack quite a punch, but they're only explosives, after all.''

"*Only* explosives?" Bravo smelled the acrid plastique vapor, the oily stench of crisped flesh. Involuntary spasm in her stump miscued the prosthesis and she kicked the cart viciously.

The car shot off into the crowd. McKay strode after it, apologized to the man it had hit, dragged it back.

"You can kick it all over. It'll come out in one piece."

Jen beat back the panic. When her throat loosened, she said, "What did you mean, only explosives? They've destroyed the cities, disrupted communications and travel, driven our larger populations underground. Doesn't sound 'only' to me."

McKay shrugged. "Twenty years ago, they might have been nuclear weapons. Thanks to the famines, nobody's crazy enough to risk contaminating viable farmland. Excuse me, Ma'am, but it looks like I've got a customer to attend to." He strolled back to his stand, leaving Jen beside her cart in the middle of the concourse.

Over his shoulder, McKay called, "You're welcome, Miss Baker."

"Thanks," Jen replied lamely. Unable to think of anything else to do, she headed off toward the food stalls, pushing the cart.

Jen's return was much easier with the cart. McKay cranked open the outer AT door for her, blocking it with his foot as she pushed the cart through. Jen paused in the doorway to thank him again.

"You didn't seem to be using the rail as you came along."

"Being able to push the weight in front of me rather

than carrying it in my arms makes a tremendous difference.
I'm hardly tired at all.''

"Good. It was worth the effort, then.'' As Jen pushed
the cart the rest of the way onto the pressure plate between
the doors, McKay added, ''The cart might be a way to get
your neighbor to come out with you. Between those handles, with that basket like a buffer in front of her, she might
feel protected enough to venture forth.''

Jen frowned. "I don't know. . . .''

"I've had some experience rehabilitating people after
all sorts of injuries and traumas. Confidence is the key. If
it would help, I'll go see her, arrange to go along with you.
She ought to get out once in a while.''

Jen felt absurdly threatened by his enthusiasm. "She's
so afraid of people. She doesn't even trust me very far. I
don't know.''

"Ask her.'' He released the outer door.

Mrs. Werner was impressed by the cart. When Jen re-
counted McKay's parting comments, however, the older
woman was all Mouselady again, wide-eyed and agitated.
She fussed over the tea things, arranging and rearranging
them for some time. Finally she poured the tea and sat back
in her chair. Jen ate and drank alone and in silence, while
Mrs. Werner picked at a slub in the cloth. Jen found her
appetite had disappeared.

"I didn't mean to upset you, spoil your tea.''

Mrs. Werner looked up from the cloth. "It's out of the
question for me to go out. He won't really come to see me,
will he?''

"I think he could be very persistent. I don't know how
far he will press me about it.''

Jen helped Mrs. Werner clear the table, considering the
problem of McKay's philanthropic zeal. As she folded the
tablecloth, Jen shook her head. "There's only one thing we
can do about McKay.''

The Mouselady looked up, all apprehension. "What?"

"You'll have to go out." At the older woman's terrified expression, Jen added, "But not as yourself. I only spoke of a scared lady. You can pretend to be an elderly, disabled, scared lady."

"In disguise?" Mrs. Werner sounded unconvinced.

"I think the second-hand stalls in Borough 2 are open tomorrow. I'll go over and see what I can find. Listen, I was trained for this sort of thing. We can't have McKay sniffing around."

Jen was very late leaving home the next market day. She walked slowly to the AT doors, keeping an eye on the old woman who walked beside her. The oldster was swathed in so many layers of ill-fitting clothes that she rustled when she moved. She leaned on the back of Jen's wire cart, clutching the edge of the rail, her small hands covered by patched black lace gloves. She had a disreputable stocking cap pulled down over her stringy gray hair, and peered nervously over her cracked bifocals with quick dark eyes.

McKay saw them as soon as they came through the outer door. He waved broadly, motioned them to join him. He finished wrapping a purchase and had sent its purchaser on her way by the time the two had made their way across the broad concourse.

"Good afternoon, Miss Baker. I see you have company today."

"Mr. McKay, my neighbor, Miss Smith."

"Miss Smith. I should be able to remember that. I am glad to see you, Miss Smith. Like the hat."

The old woman just stared at him.

Jen cleared her throat. "She didn't much want to come. Took some convincing. We don't need much today, so I thought it would be a good time for an experimental trip."

McKay turned to straighten his display. "Good idea.

You don't want to overdo. Slow's the best way." He looked over his shoulder and winked broadly at Miss Smith.

The old woman glanced quickly at Jen. Jen raised her eyebrows, shrugged. Miss Smith nodded slightly, then dropped her head a bit and pushed the cart slowly away with tiny, mincing steps.

McKay nodded approval. "That'll do. Enjoy your outing, Miss Smith. See you on the way back."

Jen smiled. "Thank you for your . . . your suggestions, Mr. McKay."

McKay waved her off. "Don't let her get too far ahead."

They went first to the greengrocers. Miss Smith stared down into the basket. She neither raised her eyes nor spoke, even when spoken to. Jen bought some fruit and they moved on to the dairy stall. Again, Miss Smith refused to communicate. Jen gave up on the whole thing and led the way home. They managed the AT doors themselves, and though McKay watched them from his stall, he did not approach them.

The two women wrestled the cart through Mrs. Werner's door on their return. Miss Smith collapsed into a chair, pulling off her cap and hair. Jen went through the groceries, putting a few perishables into the small refrigerator. When she had finished with the food, Jen sat down opposite her neighbor. The Mouselady sat and trembled.

After a while, Jen got up and put on water for tea. The whistle of the kettle roused Mrs. Werner, and she scrambled up to get the tea things ready. As they sat down to tea, the older woman spoke. "He knew, didn't he. He saw right through me. I should never have gone out. They'll find me now for sure."

"Maybe they aren't looking any more. There is a war on."

"They're looking. I know what they're like. They're looking. I'll try to escape when they come so they'll shoot me right away. I don't want to go to prison, or have my children used against me." She was twisting a little paper napkin to shreds.

Jen felt the tension, smelled the woman's fear, knew she needed some human response yet could not find one within herself. She sat, searching for something hopeful to say, finally mumbling only, "I have to go."

"Not yet. They'll assume you know. I've got to tell you, for your own safety. I wish I could tell my children. I'm frightened of the physical consequences, of course, but the thing that bothers me most is that my children will never understand why I passed classified material to the enemy."

Jen stared at the timid little lady and laughed a sharp, mirthless laugh. "You've never been near intelligence important enough to matter to anybody."

Mrs. Werner sat up very straight in her chair. "I had classified material of a sort and I gave it to the Russians."

"What kind of intelligence? Pork belly futures?"

Mrs. Werner raised her chin. "Hope. I gave the enemy hope."

Jen's stomach tightened. Mrs. Werner believed in her crime. Maybe she was mad. Maybe not. "What kind of hope?"

"The Department didn't just sit there watching the world's agricultural system collapse. The system was a house of cards, depending for its stability on unchanging weather patterns. Agriculture saw the danger. We had computer simulations of every major weather change the climatologists could come up with: Ice Ages, Mini Ice Ages, Greenhouse Effect, Solar Hyperactivity Effect, Severe Ozone Depletion Effect, warming trends, cooling trends, combinations of various factors. What we have now closely resembles the disruptions of cloud cover, precipitation and temperature patterns predicted for Greenhouse Effect modified by a prolonged cooling trend.

"The Department was preparing for weather changes. We thought we'd have more time, though. We assumed the onset would be gradual. We never dreamed the world would lose fifteen days from the growing season the first year, another twenty days the next year. . . ."

"Preparing? How do you mean preparing?"

"All sorts of things. New planting patterns, frost-inhibiting bacteria, hybridizing food crops. Especially grains. When the Wars escalated, the Department's genetic engineers had a wheat that was producing two crops a year, a very promising rice strain in trials and a field corn that germinated in cold soil, matured twice as fast as standard corn and dried fairly well on the cob when picked early. When the cities were forced underground, the team split up and kept working in small labs all over the country. They got the corn hybrid stabilized, breeding true, and sent a shipment of about two hundred pounds of seed corn to the Secretary of Agriculture a couple of years ago. I was secretary to the Secretary of Agriculture. He'd entrusted me with keys and codes. I went in the night the corn arrived, stole as much of it as I could fasten to myself with duct tape, and gave it to the tame Russian."

"They interned all the Russians after Nome."

"Most of them. They left a few, in hopes of planting misinformation with them. The one in NewWashington we called Dmitri. I don't know if that was his real name. He went to work every day in the ruins of the old Embassy, uptop. Heaven only knows what he did there. He was shadowed, of course, except I'd heard that his uptop shadow never went down the shafts and his downbelow shadow wouldn't go up top. I waited in the corner of the uptop elevator. Sure enough, Dmitri came in alone. You know how slow those AT elevators are. We managed to get most of the grain transferred before the car got to the top. I stayed in the elevator, rode it back down. When I got off, the down-below agent was gone, so I got away clean. I came straight here. We all had NewCity housing, stocked with survival rations, you see, in case things got too bad in NewWashington. One of the other secretaries was taking cancer treatments and was expected to be off work for a long time, so I switched my key for hers and I've got her apartment. They're even paying the rent. I guess they never thought to check the keys."

Jen felt nothing. Her head was somehow too heavy for her neck, so she let it drop forward. Staring at the floor, random thoughts flashed without reason to mesh them. Her heart began to pound as a dark memory rose through the confusion in her head. A young soldier with many weapons pointed at his chest, a mumbled incantation of totem words like Country and Aid and Comfort, then a human explosion as the concussion rifles, manually corrected to focus within the target instead of in front of it, became engines of vengeance at an officer's command. In the blood, Bravo found a piece of the old magic to focus herself upon.

Treason.

Bravo stared at the Mouselady, felt the warrior face come.

Mrs. Werner looked away. "I was afraid I'd see that in your eyes if you knew. I imagine that look on the faces of my daughters. I only wanted a future for them."

Bravo forced words through clenched teeth. "A future with the Coalition?"

Mrs. Werner frowned. "No. A future without the Wars. Half the world is migrating, pressing away from starvation. Huge masses of the hungry. Rivers of infiltrators. No retreat for them. Nothing left where they were. Battles and borders are ineffectual against that kind of movement. The only way to stop the migrations is to remove their cause. I tried to give the Russians a chance to feed themselves. I hoped that they would plant the corn, increase the crop systematically, that the Wars would wind down before my own children were dragged into them."

Bravo stood stiffly. "Didn't work, did it?"

"Maybe Dmitri didn't make it back home. Or, if he did, maybe it was too little, too late. I've ruined my life and the Wars will eat my children anyway."

Bravo limped over to the door. She unfastened the chains one by one.

"Don't you want your cart?"

Bravo swung the door open and lurched out without a backward glance.

Jen didn't go out at all next market day. She watched her food supply dwindle, satisfied at the thought that the Mouselady's fresh food must also be running low. Her sleeping was roiled with wild dreams and so she avoided sleep for days, until exhaustion drove her too deep for the nightmares to reach. She awoke unrested. She pulled the carton of spices from its hiding place. She opened the tins one by one and flushed their contents down the toilet.

Eventually, hunger drove Jen through the AT doors again. On the other side of the doors was McKay.

"Good morning, Miss Baker," he said.

"What's become of your cart?" he said.

"Where's Miss Smith?" he said.

Jen tried to limp past him, but he stepped in front of her.

"Miss Baker, you don't look too well. Why don't you come over here and sit. . . ."

"Leave me alone. She has my cart and I don't ever want to see her again. Now get out of my way."

McKay stepped back quickly, startled. "I'm sorry. I thought I could help." His left hand clutched rapidly several times until he stilled it with his right.

Illustrated by Dell Harris

Jen stared at the too-smooth flesh of the spasming hand, then looked up into the man's face.

He raised his brows, shrugged. "Prostheses always choose the worst moments to malfunction, don't they?"

Jen opened her mouth, found no words there and closed it again.

McKay smiled, "I wondered if you'd ever notice. Field medic. Until I got too eager about moving the wounded and stuck my hand under the neck of a poor kid who'd been booby-trapped with a grenade. They made me a rehab nurse for a while, until I started having trouble sleeping. Then they declared me unfit for duty. I recognized what you were going through. I figured you'd been in the field, too."

Jen nodded sharply. "Special ops. My partner stepped on a mine." Her eyes unfocused. "Behind lines. I had to shoot him."

"That sounds good for a few thousand nightmares."

Jen looked into his face again, frowning. McKay shook his head.

"Field medics burn out pretty fast, too, you know. We never see the ones who walk away from a fight, rarely even the walking wounded. Mostly the dead meat."

"You made it back, though. You're okay now."

"More or less. It was hard. It took a long time."

"Yeah. Okay. Sorry I got nasty with you."

"Sorry I pushed you so hard." McKay extended his live hand for a shake. Jen hesitated, then took it. The hand of a fellow vet.

McKay smiled and pushed some more. "What about your neighbor?"

Jen dropped his hand like it was hot. Glaring, she said, "I found out what she's hiding from."

"I see." McKay headed toward his stall. Over his shoulder he called, "I take it her sins are worse than yours."

Fury twisted her face into a snarl. "Yes, by God, they are."

McKay turned back.

"Try giving Aid and Comfort to the enemy. Try Treason, McKay."

"Treason? Miss Smith?"

"Not Miss Smith. Mrs. Werner. She betrayed us to the Russians."

A strange eagerness enlivened McKay's face. "Why would she do that?"

McKay's sudden intensity made Jen uneasy. "She thought if the Russians could feed themselves the Wars would stop."

"Simple-minded idea, but it might be so if we could trust the Russians to be decent."

Anger turned the world bright. "Trust the Russians? You don't know what you're talking about. You weren't there, at the Battle of Nome. I couldn't walk yet from the mine, but I could drive so I was wired into an armored servocar in the front ranks. I fought those accursed supertanks, watched them roll over my men like they were bugs to be squashed. Watched them roll over me." More Psych programming crumbled as buried memory rushed, the shattered car, twisted metal right up to where her knee should have been, the howling agony that went on and on until a medic found her, drugged her out of her skull so they could cut most of her out of the wreckage. They'd saved everything but her leg and her sanity.

Jen was shaking so badly she could hardly speak. "You . . . weren't . . . there."

"I didn't have to be there. I know what happened. Those Russian supertanks ran out of fuel. Only half the Chinese infantry carried weapons, and those were antiques. The enemy didn't stand a chance. The whole thing was a diversion. The Coalition governments couldn't feed their people anymore, but weren't about to let them walk naked into our gunsights. Unfortunately, it worked. Something like a hundred thousand Russians, Chinese and Indians came across in the north under cover of the battle, while uncounted numbers of South Americans came across the southern borders the same day. For twenty years we'd been throwing soldiers at the migrations, but they still made it into the neighborhood.''

The shaking had subsided. ''That's a damn funny version of the Battle of Nome. Nothing like the official government line.''

''No, but it's the truth and we both know it.''

Of course, it was the truth. Still classed as active special ops, Jen had been briefed between leg operations in the military hospital. She vaguely recalled trying to use her IV tube to garrote the ghoul who'd tried to debrief her.

''How did a field medic come to know so much?''

''That doesn't matter here and now. What does matter is that Margaret Werner might run off unless she's stopped. She may be gone already. You're writing off the only friend you've got because of her own account, doubtless exaggerated, of a stupid mistake. You should try to get some perspective on it, go see if she's all right. You need her more than she needs you, lady.''

Jen felt sullen. She turned away from him, limped off toward the food stalls. Something McKay had said bothered her, but she couldn't put her finger on what it was.

The greengrocer had apples with a limit of four. As Jen looked at the undersized fruit, an old thought bubbled to the surface. Each a casualty in his own way. She bought her four apples and went looking for cheese.

When Jen returned to the residence hall entrance, McKay's stall was shuttered, even though the market was hours from closing. Jen had to wrestle the outer AT door open herself. She limped onto the pressure plate between

the doors. She released the outer door, turned to face the
inner door and saw McKay standing against the wall
between the doors. He stepped around her, catching the
outer door with his foot before it could close. His face was
grim.

Jen frowned up at the security camera above the inner door. "The alarms should go off with you hiding between. . . ."

"Give me those." He pulled the bags from her hands.

"I figured she'd be low on food, so. . . . "

"Listen. Just after you left, some spook-types came
around asking questions. They had a picture."

Jen's eyes widened. McKay nodded once.

"Somebody, a bunch of somebodies, went in here a few
minutes ago. I'm not sure who they were." He set the grocery bags down against the wall.

"Let's find out who they are." Jen turned to face the
inner door. McKay released the outer door. It swung shut.
The automatic lock engaged. The inner doors slid apart.

Haze hung near the ceiling. A concussion cannon sat
halfway down the hall, still pointed at the door it had buck-
led. The gunner stood beside his weapon, intent upon something inside the blasted room. A knot of people stood beside
the twisted doorway, also watching the action within. None
of the onlookers looked like residents of the hall. The
vaunted bomb alarms were silent.

Jen slid over to the wall behind the gunner. McKay was
at her back. They moved slowly down the hall. They had
crept to within a few strides of the gunner when Margaret
Werner was dragged out into the hallway.

Her face was lumpy, already purpling, thickening
blood still oozing from her swollen nose. Her right arm
hung loose, strangely angled from a break well above her
elbow. She was clutching her abdomen and fell heavily to

the floor when the woman supporting her abruptly stepped aside. There was a buzz of chat, some laughing.

Jen's heart raced, her fingers tingled with cold. She couldn't breathe. There was wrongness here. She couldn't get hold of why. It was there, inside, somewhere deep. She had to find it. She reached past the Psych's control, past the pain to the buried place and drew the why forth.

The. Code. Calls. For. A. Clean. Kill.

Never break the Code. The Code is the only sure thing in a world gone mad with conflict. Those who are with you keep the Code. Those who do not keep the Code are not with you.

Torturing mothers of teen-aged daughters was not in the Code.

Calm washed over Bravo. Her pulse steadied. She felt her eyes narrow as a crooked smile tightened her lips. For the first time in a very long time, she knew where she stood, what to do and how to do it. The rush came, not the cold fear, but the hot glory and it felt good.

She glanced at McKay. "Stay out of my way," she whispered.

He reached out, grabbed her arm. She broke the hold easily.

The Code.

Completely sure on her feet, Bravo Baker stepped up behind the gunner and hit him with the side of her hand. He crumpled soundlessly. She rolled him over, pulled his side-arm from its holster, knelt beside the cannon. Her left hand caressed the membranes of the cannon's touchplate. The power display lit up.

"Move and you die."

Heads swiveled in unison. Eyes widened at the pistol pointed toward them. Nobody moved.

"Cannon's armed. Hands on heads. Back down the hall slowly, every one of you."

Still nobody moved.

"McKay, you get out there where I can see you."

"Miss Baker, I'm your friend."

"Move. Down the hall with the others before I make an example of you."

McKay stepped away from the wall, raising his hands above his head. He backed away from Bravo, keeping his eye on her trigger finger. "Don't shoot, Ma'am, for God's sake." As he moved past the people gathered around the door, McKay said loudly, "Ex-commando. Crazy. Better do as she says."

The rest stood their ground a moment longer, then followed McKay, backing off slowly with hands in the air. When they were a safe distance off, Bravo ordered them to spreadeagle against the walls on either side.

"Eyes on the wall right in front of you. Move a little and the pistol takes you and maybe the Comrade beside you. Move a lot and the cannon takes out the bunch of you."

McKay turned his head very slowly, until his eyes met Bravo's. She waggled the pistol warningly. McKay didn't look away, but he didn't move any more.

Keeping one eye on her prisoners, Bravo touched the release switch for the electonic gun mount, wrapped her left arm around the ceramic barrel and stood. The prosthesis sang under the weight of the gun, but it held. Bravo staggered across the hall to where her buddy sprawled.

"Charlie, you awake?"

Charlie was got up to look like a woman. Charlie was crying.

"I think you're in serious trouble, Charlie."

One of the prisoners shifted his weight and Bravo fired the pistol just over his head. He stilled.

"They think I'm part of a plot. They won't believe that I did it by myself. They want information I don't have. I don't even know how to make it up. I hurt so much."

"You'll hurt more before they're finished. I have to get you away."

"Get me away? How? To where?"

"Damn, I can't remember the extraction point for this mission. Never forgot the extraction before."

"Jen, you're not Bravo. You don't have to be any more."

"Charlie, I never have been, not as completely as you wanted me to be. But enough that I won't leave my buddy in the hands of the enemy. You know I can't let the enemy take you prisoner." Bravo's eyes never left the group of hostiles down the hall.

"They aren't the enemy, Jennifer. They're ours."

"They'll take you to some hell-hole, lock you up and throw away the key. Drug you. Wire you up. Beat you senseless forever. Sound good?"

"Of course not."

"Well, then."

One of the prisoners shouted, "It's dangerous to fire that cannon unmounted."

Bravo laughed. "I don't care, now, do I? As long as I take a few Comrades of the Coalition with me."

Charlie tried to move, gasped with the pain. Bravo looked hard at Charlie. Charlie didn't just look like a woman. Charlie was a woman. Could that be right? Then Bravo remembered. Charlie-Mark was dead. This was the new Charlie. Coded Mouselady.

"What will happen to you, Jen?"

"I'll be okay. I'll survive. Surviving I'm good at. Surviving and paying the price. You're the price for Mark. The price for you is truth. Truth here, truth outside. I'll need your family's address if I'm to get word to them. Take word to them."

"Bless you, Jennifer Baker," the Mouselady said. She recited the address slowly.

Bravo nodded. "I know that town. It's a couple exits

before my parents' place on the Interstate." She looked away from the spreadeagled hostiles, into the battered face of the Mouselady. "I bought apples today, Mrs. Werner, and some cheese. Just like that first day. Remember?"

"I remember, Dear. That was very kind."

The pistol swung down toward the Mouselady's forehead.

McKay stepped away from the wall. "Lady, don't!"

There was a muted thump as a concussion pistol blew a head apart. The pistol swung toward McKay. He raised his hands.

"Come here. Stay close to the wall."

McKay approached slowly, his gaze fixed on the pistol. When he was across from the ruined door, Bravo gestured for him to stop. He stood, hands still in the air.

Watching the prisoners at the end of the hall, Bravo said, "I never break the Code, McKay, even when it's hard. Look at poor Mrs. Werner, now."

McKay didn't look.

Bravo shortened her focus, glared at McKay. "I told you to look at her."

McKay turned his head slowly and looked at the corpse. He drew a sharp breath, the color drained from his cheeks, he swallowed noisily. He closed his eyes.

"Squeamish, McKay? Surely a field medic sees a lot worse than that. That's a fairly neat decapitation, nothing left that's big enough to recognize, just little bloody bits."

He turned toward her, opening his eyes, face contorting as he swallowed and swallowed and swallowed.

"Maybe you should try to think of something else, McKay. Like how they managed to locate Mrs. Werner so fast. I tell you who she is and what she did on my way out, and before I get home the bastards have found her, blown her door in, beaten her half to death. Have your own comm link, did you? You shouldn't have called her Margaret when I only called her Mrs. Werner."

McKay just looked at her.

"I never felt easy with you, McKay. Always watching everything, always talking to everybody, so damned interested in people you've never even seen. I should have trusted my instincts. Truth time, McKay. How did you really lose the arm?"

"I told you, I was a field medic. . . ."

Bravo dropped her aim. "I'll start with your kneecaps. Might blow your legs clean off, of course, but then, I'm not feeling too particular this morning."

"Defusing a bomb. I was on the anti-terror squad at first. I managed to get the main charge disconnected, but the detonator went off in my hand."

"So when the terrorism died out you were out of a job. Too bad. Anti-terror is an honorable profession. Informing is something else again. Going to collect some reward money, are you?"

McKay lowered his hands deliberately. "No. I'm a pro. Internal Security. I might get a promotion, though, for a spy."

"I doubt that, McKay. Please turn around. No need to raise the hands again. Just turn. I doubt that you'll be in any position to be promoted, McKay. See, the Code doesn't mention Internal Security, but the Code is very clear about informers." She dialed down the power on the pistol. "The Code says informers are spineless."

She fired at the middle of his back. The shock wave threw him forward. He landed like a crumpled toy beside Mrs. Werner's body, blood seeping through the back of his clothes from collar to belt. His scream was a thin, reedy sound.

Bravo angled the cannon toward the ceiling above the enemy prisoners and fired. The concrete began to fall in large chunks with the third blast. The bomb alarms finally went off and the AT doors sprang open to allow the tenants to escape. Frightened people boiled out of apartments up and down the hall. Bravo dropped the cannon, tucked the pistol into the waistband of her jeans, let the crowd carry her out the doors into the concourse beyond.

Rising slowly to the surface in the armored uptop elevator, Jennifer 'Bravo' Baker planned her route out of the city, along the highway to the satellite town where the Werners had lived. An unwelcome image of the big house two exits further along formed and she pushed it away as she stepped from the elevator into the long, winding access tunnel. An old thought tried to surface as she made her way among the blast baffles toward the light. A fresh breeze ruffled her hair and freed the thought.

Each a casualty in his own way. Each. Even her parents.

She reached the mouth of the tunnel, looked out over the devastated city. Bombing had reduced the tall buildings to rubble, but the streets had been largely cleared, supporting McKay's contention that there had been no bombing for some time. The ruin was wonderfully quiet, the air smelled sweet, the sun was shining.

I should have said goodbye to my folks, she thought.

I wonder if the migrants have come this far yet, she thought.

I wonder if they're friendly, she thought.

She stepped out into the sunshine.

Despite and Still
by
Marc Matz

About the Author

Marc Matz supervises the financial management of his family's cosmetics company and lives in California. His background is in entrepreneurial commerce. How, then, did the following story come to life? It's a fantasy, of a subgenre that verges on being historical fiction except the history is not always exactly like ours. There is magic in it, for one thing, and we all know that magic has never worked in our world. Thus, all the people in cultures that have lived by depending on magic rather than science have been wrong... multiple millions of people over hundreds of thousands of years. It's incredible they survived long enough to give birth to our enlightened generations.

Be that as it may, people survive by being smart, self-disciplined, and persevering at the essentials... no matter what their occupations or beliefs. And works of art—that magical result of creative engineering—speak best to their audiences when they are wise, purposeful, and unfalteringly delineated, despite and still....

She died just before dawn. I closed the book I had been reading—Estavio's *Moral Tales*—**and placed it atop the pile of** volumes that leaned perilously against my chair. I slowly rose and went to the windows and drew the heavy drapes closed. We had wanted to see the sunrise, but now I had no affection for that sight. Finally I came to her bed. I stared at her still form for a long moment, then I reached under her and changed the soiled sheets, straightened her thin limbs, and, dipping a towel in the wash basin, softly wiped her face. From the night stand I picked up a hairbrush, her favorite one, whose carved rosewood back featured a frieze of nymphs and satyrs—a very unofficial birthday gift—and used it to smooth her long white hair. After I finished, I pulled the satin quilt to her quiet breast and left the room. I did not look back.

Silence fell when I entered the crowded antechamber. They were arrayed in ranks of precedence: her sons and the other Princes of the Blood in front and, behind them in increasing number and descending rank, the Lords and Ladies of the Realm of Mistrel. I nodded to her priest and her physician, and bowed to Giovan, her firstborn and heir. The boy's face was frozen in a perfect mourning mask, but how his eyes were rich with exaltation! I hid my shudder, and passed through the entourage.

Hardly a few looked at me; too much grief, I supposed, or too much malice. Only at the rear, among the Officers of the Court, those without the privilege of birth, did

Illustrated by Lawrence Stewart

someone clasp my shoulder and stop me: the old General. He took my hand in his and tightly held it, our rings of shell brass linking together.

"Are you going to be all right?" he asked in a gruff whisper.

I shrugged.

"You served Her well."

That got a wry grin from me. "Some would say that is mine only virtue."

"Some are fools. . . . Where will you go, Damiano?"

I shrugged again. "Don't know."

He searched for words. ". . . I'll miss beating you at chess."

"I'll miss letting you win."

He glanced toward the Princes. They had entered her bedroom, except for Loren, the youngest, who had stopped by the doorway and was staring at me. The old General hardened his jaw and with a loud voice said, "Godspeed then, you . . . and Her."

"Aye . . . farewell." I took my hand from his and slipped away.

I went directly to my chambers. Freylo, my valet, had packed my bags and was gone. I did not blame him. I looked at the pots that lined my window sills, checking the soil in each, giving water to those that needed it. Done, I fished a couple of books from the shelves and stuffed them into a satchel: the Canon Arcana and my worn copy of Yailo's "Plantcraft." I used the mirror to properly wrap my cloak around my shoulders, lifted my bags, and left what had been my home.

I took my dappled pony from the Grand Stables and spurred him eastward until I reached the top of the Aern hills. I heard the slow steady cadence of the cannons. I twisted in my saddle and saw the sun turning Aerile's red-tiled rooftops into gleaming rubies, watched the thin spires of the palace flare with burnished light, and listened to the cannons roll off the years of her life. When it was over I gently urged my pony down the far slope. Only a fool would linger; there was no place for me in Aerile any more, no place left for the Queen's whore.

When I made camp that night I reflected on the truth I had told the old General. I had no idea where I was going. The thought that I could take any path, be anyone, was new and strange.

For as the God had shaped my beauty, so women had always shaped the direction and goals of my life. From Sage, the hedge-witch who took me in when my parents died (funny, to this day I cannot remember my mother and father without seeing them laid out on a dirt floor side by side, black boils on their faces); to Lila, the Warden's lady who took me to comfort her while her husband chose to enjoy the pleasures of the capital instead; to Lila's fanciful sister, Adriana, who took me to Aerile; on to all the farm-fresh chambermaids, artful daughters of the night, and sleek mistresses who graced my bed; to the sad-faced Countess, Sara, who brought me to the Court; and, lastly, the Queen who took me to her heart.

All of them, like water on a stone, shaped me, moved me. But now I was free to make my own life—if I knew how.

I heard the snicker of the horse before I saw the rider. He rode slowly, making his way carefully through the shadows and moonlight. Sighing, I stirred up the fire. It was not until he was quite close that I recognized Prince Loren. I stood, he stayed on his courser.

"I have a message for you," he said without preamble.

"When does a prince become a herald?" I asked in a light voice that hid my fear.

"When the message deals with family." He reached

toward his hip. Running was futile; I turned my face and braced for the sword thrust or pistol shot.

"Here."

I opened my eyes, a scroll was in his hand. I took the scroll with a quiet hand and unwrapped it; a ring fell into my palm. I read the words on the creamy vellum:

> My mother instructed me to take care of you, to give you a worthy station. Her will be done. Under my hand, by the power granted me by the God and the Peers of the Realm of Mistrel, I name you Warden of Salentina, to hold, protect and maintain, for the rest of your days.
>
> Giovan

I examined the ring, white gold set with engraved coral —a Warden's signet. "Do you know where this Salentina is?" I asked Loren.

"On the northwest coast," he answered slowly, "past the bogs and fens of wild Cataeleona."

"At the end of the world," I murmured. I touched his mount's sweat-foamed flank. "Do I have any choice?"

"Damiano, I had to *beg* my brother to honor her wishes. Giovan would . . . would do terrible things to you if you stayed within easy reach."

"I see. So be it. I thank you, my Prince."

He pulled so harshly on the reins that his horse reared and spun. "Do not thank me; thank Her." His voice broke on the words as he rode away.

Thank her. She had always refused to grant me lands or title; she would always say "Ah, Damiano, my Realm is not nearly enough for my love and a barony is far too much for my gardener . . . and he is worthy enough for my love— regardless, despite, and still."

'My gardener,' that is what she liked to tease me with. She never did understand my passion for herbs and wild flowers. The simple truth was, she was afraid if I had a place and role separate from her, I would leave her. In some ways, regardless of her years, she had stayed very young.

I smothered the coals and broke camp. It was a long way to the northern coast—and I believed Loren.

Marshes and long rolling sand dunes bordering a steel-gray sea. A spit of land curved to form a small cove. Boats nestled against a quay. A lonely village sheltered in the lee of the hill, and at the hill's crest, a ruined watchtower—Salentina. I sighed.

As I rode along the beach toward the village I came across a copper-haired child gathering marram grass. My long shadow must have startled her, for she dropped her bundle of leaves and whirled around to stare up at me open-mouthed.

"Are ye an Angel?"

I started to laugh, then stopped. My hair is long and very fair and the sun was riding on my shoulders; I was wearing my cloak of silver thread and my shirt of silky violet and then there is my face. Well, when I was that child's age, I would have seen an angel too.

"What is your name?" I asked.

"Charali," she replied in a trembling voice, pushing windswept hair from her eyes.

"Charali—Bright Heart—no, I'm not an angel. I am the new Warden."

She cocked her head at me, "The Cap'n? But yer young."

Cap'n, all right. "A Cap'n can be young. Why, I've heard of some as young as you."

She regarded me dubiously, with the air of someone

who suspects a fib. I gave her my most serious and honest expression, "Charali, by the Two who are One, I swear to you I am the new Cap'n . . . no more, no less."

I slipped off my pony and smilingly started picking up the sheaves of pale green leaves. "When we've gotten all these, will you take me to your people and introduce me?"

She nodded shyly and took my hand. We walked together to Salentina, the horse trailing us complaisantly and gazing about it as frankly as I would have liked to.

The villagers of Salentina accepted me easily enough. Their last Warden—Cap'n—had died childless nearly two years ago. They missed having a lord about.

Their lives were simple; the young took their boats out each morning, father and son, husband and wife, working together while the older women cared for the little ones and plaited marram grass into baskets and shoes. The old men, few as they were, mended nets, smoked fish, and taught the children the secrets of the sea.

They had a headswoman named Zola with arms as thick as my waist, children she counted by the handful, and soft hazel eyes that missed very little. She settled Salentina's quarrels and divided the daily catch into shares for the orphans, the bedridden, and the Cap'n. I had sat at my Queen's feet too long not to learn when to leave well enough alone.

The old Cap'n had lived in the largest house in Salentina, a two-story half-timber affair, shutters and frame turned gray as the sea. As my Queen would say, not enough and too much. . . . I gave the house to Zola and moved to the watchtower. It took a lot of work to restore it, but time was something I had in full measure—and sometimes the helpful hindrance of Charali. She swept and scrubbed, I lumbered cypress with a tired saw, hammered wood, and hauled stone. Easily done save for broken nails, and an aching back not built for this kind of punishment.

As I told Charali one day while we lunched precariously on the tower's crenelated top (her idea, not mine), and black-faced terns made excited passes at our food—the tower had probably been built two centuries ago at the tragic end of Aladon's reign.

Aladon, the Summer King. My Queen's beloved ancestor. For most of his life, it was as if he and Mistrel were blessed by the biune God. The winters became mild beyond memory, the spring rains soft and regular, at harvest time it was always clear and dry. The Realm prospered as it never had before or since. The crops became so abundant that the granaries groaned full and we traded rivers of wine and sweet oil for exotic treasures: buckets of pearls from far off Kandahar, cinnamon and cloves from the Isles of the Sun, and whole bolts of spider silk from the pugnacious gnomes of the Elder Hills.

But Aladon did not squander the new wealth of his kingdom; the Summer King also sponsored learning and exploration that brought greater riches to Mistrel. It was in Aladon's own factory that Saint Bartolo developed the printing block and thus gave us the chance for wisdom. With the discovery of the Great Wyvern deposits, giving Mistrel an almost limitless supply of saltpeter, the Alchemy Guild learned first how to precipitate the creation of sulfuric acid, and then, a few years later, nitric acid. From that achievement came fertilizer for the mountainous western provinces that were so poor in land; brilliant dyes and lacquers that gave our artisans a new rich palette; and not least, better explosives that enabled Aladon and his knights to root out the petty bandit states whose castles had been a canker on our frontiers. And with the long summer came a long peace for Mistrel.

Until the Sea Dragons and their hell ships came.

They struck hard and fast with their war galleys. We had no navy of our own; our gunnery had always been sufficient against the rare pirate. But the Sea Dragons wore cuirasses, had shields and helms that could easily stop a bullet. Our cannon could sink their ships, shatter their arms, but those bombards were large and heavy and the Sea Dragons moved like the wind, and fought like madmen.

It was not until the last year of Aladon's life that he was able to create a force to beat them. The cannonsmiths at their foundries turned out light, mobile artillery that could match the Sea Dragons' pace. Solid shot, chain shot, grape shot, with marksmen behind the cannon capable of hitting hands, feet, and faces. And mages to the rear of all, who, for a heavy price, flung lightning from the sky. Aladon made the Sea Dragons confront a horrible and unprofitable war; they left.

Or maybe it was as the priests claim, an Act of the God that made them leave us alone. And God's Instrument was the weather; for the sea storms came, hail that turned the Realm into fields of churning mud, and early snow so heavy it could drown horses. Maybe that is true, but long after the Sea Dragons stopped their marauding the weather stayed bad, and it never again became as good as it was during the high summer of Aladon's reign. Nor did our lives ever become as good. (But my Queen tried, how she did try . . . !)

I went out on their fishing boats, long shallow-drafted skiffs, learned how to trim the sails, how to maneuver into the wind, to throw a net cleanly across the water. But alas, my stomach and the sea could not reach an understanding. My fisherfolk were amused.

After that I explored the fens and salt marshes that comprised the bulk of Salentina, discovering some varieties of glasswort unrecorded by Saint Yailo. I was amazed at how happy that made me.

• • •

"I thought your babes knew how to swim, Zola."

She threw me a bemused look. "Huh?"

I nodded at the flailing limbs. "He does look like he's drowning."

Zola grunted and pulled her fifth, or was it her sixth, son out of the washtub. The lad jerked and splattered water about while she worked on his ears. Done, she wrapped him in a towel, swatted his rear and sent him off running. She wiped her hands and gave me her pigeon-toed curtsey.

"Yes, Cap'n?"

"I found some new saltworts—glassworts actually— which I think we might be able to use."

She looked at me as if I were one of her slower children and picked up a bar of soap. "Cap'n, we already use the wort to make this."

"Right, but *this* plant can be used to make glass."

". . . Glass?"

"Glass, bottles, cups, maybe even colored panes to grace the God's chapel."

I started to get excited: "Things we can trade with. I will need an apprentice, someone with good lungs and a strong back and half a quick mind. Zola, find me such a youngster and in a few years I'll give you—well, not riches, but a chance to do a little better, be a little happier."

Zola tilted her head at me. "Uh, Cap'n, how do ye know 'bout glass-making an' such things. I didn' think such are learned at Court." She said that last word with the upward inflection that the villagers only use when speaking of things beyond their ken: storms, God, the Northern Lights, and, since my arrival, the Court. The fact of her question startled me. The villagers of Salentina are as curious as any other folk, but—as familiar as they would be with me in casual ways—when it came to my past they remembered their place and had stayed fiercely polite.

However, they could not help but gossip. According to Charali—children make the best spies—the consensus of the majority seemed to be that I was an "embarrassment" of some major Lord, sent here to Salentina to avoid marital discord.

"I was a . . . gentleman of the Court at Aerile. Man and woman, we were expected to be knowledgeable with all the arts: mathematics, dance, languages, magic, and music. (And also how to lie with your eyes, and to be able to taste the finest trace of poison. . . .) For a while it became a fashion to learn a craft. Even those of the Blood took part. Why, Prince—no, his Majesty—Giovan learned how to be a decent farrier. I chose a less strenuous craft. Besides, glass-making fitted some of my other interests."

Zola digested what I said for a while, trying to sort out what was real to her and what was fantastical. "I see. Yes, well, there be Aggi's lad—he'll do for ye."

"Can his father spare him?" I asked.

She chuckled. "Aye, easily enough—he's like ye."

"Zola, I said I wanted a worker, not a pretty."

"Cap'n, now don't be bruising yerself," she gently chided me. "I merely meant the lad's got a weak belly."

I turned and coughed. "Send him around in the morning."

"Cap'n?"

"Yes, Zola?"

"Why?"

I looked into her hazel eyes and saw how tiny flecks of amber danced along the edge of the iris. Good eyes, and very sharp. Why me, and why do I bother? I tried to think of an answer both of us could understand.

"Let's just say it comes down to a matter of worth."

She nodded and then it was her turn to cough and look away. Smart woman, Zola.

The women. I smiled at the women of Salentina and did nothing but smile—or at least until I learned that in Salentina they kept on the custom of the Widow's Consolation: If a woman of child-bearing age lost her husband, on the anniversary of that loss she would spend the night with the Lord of the Domain. The village had its share of widows.

When a woman came to me with a sorrowful and downcast face, I would take her for a long walk along the dunes, then, as the moon rose, I had her drink an infusion of hops laced with brandy from my small stock. While the drink took its slow effect I'd show her a little piece of magic. A shard of rose quartz would spin and rise into the air so that it danced before her eyes. A few whispered words and she would fall soundly asleep. In the morn, lingering memories of fanciful dreams gave her a smile as she left my tower.

As for those who came to me with eagerness in their footsteps, well, I liked to think that they, too, left with upturned lips.

Most nights I was alone. I would read by rushlight until my eyes would give way. I would say the catechism: *Father sun, Mother moon, both are one. My soul is your soul; my heart, your heart*—and fall into dreamless sleep.

The years passed faster than I had thought possible.

It was the spring of my fifth year in Salentina, just before my twenty-ninth birthday, when the Sea Dragons came back.

At first, their raids on our coast were sporadic; little pinpricks of butchery. We heard the tales of horror from passing mendicants and shuddered. In the summer, the flood came.

As Mistrel had learned, so had they. This time their warriors carried huge curved bows made from horn, and our knights, cannoneers, marksmen, and mages fell under the onslaught of black arrows. I heard that Loren died on Midsummer's Day in a field of wild poppies. . . .

Salentina was lucky. I saw their needle-prowed galleys on the horizon nearly every week of that terrible summer, but they never pulled into our cove to turn our village into fire and grief.

Giovan sent me no warriors to man my watchtower, only a box of flares to mark which direction the galleys were headed; yellow for east, red for west.

But we did not escape unscathed, for when they came upon us fishing the banks, they took us; only a few, but enough. They took our boats, our people—my people.

On the last day of summer I called together the elders of Salentina and sat with them and told them what I planned.

We sat on the beach in silence, watching the waves break.

Fario, Charali's mother's brother, blew on his hands and rubbed the pain from his swollen knuckles. "Only a fool or a saint casts his net in strange waters." His words were etched with care: "Do ye think yer that good?"

I smiled at him. "Keep on using that cream I gave you for your joints. . . . Fario, it's not a saint's task I've set. I've got some skills I can exaggerate—and one singular talent. . . . For a time Fario, I was the best."

Zola finally spoke, "Ye kin not take a boat by yerself; they'll n'er believe that or ye." She looked at the others for confirmation, they all nodded. "Olegio will go with ye."

Ancient Olegio, toothless, half of his right hand missing —some say to a shark, some say to shame, but Olegio and his sea-dead wife would not tell—his youngest grandchild had just married Zola's third son. He was sucking on his pipe and staring at the sand. Zola read my face.

"Think us not cruel, but he is the least we can lose an' he kin still handle his boat well enough to help ye."

I went and sat by him. "You know the Sea Dragons won't take you as a slave."

He rapped his pipe against his knee, ashes like snow spilled across his lap. "Bring some of that sweetweed, Cap'n?"

"As much as you can smoke."

"Then when do we shove off?"

"On the morrow."

I spent the evening composing a letter to the old General. When I was done I sealed it with my Warden's signet, the only time I had occasion to employ it. I dropped the ring in a box where Zola would find it and give it to my successor. I called for Rebecca, a young widow whose husband had a few years back taken her inland while he tried his hand at city work. She knew how to read and write, and was the only one in Salentina whose experience passed into the outer world. I gave her the letter and, after explaining what I wished her to do, handed over a small bag of coins and my own old ring of brass.

"Should you have difficulty in seeing him," I said, "send a note with this ring. The General has its twin."

Rebecca nodded and took the items. She started to leave, then looked at me from over her shoulder. "Ye shouldn't have made me sleepy."

I laughed for the first time since Spring. I found the crystal in my pouch and showed it to her, saying, "We could always try again . . ."

In the morning Charali was waiting for me by Olegio's boat—when did she get that tall? Her eyes brimmed with tears. Before she could speak I laid fingers on her lips.

"Do I still look like an angel?" I whispered in her ear. Her mouth moved softly against my hand. "Yes."

"Then, Bright Heart, there's a chance." I replaced my

hand briefly with my lips. "On my bed is my silver cloak. Long life, Charali, happy life."

I turned my back and boarded the skiff. I hoisted the sail as Olegio pushed us off. We took the outbound tide and headed for the fishing banks. I did not look back.

I stopped throwing up after the third day. Olegio and I kept a taciturn space between us; he just smoked my weed and hummed wordless songs through his gums. I checked and rechecked my tightly packed sack of herbs, flasks and vials, especially the little purple one. The fishing was good. We caught cod and mackerel and what we did not eat we gave back to the sea. It would not do for the Sea Dragons to find us with a hold full of fish and still out.

It was on the eighth day that they found us. The war galley loomed out of the morning fog, foam spewing over the rusty iron of its ram, carmine sails billowing, and massed banks of oars cutting through the water in endless rhythm. The ship closed within moments. They threw a line off the bow and we warped alongside. Grinning faces peered at us over the gunwale and then with no warning a spear flew. It caught Olegio in the gut and without a cry he folded over and went into the water.

Mother of waters, take him into your embrace.

A rope ladder was let down. I slung my sack over my shoulder and climbed up. On the foredeck were two warriors—taller than I, and I am not small; they crowded me and knocked me down. One of them grabbed my sea bag.

"What's this?" He spoke Alashai, the old elven trading language. Perhaps there was truth to the tales that claimed the Sea Dragons were spawn of the Exiled Ones.

"Medicine: I'm a healer."

He quickly drew his blade and made a warding gesture. "A witch!"

Damn, Alashai was not a language I ever had cause to cultivate, too many awkward consonants and too few words for love. "No, a healer, a nurse. I can cure wounds, uh . . . purge bowels, ease fever and pain . . ."

The bag was swaying dangerously over the side.

"Hold!" A gray-haired giant of a man called out from amidships. For all his age he nimbly jumped over the banks of rowers to the bow.

"You say you can cure wounds?" His voice filled with scorn—and desperation.

"Aye."

"Come." he took me in an iron grip and half dragged me the length of the galley past an open hold where women, naked and bruised, huddled under a tarp, to the stern where, under an awning, a boy lay on a pile of priceless furs and rugs.

"Him."

I knelt beside the boy. His left arm was wrapped in blood-soaked bandages and it appeared someone had stuffed some sphagnum under the bandage. Good, they knew something at least. (I remembered, long ago, Sage telling me how deer would sometimes drag wounded limbs through the moss.) I looked at the boy; sweat was pouring down his face. He could not have been more than fifteen. I tried to be gentle as I undid the bandages. He tried not to shriek.

His elbow was shattered.

"How long?" I asked.

"Four nights," the man answered.

I leaned back on my heels. "I cannot do anything for the bone; it would be best to take the arm." I closed my eyes, they must know how to do it, dear God, please, not I.

"No! We are Kurig. My son must be whole."

His son. I spoke with measured words. "To save the

arm may mean losing the boy. Even if I can save the arm, he'll never be able to use it.''

"He's a warrior, not a boy, and 'tis not his sword arm. He must be whole and alive; that's all that matters. Prove your words and save him or the sea will have you.''

"As you will, my Lord . . .?''

"Mogare.''

"My Lord Mogare, I will need my bag and a basin of hot water.''

"Done.'' He started to move, then paused and made a helpless gesture. "His name is Jonalth. . . .''

I made the poultice thoughtfully; for the infection some mold scraped from hyssops, figwort to cleanse the wound and help with the pain, and some comfrey to help draw the tissue together. I gave the boy an infusion of linden tea with twenty drops of passion vine for the pain.

The first day Jonalth slept, on the second his fever broke, and at the dawn of the third day I knew we would live.

It was on the fourth night of my captivity that Mogare came to me as I slept near his boy and, waking me, took me aside. He held my face tight with his fist and stared at me.

"You're not a fisher,'' he rumbled.

I spoke through clenched teeth. "As I said, I'm a healer. I was helpin' my grandfather.''

He shook his head. "I know fishers; you're not of their stock.'' He grabbed my hand, examining the palm. "Not a warrior, maybe you are a witch. . . . Bah! It does not matter, now you are a thrall. A Kurig thrall. Do you know what that means? You belong to the firstborn of the Sea Dragons. You will do as you have done for my son. Serve us ill and I will feed your saucy eyes to the gulls. Do you understand me?''

I managed to nod. He released me and went to stand

beside the stroke, his face as expressionless as the drum-beater's. The Kurig, chief clan. I might do more than I had hoped.

The lands of the Sea Dragons had a raw beauty: homes built into cliffs of golden limestone and beyond the cliffs a forest of dark evergreens rising in waves up to snow-capped mountains. Narrow bays studded the coast; in each, two or three galleys would be moored. We followed the shoreline for two days and then we entered a crowded fjord. A score of galleys were lashed side to side. Overlooking the ships was a huge outcropping of stone that had been carved into a city crowned by soaring hawks: the Citadel of Kurig. We had arrived.

The women and I were taken ashore. They were soon separated from me and herded away into some kind of stockade. There they would be counted along with the other spoils of war and divided among the warriors. I did not see them again. I was led inside the city down a long, winding tunnel until they brought me to a damp, windowless cell and left me there in the darkness.

The following morning, two men took me from the cell and marched me to a room where boards had been laid on low trestles. They held me down and one, with a piece of sharp flint, cut the back tendons of my left ankle.

Afterward, I learned that they did this to all their slaves, their thralls. They were not needlessly cruel, like civilized men sometimes are—just indifferently so, like predators. They waited some days until my wound had healed and then Mogare put me to work.

The Sea Dragons were adept at setting bones and dealing with other like injuries, but not much else. I was to be summoned to alleviate such things as fevers and gout—which apparently many of them suffered from—but my major work was to treat the deep festering wounds that the young men of the Kurig clan often got when engaged in their favorite sport; armed only with double-bladed daggers, they hunted bears.

(Once, I found myself treating again the ripped body of Jonalth . . . What children do to prove their courage!)

Never did the women of the Sea Dragons summon me. At first I thought it was because the men saw my face and worried—an old, familiar emotion. Yet it was not so. The thought of a thrall being any sort of threat was beyond their ken. No, it was that the Sea Dragon women led a life segregated and sheltered from their men. And I was a healer to warriors, not to be bothered. As for the thralls, only if the life of a child was threatened did they call me, and then too often too late for my simple herbs.

This inaccessibility of their women meant that when my chance came, I would have to be very sure and very fast. I tried not to think of what I would do if chance never came.

Every now and then I would see some of the Sea Dragon women in robes of looted glory drifting through the corridors and high-vaulted halls of the Citadel. And I knew that they saw me. There are silent tricks to being noticed: how to stand, move, gesture, sidewise glances, how to go from humble to proud and back in one easy pose. I had studied with masters, worked my way through a company of professionals. The Sea Dragon women saw me.

However, as the days wound into weeks I caught nothing more than stares. A little knot of fear began building in me. I might have to make my own opportunities, the worst gambit for someone in my position. I began to keep a log of the women, like a stargazer, writing down every scrap of information I could glean from the too-brief moments of clear observation. Patience and luck, the twin virtues of my life. I found a possibility, a perhaps. There was an older, portly woman always cheerfully bustling about. Her freckled skin and gray-streaked auburn hair marked her as not being native Sea Dragon. Perhaps she came from one of the inland tribes that lived amongst the mountains and the snow. She appeared often in the lower levels of the Citadel, especially in the vast kitchens. Her name was Briga—told to me by a thrall in exchange for a kiss. I saw how frequently Briga was out of breath and how she would sometimes stop, and grimacing, clasp her left arm. I recognized the signs. My Lady Sara had had the same symptoms. I dug deep into my precious sack and thankfully found the right tablets.

I had been given a larger cell with a small, high window that gave me a measure of light. There was room for a workbench and some storage bins. I was allowed to go out into the sun-warmed meadows and cool forest to gather my herbs and flowers before the frost came. As a mark of my value to Mogare, not as a precaution against escape, when I was out I was always shackled with a long length of bronze chain to another thrall who would help carry my sacks.

Usually, that was a boy named Teal. Happily plump, he had been born a housethrall of the Kurig clan and proud of his fate. He was soon bored with the chore of accompanying me as I made my rounds of the woodlands, and not very interested in my home or my past. But he loved to talk. An idle question while I picked some berries or harvested some plants and he was off and running. On any subject a housethrall might know and some that I was surprised to learn about from a slave.

It was Teal who freely told me how the fabled Sea Dragon armor was made. The great oceanic serpent, from which these people took their name, was hunted in the early spring—no light task, for those monstrous snakes took down great blue whales with the ease of a wolf taking down a yearling—the monster's teeth and skin were culled and, with a stone mill, slowly ground into powder. Resin and heavy sap from the ironwood tree was mixed with the powder and the whole was poured into molds that were fired in huge kilns. Poor Mistrel, I thought after he told me, this formula would be little use to a land where there was only one tiny stand of ironwood trees in the entire Realm and sea serpents were a myth.

But the most important thing Teal talked of was what I needed most to know; he told me about the Kurig women. He told me about Iona.

The young wife of Reaxalth, chief of the Kurigs, King of the Sea Dragons. She was his favorite and not simply because of her beauty or her sweetness, qualities that Reaxalth seemed uncaring about, or that she was Chyan and her father Lord of the Dark Mountains—a powerful ally. It was because she had dreams, prophetic dreams. Reaxalth followed her dreams and grew mighty.

And Briga was Iona's old nurse and now her dearest handmaid.

Patience and luck, I reminded myself, patience and luck. . . .

My chance came at the Feast of Imbalc, when all of the Sea Dragons, men and women, celebrate the winter's leave-taking. Most of the remaining wine taken from Mistrel would be brought out and to music, diatonal, heavy with horns and pipes, the Sea Dragons would dance in the dawn. Kurig's housethralls were permitted to attend the feast, raise voice, and share in the wine. I would be there waiting, hoping.

My eyes were supposed to be only on Briga that night as, despite her age and weight, she spun in the wild flings that the Sea Dragons call dance. Yet, as I stood in the shadows of the great hall, my gaze kept flickering to the slight figure of a girl in a dark green gown, with tresses like maple leaves in autumn's splendor, swirling and laughing in the midst of the dancers.

I heard the crash. As the music fell away I pushed my way to where Briga lay. She was sprawled on the floor, unconscious. I went to my knees, opened her mouth and placed a tablet of pellote under her tongue. I tore open her bodice, listened to her heart, cursed, and began to pound her chest. Someone tried to pull me away, but Mogare roared and I was released. I went on pounding. A girl knelt beside me. On the edge of my vision I saw her gown of green. "What are you doing?" she cried at me.

"Arguing with death." I put my ear to Briga's breast. There it was, faint, but there. I found the pulse of her neck— steady. ". . . and winning." I stood. "Carry her gently to her bed and give her some tea."

"She is mine and I will see to her."

"Then do so." I turned. . . .

That her eyes were the color of faded violets did not surprise me. That they looked like the bruised eyes of a fawn, did. It was going to be harder on me than I thought.

Over her shoulder I saw Mogare and next to him a silverbearded man wearing wine-stained furs. Upon the stranger's head was a circlet of ivory and gold. Swiftly, painfully, I fell to my knees and bowed my head. "I was only trying to serve you well."

Reaxalth spoke, "You are Damiano. My kinsman has told me of you. You have done right."

I kept my head down.

"Speak," he commanded.

"I thank your Majesty. May I continue caring for the injured lady?"

A moment's silence, then her soft clear voice, "Reaxalth . . ."

"You may see to my wife's maid." Reaxalth held out his hand to his wife. "Come Iona, the dawn is near and we have Imbalc to complete." She looked down at her nurse and started to speak.

"My husband—"

"I said come!" His voice cracked across her face like a slap. She turned her face to me, her hair falling like a cloud across her shoulders. "Take good care of Briga."

"I can do no less ... my Queen."

I came to Briga's room each morning for a month. She was an ideal patient, grateful and without complaint. I confess, I began to take personal satisfaction in saving her.

And every day Iona would be there too, silently watching me as I ministered to her old nurse. I knew better than to speak to her unbidden, but I could feel her eyes on me.

I had discovered that Briga was exceedingly fond of music and had a cache of instruments. With her permission I searched among them and found an old gittern. Then after seeing to Briga's health I would sit by her bed and, with rusty fingers, play for a while, singing the songs Lila had taught me. The old, achingly sad and sweet songs that lovers teach each other. Briga did not understand the words, but she did not need to; I could see her face. And without looking, I knew that Briga's face mirrored Iona's.

A few days after she was back on her feet, Briga appeared at my cell. She stood in the doorway and, while staring curiously at the clutter, ordered me to accompany her. I quickly washed my hands and followed her. She led me through passageways I had never seen before. Past guards that were women, not men, with naked swords resting loosely in their hands. High to the top of the citadel we climbed until my ankle ached in protest. We stopped at a door bound in bronze. There was no guard. Briga opened the door and ushered me in.

The room was low-ceilinged and large. A cold wind blew off a long balcony that ran the length of one side. The only furniture was a magnificently lacquered chair (from Mistrel's sister realm of Alencu—I knew the work, I could guess the rape), a small table laden with rings, pins, and combs, and a mirror in a gold serpentine frame. The bed was simply layers of ermines and sable. A wall-hanging, its hues so faded that the figures seemed like ghosts, hung opposite the balcony. A fireplace was crackling fitfully in a corner. Iona stood alone in the middle of the room wearing a close gown of russet—severe and beautiful.

Briga stepped back into the corridor and closed the door behind her.

Walk carefully, Damiano. I thought. Walk very carefully.

"I wish to thank you for Briga's life."

I laced my fingers together and shrugged my thumbs. "Her life is her own destiny, I just helped steady her course."

"They were right about you."

" 'They,' my Lady?"

"My clanswomen. Did you think that the women of Kurig are ignorant of who and what goes about in our Citadel?"

"Nay, my Lady. I try never to presume about women. What may I ask is their judgement of me?"

She walked over to the tapestry, her fingers finding the pattern of the weave. She spoke to the wall, "That you are like a song come to life. . . . Not a warrior, you walk without fear. You speak like a Prince, yet we found you on a fisher's boat. You can deny Death with your hands. . . . You look . . . you look like the gods that walked with us when we first came to this land."

I shifted to Olavi, the silver tongue of the Exiled Ones. "Thou art kinder than kindness need be, my Lady."

She spun about and looked startled, then replied in the

same—with an accent better than mine. "'Tis kindness girded with truth. . . . I have need of thy magic."

"'Tis not magic, my Lady, merely a little knowledge and skill."

That got me the sharp edge of a smile. "Thou needst not dissemble with me. The Chyan are not skittish of mage-craft like our cousins of the sea. Our mountains hold many old secrets. . . . Call it what thou wilt, I have need of thy skill and thy aid."

"I serve my Queen."

She paced the room. The words coming only when she was farthest from me. "I am nineteen and have been a fair wife for three winters . . . I am still without child . . . I must have a son."

"My Lady, surely thou must know that all women have their own time, their own rhythm of life and birth—"

"—Thou dost not understand; mine husband, Reaxalth is . . . is no longer young, and he hath no heirs. I must have a child and soon."

And if you do not, Reaxalth will take another wife, not-withstanding your value or your beauty, and you will not even have the paltry comfort of your position. "I am sorry, my Lady, but I do not think I can help thee."

"Thou canst and wilt—I have seen it in my dreams—I dreamt of a man with hair like sunlight, standing alone in the woods. He stood with his bare back to me and the air steamed about him. I came to him and saw that he was cutting wood with his bare hands and planting the bro-ken boughs deep into the snows. And from the planting a sapling greenly rose. 'Tis clear to me, the night thou saved my Briga I knew the man was thee—and my dreams nev-er lie."

She stood close to me, too close. I had to back a step. "Yes . . . well, I can prepare a drink of juniper berries for thee and thy lord. It is known to quicken desire, heighten passion—"

"—my being barren is not for a lack of trying." She had a most extraordinary blush, pink lavender and pale rose.

"No, I am sure it is not." I looked away, into the mirror. To my chagrin, I was finding that I could not face Iona's eyes and lie. So I thought of Charali, of Salentina— the truth then, wherever it takes me. . . . "There is a ritual used by the witches of Cataeleona—'tis a fey and feral province of my land. It doth involve magic, real magic, and . . ."

"What else?"

"It requires thy being touched."

I blushed before she did. The air felt clotted and charged as it does before the coming of a storm.

"Leave me," she whispered.

I spent a restless night in my cell. I knew she would call for me; her need, and what she felt beneath her heart, would see to that. What kept me awake was not success, but its cost. Magic is easy, but it has a price, one not measured in gold. And life magic has the heaviest toll, one we both would have to pay. I had expected many things, but not regret.

She was standing on the balcony, her back to me. "Reaxalth leaves for the Dragon Hunt in two days. Make thy preparations . . . I will send for thee when it is safe."

I brought what I needed on a wide tray: four candles, a piece of chalk, a cup of medicated wine, and two bowls —one holding pure olive oil, the other the blood of a newborn lamb killed by my direction with a single blow.

Heavy curtains closed off the balcony. She was sitting in the chair near the fireplace, her face hidden in shadows.

"What must I do?" Her voice was clear and controlled.

"Put up thy tresses."

As she took some combs from the table and began to

pile up the massy richness of her hair, I drew a wide circle with the chalk. At each cardinal point I placed a candle and with a taper lit the wicks. I gave her the cup of wine.

"What is this for?"

"To put thee at ease."

She tossed the wine into the fire.

"Remove thy gown and stand in the center of the circle."

She stood and undid the pins on her shoulders. The gown fell rustling into a pool at her feet. The candlelight gave her skin the hue of honey. I was fine until she moved —and took my breath away.

She waited for me in the circle. Her eyes stayed unwaveringly on mine. I nudged the bowl of oil with a finger. The bowl rose from the tray until it floated above her. Slowly it tilted and the oil flowed down onto her shoulders, breasts, stomach, and thighs. She trembled as the oil caressed her, but her eyes of violet did not leave me.

I willed my memory and said the words. The power came to me. It started in my chest and coursed through my arms to my wrists, my palms, fingertips. My nails glowed like coals. I dipped my left hand in the lamb's blood and walked into the circle.

Where I touched her I left a trail of fire. She stood motionless, like a perfect statue, like a startled fawn. From the slope of her breasts to the slender curve of her hips I drew blazing lines. When the lines were joined I touched her forehead and left a star on her brow. "Think and say thy heart's desire."

"A son."

I touched her lips with my fingertips and, reaching down, touched the center of her. She gasped and the fire on her skin became rainbows of blinding light.

"Done."

The lines faded like mist in the dawn. I stepped back and picked up her gown. "We are finished, my Lady."

She came to me and cupped my face between her hands. "No, we are *not* finished." Her mouth found mine.

A harsh war must have been waged in Briga's heart between devotion and gratitude, between outrage and fear. I have fought in that war myself, and I recognized another veteran. How hard it must have been for her, I could easily guess. But with the resolution of her heart came seven nights that she managed to escort me from my cell to Iona's high chamber without a soul seeing us. Each night she closed the door behind me and stood watch with her self until sunrise.

I made love to Iona as if each night was the first time in my life, and the last. And for a while I took the bruised look from her eyes.

On the sixth night, as we lay entwined on her sable bed, she told me that Reaxalth would be back in two days, that we would have only one more night.

As we lay together on the seventh night I gave her a cup of wine. She laughed and clung to my neck. "A kiss from thee and I'll have no need of wine."

"'Tis from my birthplace; I want to share that memory."

She sat up, her breasts like summer apples swaying in the breeze. "As thou wishes . . . I will take every part of thee," she said, and, throwing her head back, drained the cup.

I took her in my arms and afterward held her until she fell asleep. I watched and when her eyelids began to tremble and her legs kicked gently like a swimmer against the sea, I knew that the tears of the poppy had taken effect. I pushed the hair from her ear and softly spoke to her of treasure and mountains and mystery.

• • •

At Beltane, after the spring planting, when the war chiefs of the Sea Dragons assembled at the Citadel of the Kurig to plan their raids, Reaxalth told them of two great things. First, that all the bands of the Sea Dragons were to join on a raid of the Shrine of the Moon high atop cloud-shrouded Mount Tyskia by Mistrel's western shores. For there, unknown to the world, Aladon of long ago had hidden the hoard of the Great Wyvern.

Second, that Iona was with child.

The Citadel shook with Sea Dragon yells.

I awake to the sounds of weeping. I stay on my cot and listen to the Citadel echo with cries and lamentations. When I am sure of what I hear, I rise and find my little purple vial. I pour its milky contents into some water and drink. I make my way unattended to Iona. She is waiting for me, a double-bladed dagger in her hand.

She speaks tonelessly, "They went up Mount Tyskia and the mountain shattered and fell down on them and buried them with stone. Reaxalth, Mogare, and all their kinsmen. . . . The thunder weapons of Mistrel were brought from hidden places and the ships were broken like twigs for the fire . . .

"My dreams never lie, but I did not see this. Tell me, Damiano, how is that? My dreams never lie. . . ."

I limp to the balcony. In the half-light I see one battered ship riding low at its anchor. The masts are gone and the stern is scorched wreckage.

"Thy dreams do not lie, Iona."

She runs to me and pushes me against the ledge, stabbing and slashing at my arms and shoulders. She keens and curses as she raises the dagger, again and again. But the cuts are not deep and the pain I feel has nothing to do with my wounds. When she stops, her eyes are blurred with tears.

She hands me the dagger. "Kill me, for I cannot kill thee."

I drop the dagger over the ledge. "Nay, my Queen, I *chose* another path." I hold her in my arms as she cries for rage and grief and love.

My legs begin to tremble. "Help me to the chair. Iona, please . . ."

She holds my head in her hands and stares at me, her face suddenly pale. "What other path? No, Damiano, no . . ."

"The chair . . . please . . ."

Leaning on her we make it across the room. I twist the chair so that I can see the sky. I want to see the sunrise.

She sinks to my feet. I stroke her crimson hair, my hands are becoming numb.

"Why? Thou must have known I could not—"

"—We could not. But if we were together they would find us out and thou wouldst watch me die badly . . . before they tore thy child from thy womb.

"Apart . . . I cannot bear to lose another . . . thou wilt have a beautiful son. Take him to the Chyan, to the mountains . . . keep him from the sea. . . ."

She says things to me that I always wanted to hear.

It begins to get very cold.

"I love thee, despite and still."

I force my eyes to open, but Iona's face is the only one I see.

'. . . Aye, and I always serve my Queens."

A Walk by Moonlight

A Folktale of the Present Day

by
Mark Anthony

About the Author

Yes, it's his real name. Mark Anthony is about to receive his degree in anthropology from the University of Colorado and is applying to graduate school in order to study human paleontology.

He pursues hiking and, sporadically, running. He has loved to read since spending early summers in a mountain cabin and still considers it one of his major avocations. He has written a novel based in part on his story here and submitted it to a publisher. Other than that, he points out, he has lived remarkably free of picturesque experiences.

In which case, the following story testifies to a rich interior life. It was the first story he ever seriously drafted for submission anywhere. We may safely assume that others will follow. . . .

Nicholas Grey lived in a drab brownstone on a drab street in a drab part of the city. At least, that is, until tonight. But now he was leaving. As he locked the door, almost on an afterthought, he realized he had no idea why he was leaving the apartment. All he knew was he couldn't stand to stay inside its four dingy walls any longer, staring at the peeling, pink wallpaper in the dirty glare of a bare 60-watt bulb.

He changed his mind about the door and jerked his key from the lock before he'd slid the deadbolt home. Why not leave it unlocked? Nick didn't feel like a person who was planning on coming back home, except perhaps to crumple a few clothes into a duffle, and every moment he felt even that possibility going the way of dishwater swirling down the drain.

Besides, what was there for anyone to steal? Certainly not the T.V. No, that was the latest thing to turn traitor on him today, blowing out its electronic entrails in a gout of sparks just as Nick was hoping to sink into mindlessness and forget the rest of today's betrayals. He really should have been expecting it. After all, three was his lucky number. First he'd walked into the Uptown Insurance Company this morning, neatly attired as usual in his dark brown suit, and plunked his battered briefcase onto his desk only to find that it wasn't his desk anymore. Over the weekend, some fresh, pimply kid had slithered into the office and taken his place. His name was Wendell, Nick had learned while breaking the kid's plastic nameplate in two.

"Sorry, Nicky," the plaid double-knit manager of Uptown Insurance Company had said, patting the shoulder of Nick's brown suit. "It's a figures game. You know that. And you just haven't been putting out the figures."

Nick had dropped his briefcase then, maybe not meaning to score on the manager's toe, but probably. He had walked out with as much dignity as one could after getting booted from a place the caliber of Uptown Insurance.

Next, he had promptly discovered his car was gone.

"Yeah, it's a figures game," Nick had said, double-checking the parking space. "And this really figures." But there had been no metallic blue '74 Chevy Impala anywhere in it, only the fuzzy green whatever-it-was mutant thing he'd won at a carnival and kept on the dash. His mascot. Nick kicked it into a storm grate and caught a bus. He never could afford a cab.

And so he'd come home to find that even his meager hopes of *I Love Lucy* were to be denied by the capriciousness of electrons, and Nicholas Grey decided the entire universe might as well be giving him the finger.

So Nick decided to take a walk. Where to and how long were unimportant variables. He pulled his dull trenchcoat around his thin frame and picked his way down the brownstone's crumbling steps into the cool, late-spring night air. The full Moon was just rising over the dull edges of a brick tenement across the street, casting its beams carelessly about the neighborhood. But the light didn't give a smooth, silvery cast to the squat buildings as moonlight was supposed to do. Instead it highlighted every dark crack in the brick and stone, deepened every pothole in the street and cast a livid aura about every piece of litter that clung to the gutter.

Nick stopped for a second, realizing that he'd never really seen these buildings out of daylight. He always kept the curtain of his one square window drawn, and this wasn't the kind of neighborhood where hanging around on street corners after dark was a good idea. Nick even thought for one giddy moment that by mistake he'd stepped out of his familiar door into a different world. But then a pair of unbalanced headlights seared his retinas, and he blinked, shaking the notion out of his head.

He stood transfixed only a moment longer and then walked out into the night, his shoes grinding on the shadow the Moon cast before him. The air was gentle on his cheek but slightly fetid in his nostrils—the scents of cooking, of sweat, of car exhaust, of the dark oily water that stood in potholes blending with the faint, pervasive stench that could only be termed *city*.

After a few minutes his steps fell into a rhythm, each beat jarring something loose from his brain and sending it spiraling to the sidewalk. Soon he began to unhunch his shoulders, as he passed street lights, people, deli's, and X-rated theaters, letting his coat hang open as if to let the darkness come closer to him. He was even beginning to decide this walk had been good for him, and that maybe now he could go back and sit on the sprung cushions of his couch and have a cup of coffee.

And then Nick saw the old black man.

He was sitting under a street light, playing something on a tenor saxophone. It might have been "Amazing Grace" he was playing, but then it might have been "When the Saints Go Marching In." It was hard to tell, and Nick wasn't really listening anyway. He was watching the old man's fingers. They were dark and scaly, knuckles swollen, but they danced up and down the sax, weaving so they should have tied themselves in knots. One second Nick thought he was standing on the opposite corner, just staring, but the next he was standing in front of the old man, so close he could have touched him, so close he could see the white scar tissue that sheathed his eyes.

The old man played his song a bit more, breaking up the riff and then letting the last note wail as it died slowly on the air. Then he pulled a rumpled handkerchief from his breast pocket and dabbed his leathery brown lips.

"Glad you could make it, son," the old man said in a voice as rich and husky as the sax's while he reached down for the instrument's battered case propped up against his folding chair.

It took Nick several moments to swallow. The air around him had suddenly gone thick and warm. The light of the street lamp was honey gold. "Make it?" he finally managed to ask.

"Sure, son. Been 'specting you all night. Hope you don't mind my saying, but you're a trifle bit late." The old man's blind fingers slipped the sax into its felt-lined case.

"Late?" Nick asked, squatting down some to be more on a level with the old man's face. It was a rough, weathered landscape, and the dusky brown ridges and crevices could have hidden a hundred histories, which Nick supposed they did. And the eyes didn't seem so much blind as just looking elsewhere. "What am I late for?"

"You don't know?" the old man said softly, more to himself than to anyone. "Of course you don't know," he said loudly then, slapping his bony knee through his faded twills. "Old Scrounger, you get slower than snot in January with every passing minute." He turned his face to Nick, who had the disconcerting impression that the old man was somehow studying him. "Course you don't know. *We* was 'specting you, but you wasn't 'specting *us*. Well, I reckon I'd better introduce myself. Scrounger's the name—Old Scrounger." He thrust out his hand and Nick caught it. The grip was warmer than he thought it would be, and stronger, and the skin was as smooth as old leather.

"My name is—" Nick started to say.

"Nick. Nicholas Grey. You live—or up until a little

while ago you lived—at 1762 East 71st, Apartment Three. You're six feet even, need to put a bit of meat on your bones, got brown hair and eyes the color of your name. Son, you got the looks to do right with the ladies if you just weren't so damn serious all the time." Old Scrounger sat back in his chair looking just the slightest bit pleased with himself.

"You're not blind, are you?" Nick accused, standing back up. But the old man rolled his pale orbs in their sockets, and Nick knew that wasn't true. After a minute he squatted back down. "How do you know all this?"

"My eyes may not work, son, but I can still see." Old Scrounger pulled a small packet out of his pocket. "Want a Juicy Fruit?" Nick nodded dumbly and accepted the gum, hardly noticing the taste as he shoved it into his mouth. "I can see all that just like I can see you're the one who was supposed to come tonight. Gonna stop Black Gutter Jack, you are," the old man said, baring surprisingly white, even teeth as he grinned.

"Stop who?" Nick asked, telling himself he'd found yet another street-corner weirdo, though he knew all the same it wasn't true. "I'm not doing anything tonight. All I came out for is a walk. That's the only reason I left my apartment."

"And it's a damn good thing you did leave it, son," Old Scrounger said, suddenly leaning forward and poking Nick's shoulder with one hard fingertip. The smell of Juicy Fruit, cigars, and muscatel wafted sluggishly around them. "If you were still there then you'd be deader'n a rat in a cat's insides. Gutter Jack, he knew you were coming, just like the rest of us. But he couldn't do anything, not 'til the Moon had risen. She's his power, you know."

"But what am I supposed to do?" Nick asked. The old man was silent for a moment, and Nick listened to the distant sounds of sirens and laughter.

"You gotta get the talisman, that's what, son," Old

Scrounger said, his voice suddenly low and conspiratorial, forcing Nick to bend closer. "You get that, and Gutter Jack, he's nothing more than a dog's squat on a fire hydrant." At that, Old Scrounger cackled and slapped his knee again.

"And if I don't?" Nick asked, suddenly feeling light-headed.

"Then Gutter Jack gets us all—including you—to do his bidding. And mind you, it ain't going to be picking posies in the garden. Gutter Jack—now there's a dark soul if ever there was one. And believe me, son, there's been plenty."

"Who do you mean, 'all of us'?" Nick asked.

"Ain't you got nothing in your head 'cept stuffing and questions, son?" Nick shook his head sheepishly. "All right," Old Scrounger said, "one more, and that's it. Let me just tell you, boy, there's a lot of us out here you don't know about. Oh, you probably seen us. Every day, people like you just pass us by, hardly ever noticing us. And if they do, then they never give us a second glance but just turn their thoughts back to their business lunches and dry cleaning they got to pick up. But we're here, and sometimes what we do keeps their cozy lives in those cozy tracks they're so damn used to. Not that they ever thank us. No, we're the loonies, the sweatshop stiffs, the bums." Old Scrounger let out a dry, high-pitched laugh at that. "But on a night like tonight, it's their butts in the sling as much as ours. And it's up to you what happens, Nick, my boy."

"But I don't know where the talisman is. I don't even know *what* one is," Nick said, standing up. "Hell, I don't know anything about what you're saying."

"That's all right, son," Old Scrounger said, grinning as he picked up his sax again. "Just start walking. Toward downtown. You'll get there. You just watch out for what old Gutter Jack sends after you." He put the sax to his lips and the tune Nick couldn't quite pin down started spilling out again. Maybe it was "Oh! Susanna."

"What do you mean?" Nick demanded. "I don't understand." But the old man just kept playing and staring into that other space with his dark eyes. Finally Nick gave up and shuffled away. He started walking in the direction of his apartment and then turned to have one last glance at the old man. He stopped when he saw the circle of brightness under the street light was empty. But he was sure he could still hear the voice of the sax, distant as an echo, speaking in its own tongue to the night.

Nick shivered slightly and pulled his coat tighter around him as he turned back and started walking once more, this time in the direction of downtown.

Nick walked. He walked down narrow streets that twisted amongst crowded apartment buildings. He walked down wide avenues past poplar-bordered estates. And while he walked, the Moon rose higher in the sky, casting its loose gauze over the city. But he didn't meet anybody as he walked. Not old black saxophonists. Not Gutter Jacks, whatever it was one looked like. There was nothing strange about the walk at all until Nick realized how strangely empty the city was. It was as though everyone was indoors, waiting. And every once in a while, he heard the laughter. It was high and distant, and Nick couldn't shake the impression that it was mocking him, that maybe it was following him.

When he finally passed a diner in which there were actually people eating in the neon and fluorescent radiance, he decided to take a break and have a cup of coffee. Nick distinctly heard his feet groan as he sat down in the vinyl booth, kicked off his loafers, and rubbed his toes. After a minute, he glanced around at the other customers in the place. There was a pinkish old woman sitting at a table with a small pinkish poodle. A pair of truckers sat at the counter, laughing coarsely, and a young Chicano couple sat in a booth, holding hands across the white Formica table.

"What can I get you, hon?" a voice asked, and Nick looked up to see a vision in pink polyester hovering above him. Her name was Rosa, by the name tag embedded in a mass of lace and ruffles on her breast. She smiled at him with bright red lips, never missing a beat as she chomped on what must have been a very good piece of gum.

"Uh, just coffee," Nick said.

"O.K., hon," Rosa said. "You wouldn't want a nice apple Danish, would you? Fresh even, can you believe?" She laughed and Nick nodded. "Be back in a flash, hon." Rosa said, scurrying off behind the bar.

She brought the coffee and Danish in a few minutes and told Nick in a warm voice, "Now just let me know if you need anything else, hon." She turned to bus another table, but Nick had the odd notion that, before she did, she'd stared at him just a moment too long. On impulse, Nick glanced about the diner and saw that everyone was just turning their heads, as though they'd all been staring only a second before.

He ate his Danish and drank his coffee, and pretty soon his feet started to uncramp, so he slipped his loafers back on. "Can I get you anything else, hon?" Rosa asked him. When he said no, she laid his check on the table and told him, "You can pay it when you're ready, hon. Thanks."

He swilled down the last of his coffee and went to the cash register. Rosa was manning that, too, and she rang up the total and took his cash. When she was handing him his change, she asked, "So, where're you headed tonight, hon?" Suddenly the diner was silent except for the clank of a single fork hitting a plate.

"Uh, nowhere, really," Nick said. "Just out for a walk."

"Uh-huh," Rosa said, nodding as if Nick had just confirmed something. "Now listen, hon," she went on, leaning toward him over the cash register. She smelled like soap and cigarette smoke. "It might not be any of my business what you're doing tonight, but then, it might be. Just take my advice in any case. If you meet up with one of a certain someone's flunkies, and if he asks you something, just remember, the answer may be that there ain't no answer. Got me, hon?" she asked, winking at him.

"Uh, yeah," Nick said. "Thanks."

"No problem," she told him. "Like a mint?" She held out a basket and Nick took one. "Thanks, hon," she said. "Come again."

"Sure," Nick said as he walked out the door. He was positive every pair of eyes in the place was on him, but he kept his own straight ahead until he was well out into the night. When he finally looked back, the diner was just a brilliant island of chrome in the darkness. The Chicano couple were still holding hands. The truckers were laughing over a new crudity, and Rosa was giving the pinkish old lady her check. But for the Danish sinking in his stomach, Nick would have said he'd never been in there at all.

He turned to continue his walk—and bumped promptly into a stone column. Stars shot across his vision as he gripped the massive girth to keep his balance. It took him a few moments to notice that the stone wasn't cold. In fact, it was warm. And suddenly the column let out a chuckle like a low rumble of thunder. Nick let go and skittered backwards. It wasn't a stone column he'd run into after all, just the human equivalent of one. The man—Nick supposed that was the only thing one could call it—was at least seven feet tall and all big bulges covered with short bristling hair. He was wearing a black T-shirt with a faded glittery picture of Barry Manilow.

Nick, though, wasn't about to comment on the thing's

musical taste. Instead, he backed away slowly—and then heard laughter behind him. Nick spun and saw a thin, weaselly man dressed all in white with at least a pound of gold chains dangling around his neck. Two scantily Spandex-clad women hung on to him, one on each side, giggling at Nick as he jerked his head wildly from side to side, looking for an out. There wasn't one, of course.

"Well, well, well, what do we have here," the pimp—he couldn't have been anything else—said in a grating voice. "Looks like a Nick-rabbit in a snare." He laughed at that, and the two prostitutes joined in, but his laughter stopped abruptly. "Hey, broads, shut up," he barked at the women when they didn't stop their own musky mirth fast enough. "Well, Nicky, my boss sent me to come take care of you." He drew a small vial out of his breast pocket with a ring-encrusted hand and held it to his nose, sniffing delicately before passing it on to the women. "So what is old Cy going to do with you?"

"Let me go?" Nick tried in a small voice, but Cy shook his head slowly and grinned. Light glinted off his gold front tooth, and Nick could see his face was cratered like the moon with acne scars. Sweat began running down Nick's sides.

"No, Nicky, I don't think that would please Gutter Jack at all," Cy said, coming closer, shrugging off the women like a fur coat. "I could just give you to Sammy—" Nick heard a low grunt behind him. "But that wouldn't be very sporting of me, now would it?" Cy asked. Nick could smell his cologne now, an odor that reminded him of the oranges that had been sitting on top of his fridge for a month. Suddenly, he heard a small *snick* and felt a cold sharpness against his stomach.

"I could take you myself," Cy said, "but that wouldn't be too fair either, huh?" Nick shook his head in a definite no. The grease Cy used to slick back his hair was exuding a smell like toxic waste, and Nick was biting his bottom lip just to keep from throwing up. "No, it wouldn't," Cy said, easing off the switchblade and backing away. He pointed to a small trash can, and one of the women—a leggy redhead— took off her coat and spread it over the top. Cy sat down, lit a cigarette, and offered one to Nick, who refused.

"Tell you what, Nicky," Cy said between puffs, "we'll make it a little contest. I'll ask you a riddle, and when you can't answer it, you can decide if you'd rather be killed by me or by Sammy." The grunt again.

"Boy, does that ever sound fair," Nick said, his voice croaking like a dying frog in his throat. "But what if I answer it?"

"Oh, you won't, Nicky," Cy said, and the prostitutes giggled again, sauntering up behind him to drape themselves about his narrow shoulders again. "But just to make you happy, if you answer it, you can go, just like you asked so nicely to do. Now, you ready?"

Nick nodded jerkily.

"All right then," Cy said, smoothing back an oily wave of hair. "Answer this one. What's my middle name?" Cy puffed on his smoke smugly while one of the women crooned to him what a brilliant riddle it was. Sammy was silent, but Nick could feel warm, wet breath on the back of his neck.

"Uh, your middle name, huh?" Nick asked. Cy nodded. "That's a good one. Any hints?" Cy threw down the cigarette butt and came toward him, grinning wider, switchblade ready and glinting in the moonlight.

"No hints, Nicky," he said. "Now answer. Time's just about out."

Something was knocking at a door in the back of Nick's brain, but it was hard to pay much attention to it. All he could think about was that gold tooth, shining brighter as it came closer and closer. For one delirious split-second he even had the wild desire to shout out *Wendell!* But then Cy pulled back his arm, ready to plunge the knife into Nick's gut. And suddenly the door burst open and Nick remembered Rosa, leaning over the cash register.

"There's no answer!" he shouted raggedly. "You don't have a middle name!" Cy stared at him a moment, rage twitching his pock-marked face, glazing his bulging eyeballs. He jerked the knife up, resting it against Nick's throat, and Nick could feel a hot bead of blood rolling down his skin. Then the knife flashed, and Nick heard it skittering along the pavement.

"Get out of here," Cy said, his voice full of venom. He grabbed the vial from one of his women and took another snort from it. "Get out of here!" Nick was too stunned to move. He lifted a finger to his throat as Cy turned away, gesturing to the women and Sammy. But the redhead hesitated a moment and then walked over to Nick. She was pretty as she slipped something tinklingly silver off her wrist and onto Nick's.

"I like you," she breathed softly. "Remember this if someone tries to hurt you like this again. And think of me, Sandra." She kissed his cheek gently and then hurried after Cy, hanging onto his shoulder again when she reached him. Nick waited for the night to swallow them completely before he finally let out his breath. His neck stung but the bleeding had already stopped, and his wrist jingled softly as he moved it. He looked for a second at the silver charm bracelet Sandra had placed there. The charms were tiny bells, and they played their music with the slightest movement. Nick tried to take it off his wrist and discovered that he couldn't. After a few minutes of trying, he shrugged and started to walk once more.

"Wait up a second, Nick," a voice said behind him before he'd gotten two feet. Nick turned around, dreading

what he was going to see this time, but the alley where
the voice had come from was empty. A trash can lid rattled, and the voice came again, small and high-pitched, but
rich and musical. "Over here, Nick, by the dumpster."

Nick strained his eyes peering into the shadows by the
overflowing dumpster. At first he couldn't see anything but
piles of old trash, but then a slight movement, near the
ground, caught his gaze. Nick stepped closer and saw that
it was just a battered alley cat licking its paw with a dig-
nified air.

"Just an alley cat? Nick, it's not polite to insult someone whom you've only just met," the cat said as it hopped
up off its cushion of garbage and leaned forward into a claw-
extending stretch that ruffled its rusty fur. The cat shook
each of its back legs delicately, gave a great yawn, baring
its white needle fangs to the moonlight, and sprang up onto
the rim of a dented trash can. It stuck a tentative paw inside
but withdrew it almost as quickly, wrinkling its nose and
wriggling its whiskers in disdain. "Nothing. Should've
figured, in this neighborhood," the cat said as it seated
itself primly, wrapped its tail about its feet, and regarded
Nick with wide, pale green eyes. "Sorry, Nick, I'm forget-
ting my manners. My name is Fishbone. Thaddeus T. Fishbone." Thaddeus extended a small paw toward Nick.

For lack of a better reaction, Nick took the proffered
paw and shook it gently but then quickly snatched his hand
away and hid it behind his back. "Uh, what's the 'T' stand
for?" Nick asked, for lack of anything else to say.

"Why, Tom, of course," the cat replied. "What else?"

"Listen . . . Thaddeus, it's been a real pleasure, but
I've got to ah, to . . . ah," Nick resorted to pointing backward and started stumbling out of the alley, but his foot
slipped in something unquestionably slimy, and he sat down
hard on the damp cement. Thaddeus strolled leisurely

toward him and hopped into his lap, purring when Nick involuntarily ran his hand down the cat's back.

"Listen, Nick," Thaddeus said, standing up on his hind legs and putting his paws on Nick's chest, "you still don't get this. You're playing along O.K., but you think it's just a game, albeit a slightly weird one."

"Hey, I didn't ask to do this," Nick said defensively. "Hell, I don't even know what it is I'm doing. I think I'm just going to go back home."

"I wouldn't bother, Nick," Thaddeus said, running his rough, pink tongue over his chops. "Burned. Gutted out completely an hour ago, courtesy of your friend and mine, Gutter Jack. Had the firefighters pretty well baffled, too. Nothing they did even slowed the inferno. Funny thing was, none of the other apartments in your building so much as got smudged by the smoke."

"Jesus!" Nick breathed as the chill leapt from the pavement and into his chest. "Cy and his goon. Now this. I didn't know I could get killed doing this. Hell, I didn't know."

"Ah ha!" Thaddeus purred triumphantly, thumping a paw against Nick. "So you admit then that you *do* know what you're doing and that you agreed to do it!"

"No!" Nick said, standing up abruptly and sending Thaddeus to the pavement with a *brrrt!* "No, I don't know what I'm doing, running around this city trying to find a talisman when I don't even know what it looks like or where it is and having to guess some creep's middle name in the meantime."

"It's a stone bannister knob, Nick, big as you can grab in two hands," Thaddeus said. "And I do mean you, Nick. You're the only one who can touch it. Old Scrounger's a romantic, so he was probably hoping you'd just stumble across the thing of your own accord. But I'll tell you where it is. The library. Downtown."

"The library?" Nick envisioned the building, the marble columns, the cyclopean staircase, the massive stone bannisters, topped with—

"The library," Nick groaned. "There's got to be a hundred of those stone things on the bannisters. Which one is it?"

"Why should I bother telling you anything more, Nick?" Thaddeus said, coolly licking a paw again. "You're probably not going to do it anyway. You're going to go back to your safe little apartment. Only you'll find it's a burnt-out husk. But even if you change your mind then, it'll be too late."

"All right, I'll do it, I'll do it," Nick said in exasperation.

"Promise?" Thaddeus purred.

"Yes, I promise. Now which one is it, for chrissake?" Nick demanded.

"Oh, that," Thaddeus said, sounding disinterested as he hopped to his feet. "I haven't the faintest idea. That's one you'll have to figure out for yourself. But you've only got until moonset, Nick. If you don't have the talisman by the time the Moon dips below the skyline of the city, then Gutter Jack's free to do what he wants. Forever. But don't worry about it, Nick. You won't suffer too much. After all, you'll probably be the first one he destroys." With that, Thaddeus turned about and padded down the alley, his tail waving back and forth in the air, and Nick just stood there, unable to get his jaw back up where it belonged.

Just as the small form disappeared, Nick heard the cat's voice drift back. "Don't ever forget, Nick. This is real. No matter what you think, Gutter Jack can hurt you and all of us. Remember. . . ." But the rest turned into a distant *meow* that faded into the darkness. Nick sank back to the pavement, sat a minute more, and then took a deep breath, stood up, and glanced at the sky. The Moon had just begun its descent as he started walking once more into the city.

The skyscrapers of downtown were beginning to loom over him, onyx sentinels that kept making Nick think of the monolith in *2001*, when he reached an intersection that was particularly devoid of both traffic and people. Nick felt his lips say *uh-oh*, but no sound came from his mouth as he took a tentative step into the street. Nick could tell as well as anyone else when lightning was about to strike.

And then it struck.

A manhole cover next to him burst out of its socket in a blast of smoke and white-hot sparks, spinning in the air like a titan's Frisbee until it crashed thunderously into the street. The most disconcerting thing was that Nick was positive there hadn't been a manhole there a moment ago. But he was good at taking hints, and he tried to make a break for it, dashing to cross the intersection as fast as he could. But then another manhole cover that hadn't been there before exploded furiously in front of him, and Nick dove for his life.

As he rolled, he heard the mocking laughter that had followed him earlier. Now it was bubbling forth in front of him. Nick scrambled to his feet and for a split-second saw a slim figure on the sidewalk. He caught the gleam of the street light off black leather, off a metallic mohawk, off something small and silvery dangling from one ear. But the figure gestured abruptly with a spike-gloved hand, and manhole covers went whizzing through the air all around Nick, one missing his head by inches.

Then smoke choked out all of the air, and the figure disappeared from sight. Nick couldn't even see the opposite curb as he threw his body to the ground, narrowly ducking thirty pounds of flying iron.

His face didn't hit pavement, though. Instead, he was staring into the jet blackness of one of the manholes. Another cover clattered uncomfortably nearby, and Nick

Illustrated by Denis Beauvais

remembered Thaddeus's advice. He could die. Horribly. Without a second thought, Nick went for the only out he could see and jumped down into the manhole. He heard a shriek of rage follow him, a shriek that suddenly transformed itself into satisfied laughter.

Nick fell a whole lot longer than he thought he would, and landed a whole lot harder, too. He floundered in murky water and thought he was drowning because he couldn't breathe, but then paralysis loosened its grip on his lungs and they drew in a ragged, shuddering breath. He sat up straight and realized the water wasn't more than a foot deep. The stench, though, was enough to drag him under, and small blobs of things he didn't even want to think about bobbed and floated against him, making him stand up with a hearty *eeyech!*

It was then he realized that he could see. A faint, livid illumination came from all around, and Nick wondered for a second if it was moonlight. But when he looked up, there was only slimy tile. The manhole was gone.

"Oh, great," Nick said aloud, his voice skittering off the walls. "What could possibly be better than this?"

A scurrying and chittering in the distance answered him, and Nick figured this was a pretty good time to start looking for an exit sign. From the noise, every rat that had lived since the 16th century was back there, and all of them sounded hungry.

The water sucked and gurgled with each step Nick took, dragging his feet down. More water dripped from the walls and from the ceiling onto him until he felt the odor of sweet rot and old death had soaked into his pores. He struggled forward, but he didn't come across any more manholes, only passageways that twisted and split off at random. Soon, he had no idea if he was going in circles or maybe in figure-eights, but all the while the scraping and rustling was getting closer. Suddenly, he stumbled out into a larger chamber, a main junction of several cylindrical passageways, each spewing forth its own noxious concoction, and he gasped in relief when he saw against the opposite wall iron rungs that led up to a manhole.

"Wonder what the fire marshal would say about the way they hide the exits down here," Nick said as he started slogging through the muck. And he was almost halfway there when the alligator burst out from underneath the slime, its huge jaws snapping.

Nick stumbled backward just out of reach, windmilled his arms wildly, and then sat back into the reeking water. He could hear the rats scurrying close behind, but it looked like all they were going to get was leftovers.

"I can't believe this," Nick said as the huge creature came toward him, spreading its jaws wide enough to swallow him in one gulp. "I always told people not to flush their baby 'gators. I told them this would happen." Nick braced himself, waiting to feel his bones crushed to splinters.

But the alligator had stopped and just floated there, staring at him. It closed its jaws and Nick was positive afterward that it winked one bulbous eye at him, all the while giving him an alligator's toothy grin.

A set of small claws scrabbled across Nick's neck and he jumped up with a yelp, flinging a healthy-sized rat across the room. He flailed as fast as he could toward the ladder—giving the alligator a wide berth—and scaled the slimy rungs to push against the manhole cover. It didn't budge.

The rats were pouring into the room now, thousands of them, their small red eyes glowing hotly. The alligator had vanished, and the rats were rapidly piling themselves up underneath the ladder. Already the top of the mass was threatening his foot. Nick shoved with all his might, but the manhole cover was rusted tight. A particularly muscular rat leapt up and landed on Nick's shoe, but he managed to shake it off, preparing himself for a really big scream, when abruptly the air pressure changed.

The pressure grew higher until Nick thought his ears would burst and his brain with them. And then with a deafening *pop!* that sent Nick's blood fizzing like soda water in his head, the manhole cover burst outward, and so did Nick, in a cloud of white smoke and fiery sparks.

He tumbled and rolled on the pavement, lying there for a stunned moment, and could hear manhole covers still blowing and crashing to one side. Suddenly a heavy plopping rain began around Nick, and when he heard the squeals, he realized it was the rats. He scrambled to his feet dizzily and dashed away from the smoke and mayhem, and only when the crashing had dwindled to a faint, echoing din did he pause for a minute, hands resting on knees, to catch his breath.

The night air was cooler now, and Nick noticed his clothes were perfectly dry as he wrapped his coat tighter about him. He glanced up and saw the Moon was nearly halfway to the building tops as he started in a limping jog toward downtown.

The library wasn't more than a mile away, but Nick just had to stop. His blistered feet throbbed in his scuffed loafers, and that apple Danish seemed too many miles back. He scanned both sides of the street as he hobbled along, but every deli, every coffee shop was dark and silent, and Nick started to believe this was just another little treat Gutter Jack had arranged for him.

And then Nick saw the warm red glow of neon. *Madame Zola's,* the flashing sign read—*Fortunes Told* and, beneath that, *Breakfast Served 24 Hours.* Nick breathed a prayer of gratitude to the deity of late-night wayfarers, stumbled up the steps, and pushed through the ornate stained glass door. Bells chimed behind him as he found himself in a dimly lit, tapestry- and bead-swathed room.

Suddenly a mass of paisley and striped silk scarves separated itself from the jumble of pillows on the floor, and it took Nick several moments to realize that there was a woman inside it.

"I am Madame Zola," the woman said in a coppery Mid-Eastern voice as she crossed to him, taking his hand between hers. "Ahh," she said, throwing back her head, "I sense you come from afar, through great darkness and peril."

"Yes," Nick said, "yes, that's right!"

"It is?" Madame Zola asked, slipping into a nasal secretary's voice. "I mean," she continued in the Mid-Eastern lilt, "of course you have. Come, sit." She led him to a pile of densely embroidered cushions. "What is it you require? The cards? the crystal? No! Let me guess," she said, jerking him off balance as she pressed his hand to her forehead. "Ah, Eggs Benedict, of course!" she cried in delight, letting go of Nick's hand. He fell face first into the cushions. "You're in luck. That's the special this week. Only $3.95. Back in a flash." She disappeared in a whirl of bright silk through a beaded doorway just as Nick managed to get his head above the pillows.

He didn't say anything, though. Eggs Benedict was fine by him. Instead, he leaned back into the cushions for a few minutes until his feet had quit screaming and had settled themselves into a chorus of steady whimpering. Eventually, curiosity got the better of him, and he started poking about the room, peeking in various niches and small wooden boxes.

He found candles, incense, beads, unknown powders, and silver rings shaped like coiled snakes, and, under a black cloth on a small round table, her crystal ball. He simply couldn't resist passing his hands over it and peering

inside, and he was somewhat surprised when he saw
something—someone—within it. The image was of a young
man with a metallic mohawk and a safety-pin in his ear,
garbed all in black leather with silver-spiked trim. Suddenly, the young man whirled around and looked straight
out of the crystal at Nick as though he knew he was being
watched. Nick almost choked and jerked his head back, but
after a second, he knew by the darting eyes that Gutter Jack
couldn't see him, so he bent closer to have another look.

Gutter Jack was the prettiest human being Nick had ever seen. His features were long and smooth, his ears just
ever-so-slightly pointed, and his eyes as clear as a hurri-
cane's. Instead of detracting from it, the hair and getup only
added to his wild beauty, and Nick had to shake his head
and blink his eyes to break his gaze from the crystal.

"Hey!" Madame Zola shouted at him as she appeared
in the doorway bearing a loaded tray, "You want your fortune told, you gotta pay."

"Uh, sorry," Nick said, jumping away from the crystal
ball. He knocked something off a small shelf in the process
and quickly bent to pick it up, apologizing profusely.

"No, don't touch that!" Madame Zola yelled, but it
was too late. Nick already held the silver half-moon amulet
in his hands. Suddenly it flared blue-silver, and Nick let out
a yelp, dropping it as he flopped backward into the cushions. He heard china shatter as Madame Zola's tray hit the
floor. "It's you," he heard her say.

"Quick, get up!" she said, grabbing his hand and yank-
ing him up out of the pillows. The scarves had fallen from
her face and Nick could see she was older than he had
thought, but the lines in her pale skin and around her large
eyes lent her an air of assured beauty. "I must be getting as
old as Scrounger, thinking a regular customer was out on a
night like this." She straightened his twisted clothes and

led him gently but forcibly to the door. "You've got to hurry. There isn't much time."

"But what about the Eggs Benedict?" Nick asked, trying not to whine.

"You can think of food at a time like this?" she asked incredulously. Nick nodded, but she wasn't looking for an answer. "Here, take this," she said, pushing the cool metal of the Moon amulet into his palm. "You're going to need it."

"What's it for?" he had sense enough to ask as she pushed him toward the steps.

"It'll tell you which one," she said, shutting the door. "Hold it in the moonlight." Nick heard the door latch and the bolt drawn.

Great, he thought as he stumbled down the stairs. *I've got to save everyone on an empty stomach.* But then he looked up and saw that Madame Zola was right. The Moon was getting close to the building-tops.

"Ow! Too busy to watch out for an old man, huh?" a feeble voice groaned as Nick tripped over what he'd taken for a piece of trash lying in the gutter. "Young people," the voice muttered, and Nick bent closer to see what it was.

Underneath a layer of newspaper was the remnant of a man, dressed in ragged overalls. His purplish skin looked ready to slide off his face, and his beard was matted and the color of tapioca. "Can I help you?" Nick asked.

"Help *me*?" the wino wheezed, and Nick nearly passed out from the cloud of alcohol fumes that engulfed him. "You folk are always so darn sure of yerselfs that you just assume that *you* can help *me*."

"Oh, well, sorry," Nick said, blinking the tears back from his stinging eyes and standing up. "Well, I've got some business to take care of, so. . . ."

"So what?" the bum sputtered. "So yer business is so gol-darned important that you don't have time for an old sot like me, 'zat it?" Nick mumbled something noncommittal, and the bum took a swig from something in a paper bag. "Now don't go off half-cocked, boy. I got something here that might help you a bit." He held up the bottle in the sack, and Nick could almost see the noxious vapors curling up out of it.

"Uh, no thanks," Nick managed. "I don't really need a drink right now."

"A drink?" the old bum hooted. "I don't mean for you to drink it, boy. Darned stuff'll kill you, melt yer innards right through. I ain't got any innards left, so I'm all right, but I wouldn't drink a drop of it if I were you."

"Well, what do you want me to do with it?" Nick asked dubiously.

"C'mon, boy," the wino answered. "This ol' rotgut'll dissolve just about anything. Don't tell me yer not gonna be needing all the help you can get in a few minutes."

"Wait a second," Nick said. "Don't tell me you're in on this thing, too."

"Haven't you got that through yer thick skull yet, boy? We're all in on this. Only problem is, it's all up to a bone-head like you. Now take it, take it."

Nick reached for the bottle. It felt nauseatingly warm underneath the paper. "Uh, you really don't need this, do you?" Nick asked.

"Naw, got a spare," the bum said as he pulled another bag out from under the newpapers and took a long draw from it. "Whew! That does light a fire in yer chimney, if you know what I mean. Now get along, boy. Time's a wast-ing." Nick glanced up and sure enough the Moon was almost resting on the building-tops.

"Got to go," Nick said. "Uh, thanks," he added and dashed off into the night. When he was almost out of sight, he thought he heard the old wino mumble, "Darned young people," but he couldn't be sure.

Nick ran as fast as he could, but a career at Uptown

Insurance hadn't exactly prepared him for the First Annual Midnight Supernatural Dash. By the time he rounded the corner into the plaza that spread out beneath the library, his heart had migrated into his ears, and his lungs had just plain resigned. He looked up expecting to see Gutter Jack and an army of Gutterlings, but the plaza was empty. Only moonlight filled the space between Nick and the library steps. And there were the bannister knobs, all one hundred and twelve, if Nick had stopped to count them.

He didn't get a chance to, though. As soon as he could hear over his own wheezing breath, the sound of distant but rapidly nearing engines reached Nick's ears. He groaned and started hobbling across the plaza.

He'd only reached the middle when the Moon skimmed the building-tops and the Harleys came roaring in. There were three of them, each with a leather-jacketed avatar of the Devil himself. The bikes were beasts of dark metal, belching flame, sulfur, and ungodly noise, and the rider astride each grinned, showing off yellow fangs. Dark spittle ran down their chins. Nick couldn't move, but just gaped at them as they sped closer. He could see the steel chains they wore. He could see their tattoos, could even read them. One biker had a flaming skull etched into his arm that bore beneath it the succinct caption, *Kill—It's Fun*. The tires of the bikes tore chunks out of the pavement, and they were about to do the same to Nick.

Then Nick heard laughter behind him, breaking the spell, and he leapt aside, just after what one could reasonably consider the last moment had expired. Exhaust roasted his skin, but he was still alive when he rolled to his feet.

One of the bikers split off from the others then, revving his machine until it belched flame like a Chinese dragon. Nick watched him circle almost leisurely around the plaza and realized too late what was happening. Suddenly the other two bikers popped wheelies, tearing huge chunks out

of the granite tiles and sending rank smoke billowing into the air. They aimed their machines straight at Nick just
as he saw the third biker do the same from the opposite
direction, and he started running perpendicular to their
approaches, dodging the gaping holes in the pavement as he
made a break for the library.

But the bikers kept after him. He wasn't going to make
it, he was going to get it from both sides. *Jesus,* he thought,
I'm going to be paté faster than I can scream Cuisinart. It
felt like his heart was thumping outside of his chest. *Wait!*
Something *was* thumping outside of his chest. Nick reached
into his topcoat's breast pocket and his hand met paper
around glass. Suddenly he smiled. He had a plan. Not a sensible one, nor even a somewhat risky one. But it was a plan.
Nick spun on his heel and started running *toward* the two
bikers, turning his back on the third.

The bikers shouted like banshees, obviously pleased at
the prospect of a more head-on collision, and Nick just ran
grinning at them, hands behind his back. When combustion-
powered death was less than twenty feet away, Nick let the
bottle rip and then dived for cover in one of the tire gouges.
The glass shattered in front of the bikes, and the riders had
no time to swerve.

The Harleys' front tires hit the rotgut and melted like
jelly, sending out thick yellow fumes that made Nick retch.
The bikes swerved, the daemon bikers no longer grinning,
and then hooked onto each other as they spun out of control. They hit a black marble replica of *The Thinker* at 117
miles per hour and the night lit up like the center of a super-
nova.

Nick turned away from the blast—and there came the
other biker swinging a gigantic black iron flail, flames jet-
ting out behind him, and a death's head dangling from the
handlebars. Nick had forgotten about this one, but he didn't
even have time to scream. The biker roared as he swung the

flail to cave in Nick's head, and Nick involuntarily stuck his hand out to shield himself from the pulverizing blow. Silver flashed, metal shrieked, and ozone raised the hairs in Nick's nostrils. The spiked ball of the flail bounced off Nick's arm, not even scratching him, and into the twisted visage of the daemon biker. The bike spun wildly and then flipped, consuming itself and its rider in a gout of green flame that spurted into the sky. Nick stared at his wrist, remembering Sandra's bracelet even as it slipped off his wrist, turning into molten droplets.

And then something made him jerk his head upward. The Moon. It had sunk halfway below the downtown skyline! Nick jumped up and ran for the library's steps, dodging the smoking wreckage of the Harleys. His foot met the first step—and then laughter rang out above him.

Nick looked up into the beautiful, empty eyes of Black Gutter Jack. "I've won, Jack," Nick said, surprised at the metal in his own voice. "Get out of my way."

"Oh, I wouldn't dream of stopping you, my dear friend," Jack said smiling, his voice as clear as winter bells. "Be my guest. There's only one hundred and twelve bannister knobs. And you have about time to test out, oh, I'd say two!"

"That's all the time I need, you creep," Nick said as he pulled out Madame Zola's amulet. But even as Jack gasped in horror, Nick's foot caught the edge of a step, and he went sprawling to the marble, the amulet tracing a delicate, silvery arc as it flew through the air.

Jack's gasp turned to mocking glee. "Oh, Nick. It looks like you're all out of luck. And you came so far, too."

Nick lay face down on the steps, a pitiful figure, as Jack stepped lightly down toward him to gloat. But when Jack's fading shadow touched him, Nick sprang up with a grunt of triumph, flinging himself at the lithe form of Gutter Jack.

The two grappled a moment, Jack with the strength strange in his willowy body, Nick with the strength of desperation.

Suddenly Nick paused. "What am I doing?" he asked suddenly. "You've sent your little tricks after me, and now you're done. You can't do anything more to hurt me."

"You're wrong, Nick. You're so wrong. I can hurt you. I can hurt you very badly. Just let go of me and go on home now," Jack said, his voice full of sharp edges, but behind those edges hid a faint note of hysteria.

"You're pissing me off, Jack!" Nick shouted, anger erupting in him for the first time since his journey began, replacing fear with its hot intoxication. "Out . . . of . . . my . . . WAY!" he gritted between his teeth. And then with a grunt that would have done Cy's goon, Sammy, proud, Nick grabbed Gutter Jack's black leather jacket in one hand and his silver-studded belt in the other and heaved him down the steps.

Nick didn't wait for Jack to land. He ran and leapt forward, his fingers scrabbling for the amulet. Just as Jack let out a scream that woke the dead and knocked them back in their graves all in the same moment, Nick's hand closed over the silver metal, and he thrust the amulet into the rapidly fading beams of the Moon.

The cold silver metal hummed brightly and nearly shivered out of Nick's grasp. But he held tight as a shaft of pure molten silver shot from the amulet straight at one of the bannister knobs. Nick watched breathlessly as the stone flared brightly and then burst apart, revealing beneath its shell an orb as pale and luminescent as the Moon itself.

"Ha ha!" Nick cried in glee, scrambling over to the bannister. He hesitated only a moment, his fingers hovering over the talisman, and then he closed his hands around it. The orb was cool and slightly slippery to the touch, and it parted from the bannister with a faint *snick*. Lifting the talisman, Nick turned around to confront Gutter Jack—

—who was not cowering and groveling at all like Nick expected him to be. In fact, though he stood at the bottom of the steps and came no closer, Nick could see that he was laughing again, silently, holding onto his sides as if to keep his mirth from splitting them open.

"I must confess, you did have me worried for a moment there," Jack said, grinning broadly, displaying his white, even, slightly pointed teeth. He looked like an elfin child, Nick thought then. Pretty, innocent, and delicate. But strong. Strong and old, much older than he appeared. Older than the city, older than the people who first came. And he had never been innocent. "After all, you did manage to get the talisman, and here with, I'd say, a good minute to spare by the looks of the Moon." Nick jerked his head up at that and saw that only a thin slice of the Moon still peeked above the skyline. "But I forgot," Jack let out a small self-deprecating chuckle, "you have no idea how to use it." His mirth got the better of him then, and peals of his laughter rang out over the plaza, echoing off the twisted wreckage of the Harleys that still glowed evilly beneath their columns of thick, greasy smoke.

And Nick realized he was right. With the last few seconds slipping past, nothing he did affected Jack at all, except to make him laugh even harder. He lifted the orb over his head, concentrated as hard as he could on Jack's head exploding, said any magic words he could think of, like *abracadabra,* but it was to no avail. Quickly, he thought he could throw it at Jack, or try to touch him with it. But just as quickly he realized Jack would be able to dodge it effortlessly with a nimble little skip.

I've lost. We've all lost, Nick thought, his heart sinking into his stomach. *Why can't I think of the one thing he least wants me to do with the orb? That would have to be it. But how could I ever guess what. . .*

And then Nick had an idea. "You've won, Jack!" he called. "I've only got a few seconds left."

"Glad you've come to your senses, Nick," Jack said merrily, bowing with a flourish. "Because of this, perhaps I'll make your death a bit less hideous."

"That's too kind of you, really," Nick said, eyeing the last sliver of the Moon. "But first I want to give you a little victory present." Suddenly Jack froze, but before he could say or do anything, Nick shouted in a voice as clear as ice-water, "I give this talisman to you, Black Gutter Jack!"

The Moon stopped. The barest glowing sliver hung just over the skyline, and Jack screamed as a thin shaft of pearly radiance burst forth from it, straight from the heavens into the heart of the talisman. Nick squinted his eyes at the searing-white fire that burst forth, but the touch of its flames was cool as gossamer on his hands. And then the shaft reflected off the orb, shooting into the chest of Gutter Jack, taking hold of him, reeling him in.

"No!" Jack screamed in a voice filled with cold eternity. "No! Don't do this to me!" Sweat was flowing from every pore in Nick's body, but he kept his grip on the talisman. Suddenly one of Jack's feet jerked itself onto the first step, obviously against his will. Then his other foot stepped up, and inexorably Jack moved up the staircase toward Nick, moaning, ranting, and screaming all the while. Foam flecked his smooth lips, blood showed against the whites of his clear eyes as his delicate hands shot out before him, reaching for the now pulsating orb.

"Go on, Jacky," Nick said, grinning now. "Take it. It's what you want, isn't it?"

No. Jack's mouth kept forming the word, but no sound came out, and then his hands closed over the talisman. The Moon dipped behind the skyline and the night exploded.

The force of the shock blew Nick ten feet backward, and the agony of Black Gutter Jack's scream ripped not through his ears, but his mind. Nick watched as a pale inferno engulfed Jack's writhing form, but the blaze was too dazzling, and Nick had to shut his eyes to keep them from blistering. Abruptly, something cut off Jack's scream, and everything was silence to Nick as he lay there with his eyes clamped shut. And then, finally, the noises came. A siren. Footsteps. The passage of a car.

Nick slowly opened his eyes and was surprised to see Jack was still standing there in the darkness. He jumped to his feet, ready. And then he saw the cool marble that was Gutter Jack's face, that formed his hands where they gripped the talisman, again just another piece of stone.

Nick sighed and then stretched, arching his back. "Aagh!" he said when his feet reminded him that they still hurt as he limped past the library's newest piece of statuary and down the steps. The cool breeze blew back his topcoat, felt good on his face. It wasn't until he was halfway through the plaza that he noticed the people.

"Boy, hon, sure looks like you could use a cup of good strong coffee."

"Rosa," Nick said gratefully and smiled. "Yeah, I sure could."

"And I think you'll be needing a place to stay, at least for a while," Madame Zola said, stepping out of a shadow. "I've got an extra room. Can you wash dishes?"

"Yeah," Nick laughed. "Yeah, I can."

"We owe you a big one, son," Old Scrounger told him. "You did your job right, just like I knew you would."

They were all there, Nick saw now. The wino. Sandra. Thaddeus T-for-Tom Fishbone. Even the people from the diner.

"C'mon, hon," Rosa said, wrapping an arm around him and leading him out of the plaza. "You're one of us now."

Nick smiled. He liked the sound of that. Now *he* was going to be one of the ones people just passed by, part of the universe most people shut out behind their curtains and never bothered to see. And now he knew what all those people were missing.

"How about those Eggs Benedict, too?" Nick suggested, and everyone liked the idea.

Wisdoms & Warnings: Writing SF for Younger Readers

by
Jane Yolen

About the Author

Jane Yolen is one of SF's leading experts on this topic, being the successful author of countless stories at all lengths for readers of all ages. She has published over one hundred books, most but not all of them for younger readers. She now has her own imprint—Jane Yolen Books—for younger SF readers, from a major publishing company. She is also a past President of the SFWA.

Her many honors and awards testify that she can excellently do what any writer has to do—reach the audience. And in the essay that follows, what you will find is precise, hardedged advice on that topic.

The WOTF rules state we regret we cannot accept works intended "for children." That's true; to compete equally, the stories that come before the judges must all be presentable to the same public, which is presumed to be adult... in some sense. The distinction lies in the depth of education *assumed to lie behind it. Yet many of Robert A. Heinlein's "Young Adult" novels were quite successfully serialized to the ("Old Adult"?) audiences of* Astounding *and* The Magazine of Fantasy and Science Fiction. *We paraphrase: We regret we can only accept works intended for adults. . . .*

There is an old story told about the great man of the theater, Stanislavsky. He was approached by a young actor for advice. The actor said (and this is neither a translation nor a transcript of that conversation, but rather an artistic reconstruction): "Sir, I have always performed for adult audiences but tomorrow I must perform for an audience of children. What should I do?"

"Act as you always do," Stanislavsky counseled. "Only better!"

It is the same when writing for children, whatever age one uses to define someone whom the publishing industry identifies as not yet being "an adult."

With that initial warning issued, I'd like to add that writing for "children" is great fun; there are many kinds of opportunities open to new writers, and the rewards are long-lasting.

However—and it is a big however—there are some warnings you should be given. We are not talking about a pastel Neverneverland. Here there be sandtraps, tiger pits, sucking marshes *and* dragons.

Warning #1: "Only better." As Walter de la Mare, that consummate poet of childhood once said, "Only the rarest kind of best is good enough for children." As adult readers, we forgive even our favorite writers. We know them to be human. But it has taken us years to develop this tolerance. Young children often believe books have grown, like antic wildflowers, on the shelves of the nursery. They forgive nothing. So watch your diction, make sure your hero's eyes are the same color all the way through, and check those illustrations. If it says a *pink* dragon, it had better be pink. Older children will be quite a bit older before they become even slightly more forgiving.

Warning #2: There are any number of children's book genres that accommodate (even cry out for) speculative fiction. A children's book author is not confined to 650-page novels—except for the very rare Richard Adams' *Watership Down* or the even rarer J.R.R. Tolkien—nor forced to accept the conventions of a literature magazine.

Each of the available children's genres has different rules. For example, there is the picture book, which in print is going to be 32 or 48 pages long. The text here may be as short as Sendak's *Where the Wild Things Are* or as long as Chris Van Allsburg's *Polar Express.* These books may be characterized as stories that are completely illustrated.

There is also the storybook with illustrations, such as Jarrel's *The Bat Poet* or Steig's *Abel's Island.* There are massive story collections like Kennedy's *Collected Stories* (based on his picture books), long illustrated volumes such as Dickinson's *Merlin Dreams,* medium-sized collections such as Babbit's *The Devil's Storybook* or short illustrated ones like my *The Girl Who Cried Flowers.* There are SF poetry collections, short novels, Young Adult (YA) novels, anthologies, and even non-fiction like Georgess McHargue's *The Beasts of Never* and *Meet the Vampire.* **And every publisher is looking for these kinds of books—not just specialty houses.**

In children's books, whimsy still exists and talking animals abound, fairy tales are rewritten and reworked, old magics evoked, and children thrown backward and forward in time through essentially fantastic means. But there is also plenty of realistic science fiction, from Heinlein-type space adventures to hard-hitting dystopian novels such as Joan Vinge's *Psion;* from space trilogies by new authors like John Forrester to single novels such as Diana Wynne Jones's gnomic *The Homeward Bounders;* from picture books like Winkowski's tender *The Martian Crystal Egg* to Grahame Oakley's postnuclear holocaust parable, *Henry's Quest.* (A very important thing to remember is that publishers create marketing categories, such as "YA," and specify "reading levels," but we all know that people routinely can and do read well "above" their physical ages.)

In other words, the range is open—and endless.

Warning #3: If you are going to write for young readers, acquaint yourself with the popular authors of children's books today. If the books I have just mentioned are unknown to you, get them from the library. Also try: Patricia McKillip, Robin McKinley, Betty Levin, Andre Norton, John Rowe Townsend, Patricia Wrightson, Bruce Coville, George Zebrowski, Zilpha Keatly Snyder, John Bellairs, Lloyd Alexander, Shirley Rousseau Murphy, Diane Duane, Alan Garner, Kevin Crossley-Holland, Sid Fleischman—to name just a few, and in no particular order.

If you do not know what speculative fiction is currently being published in the children's book field, you will only repeat the mistakes that hundreds of would-be writers have made; you will not be able to aim for the "rarest kind of best." If you are unwilling to read this stuff, why do you want to write it? Only excessive and overweening pride whispering in your ear: "You're better!" How can you know you are better when you don't know what you are better (or worse) than? And can you, in fact, meet the standard cited by Stanislavsky and de la Mare?

Besides, some of the finest fantasy and science fiction being written today is in the guise of children's books, and it would be a shame as a Constant Reader if you missed out on it.

Warning #4: You must read your manuscript aloud. Children's books are meant to be read aloud—even the novels. There is a reason for this: the pattern of buying in the children's book field is an odd imbalancing act—70 to 80 per cent of all children's books are bought by schools and libraries. Teachers read the good books out loud in the classroom; librarians read out loud to school groups. In no other literature (except poetry) is this so universally true. Therefore, if your manuscript suffers when read aloud, if the writing sputters and stops, if your tongue tangles on clauses and stutters on participles, then the manuscript is not ready to sell. Reading your work aloud is one of the best ways to learn what needs to be polished, what should be eliminated. It is a slow process to be sure, but an important one. The reading eye tends to elide over weak passages, avoiding them. The speaking mouth reveals every fault.

Sub-warning: Reading your book to an eager, listening child is no absolute guarantee of its worth. A child who is desperate for attention will listen to a full rendition of the Brooklyn Telephone Directory. While a child is your final audience, your first and most critical audience must be *you*.

Warning #5: Once upon a time certain words, certain actions, certain feelings were taboo in children's books. Not now. Recent speculative fiction children's books include a fairy tale picture book in which both the child protagonist and her mother die in the last paragraph (*Dear Mili* by Wilhelm Grimm and Maurice Sendak), a science fiction picture book in a postnuclear war world in which a white king and a black queen are married (Oakley's *Henry's Quest*) and a time travel novel in which a young Jewish girl is zapped back to the Holocaust and lives out her short life in a concentration camp (my own *The Devil's Arithmetic*).

The operative phrase is: Does it work? And the corollary is: Is it necessary? If the story demands a once-taboo swear-word or action or feeling or situation, then of course use it. If it is there only for shock value or because you wanted to see if you could get away with it—leave it out.

Warning #6: Children are not casual readers. They read for their lives. They read for information about their worlds—inside and out. They do not forgive dishonesty, smarminess, condescension, or mistakes. A children's book can, quite literally, make a difference in a child's life.

I received a letter recently from a junior high school boy who had read my SF novel *Dragon's Blood* and told me that he was short and never chosen for games. But after reading *Dragon's Blood* he realized that it was what he did—not how tall he was—that mattered. And he meant it.

Our childhood heroes and our childhood books stick with us long after the most recent adult novels have passed by. I remember more about my favorite stories read in that long ago—*The Wind in the Willows, Treasure Island, The Jungle Book, Alice in Wonderland, The Secret Garden,* and *Charlotte's Web*—than I do about the good adult books I read this month: a Silverberg, a Card, and the copyedited manuscript of my own latest adult book. Which is not to say that Silverberg and Card and I write forgettable novels. Rather, it has to do with the way children take in their stories, gulping them down, then re-reading them every bedtime, every rainy day, every sorrowing time, every happy time. My middle son read *Lord of the Rings* at least four times before he was 13. My daughter re-read *Charlotte's Web*—and especially the death scene—nightly for months. (My youngest read *Peterson's Bird Guide* over and over, but that was a different kind of obsession.) Last year I received a letter from a boy who informed me he'd read *Dragon's Blood* thirteen times and "Sometimes I wake up thinking I'm Jakkin Stewart."

Therefore, to write for children is a responsibility. One should never preach, yet one must always be aware that the stories we serve up to our children have the power—and the opportunity—to make their worlds tremble.

Warning #7: Study the market. There is one out there! And, though you can rarely find word of it on the pages of *Locus* and *SF Chronicle,* there are specific places to go to learn more about the world of children's literature since speculative fiction is such a large part of that world.

Magazines: *The Horn Book, The New Advocate, Parents' Choice, School Library Journal, Children's Literature in Education, Language Arts*—the children's section of your library or your local school's library should have copies.

Books: Some of the following will give you a short but thorough grounding in all aspects of writing for children: *Writing with Pictures* by Uri Shulevitz; *Books: From Writer to Reader* by Howard Greenfeld; *The Way to Write for Children* by Joan Aiken; *Talent Is Not Enough* by Mollie Hunter; *The Children's Picture Book* by Ellen Roberts; and my *Writing Books for Children* and my forthcoming *Guide to Writing for Children.*

There is an organization that caters to the needs of writers for young readers: SCBW, the Society of Children's Book Writers: P. O. Box 296, Mar Vista Station, Los Angeles, California 90066. You do not have to be published to be an Associate Member. There are well over 4,000 members worldwide. SCBW offers reports on the market, on magazines for children, on contracts, on agents, on computers, on preparing manuscripts, etc., all free to its members. It also gives a yearly award, *The Golden Kite*, to the best books of the year. Speculative fiction has often won.

There are conferences and seminars around the country on the writing of children's books—and probably even a panel or two at your friendly local SF convention.

Finally—there are the books themselves. They—and your own heart—are the best teachers.

Warning The Last: Do not ever ever ever refer to *any* of these books as Juveniles. Not only is that a pejorative usage, a kind of looking-down-the-long-nose by writers of adult books, but, even worse, if you use it *I* will know and I will hunt you down and tear up your book-writer's card, and tell the world you are a writer of Seniles!

Starbird

by
J. Steven York

About the Author

Steven York is a member of a group called Puget Sound Writer's Cramp and lives in Kirkland, Washington, where he is a freelance technical writer. He is one of the founders of Telecommunications Users Group and also writes reviews and articles for computer magazines. He has written a number of computer software manuals and hopes someday to hold an entire SF convention electronically.

He was introduced to SF by the Young Adult SF novels of Robert A. Heinlein. At the age of fifteen, he stopped drawing homemade comic books and began writing stories. But his other interests and his career as, first, a computer consultant and then a software specialist drew him away until he attended an SF convention panel on writers' workshops, went home, and helped found Writer's Cramp.

His first entry in the Contest won Honorable Mention. Here is his second. . . .

Illustrated by Ed Kline

"**E**asy," said Teeth, his words **filtering gently through Undermind to Green Stone, "you must not warp the wing too much,** or we will stall. Recovery at this altitude would likely overtax your skills. Spreading the wing tips instead will lower our stall speed, and make the ship more controllable."

"I understand," said Green Stone. "It is necessary to anticipate the wind gusts and compensate continuously."

The deck rocked under Teeth's holding feet, *Starbird* becoming less stable as Green Stone slowed her for landing. While one pair of eyes remained locked on the unfamiliar flatness of the viewscreen, he brought the other pair around to study the young Oun in the pilot's position. Green Stone was not without talent, but his nervousness was overcoming natural ability. Teeth reached out a gripper and tapped him reassuringly on the back of the head.

"Deploy the legs now, toes spread," Teeth instructed. "The webs provide braking at the end."

"Yes," agreed Green Stone, but again he was having problems. Deploying the webbed landing gear introduced new aerodynamic forces he had not anticipated. As he struggled to adjust the trim, the deep blue surface of the lake rushed up on their screens. *Starbird* struck the water feet first, then tipped forward so that its keel belly-flopped into the water. The deck tilted wildly. For a moment, forces twenty times the force of this planet's gravity tried to tear Teeth from his position at Green Stone's side. Teeth's holding feet remained firmly stuck to the deck. His only reaction was to bend slightly into the pull. The landing had been clumsy, but well within safety limits.

"That was better," said Teeth, "I will skill you as a pilot, yet."

The primitive symbol Green Stone sent back through the Undermind was the equivalent of a human shaking his head 'no.' "If it were only a matter of knowing, we could all be pilots. This skilling is more difficult than any I have experienced. You are unique, Teeth."

"You have the talent too," said Teeth. "Give yourself time. This method of flying is such an alien one, and there are many other things to be considered in the operation of *Starbird,* such as stealth." He scuttled around Green Stone, to the control panel that rose slightly from the deck. With a few deft movements of his grippers he retracted and folded *Starbird*'s wings, restored floating trim. This done, he passed control over to the support engineer who would keep watch and maintain their camouflage. A glance at the screen showed that the other gulls in the water were the only ones who had noticed the strange visitor in their midst. In a moment, even they had forgotten.

Under the support officer's control, the churning of the landing gear propelled *Starbird* slowly through the lake's chilly waters, in search of further knowledge about the strange creatures who called themselves "men."

"Pardons," said Green Stone. "The diversity of this task eludes me. So many aspects of operating the ship involve not only the physics of our operation, but the aesthetics of our disguise."

Teeth symboled the equivalent of a smile. "That is why this lake was chosen for your lessons. It is isolated from human activity and dwellings."

Green Stone bobbed his enlarged engineer's head sadly. "It is for naught, Teeth. I will never be a pilot as you are. I might navigate *Starbird* from place to place in an emergency, but I could never fool a human's most casual inspection.''

"If you can fly in an emergency, it is something. Until you reached that level of skill, I was indispensable. It is not the way of the Oun to have an individual who is indispensable. It is not comfortable to be the individual who is indispensable.''

Teeth scuttled closer to the viewscreen and sank into contemplation. It was not a luxury he often allowed himself. Deep contemplation drew heavily on the shared resources of the Undermind. With the small number of individuals isolated here on *Starbird,* their tiny Undermind was not normally to be squandered. Now, with the ship cruising quietly through the water and most of the crew engaged in only routine tasks he allowed himself to slip for a moment.

Green Stone could fly. Not well perhaps, but enough that he might get them back to the human space complex by traveling at night and avoiding human habitation. His attempts to teach Grasp were not going as well. Teeth held little hope for improvement. Grasp seemed unable to compensate for *Starbird's* size and inertia, or of working with the external forces on the ship, rather than against them. The ship's Pinnacle would not be pleased with that assessment.

Grasp was the Pinnacle's second in command, and his personal choice as pilot. Only after Grasp had been unable to master atmospheric operation of *Starbird* had other Primes been allowed to try. To the Pinnacle's distress, only Teeth had shown any aptitude. It was Teeth's idea that Engineers be tested as well. He had been delighted when his old friend Green Stone had shown promise. The Pinnacle did not fully approve of their friendship, or the idea of a non-Prime pilot.

"You are daydreaming again!" The words boomed

through the Undermind. Teeth skittered sideways a few steps in surprise.

"Apologies, my Pinnacle. I seek only to better serve our Undermind."

The Pinnacle entered the bridge and climbed the slight incline to his perch. "Think of how to serve me, Teeth. Have you made a pilot of Grasp yet?"

"Green Stone is doing well, Pinnacle, enough so that I am at least somewhat expendable."

"I asked of Grasp, not your freakish Engineer. Must I force you to share more fully with the Undermind?"

Teeth shuddered at the thought. An individual Oun was to the Undermind as a fish is to the sea. The balance between within and without must be maintained. Without that balance, even a fish can drown. A Pinnacle, as a focus of the Undermind, could destroy that balance. The result was a loss of one's individuality and initiative. The body remained alive, a servant of the Undermind, useful for manual labor, repetitive tasks, and as an additional mental resource for the Undermind to draw upon.

Teeth sent a symbol of subservience through the Undermind. "Apologies, Pinnacle. I only wished to provide you with the good news that we are no longer totally dependent on my skill. Grasp does not fare as well."

"You declare failure then?"

"It has long been observed that certain skills are less easily learned than others. The method of flying used by *Starbird* appears to be one such skill, but to a greater extent than any in our experience."

"There are flying craft on our own world. I have flown them myself. It is not difficult."

"Apologies, Pinnacle," Teeth struggled to communicate the alien nature of the task through the rigid symbols of the Undermind. "Those craft are small, light and very powerful for their size. Their flight characteristics more resemble those of an Earth insect than the bird our ship emulates. With those craft, it is easy to compensate for lack of skill and foresight with brute force. *Starbird* is much more massive, and has considerably less power relative to weight. It is necessary to anticipate, to plan every move in advance of its execution, to ride on the winds rather than power through them, to exploit every aerodynamic trick possible just to keep it aloft and under control."

The Pinnacle shuffled impatiently. "The difference seems more of degree than kind. You have failed to demonstrate why a mere Engineer can be taught, and not Grasp, my Pinnacle-in-waiting. You will continue Grasp's skilling. You will succeed!" The Pinnacle turned and scuttled off to his chamber.

Teeth snapped his grippers in angry frustration. The proof Grasp could not be taught was in his failure to progress. Why couldn't the Pinnacle understand that? He lashed out at the air with a gripper, then caught himself. Teeth had never harbored such thoughts of conflict with any Pinnacle before. Amazement replaced his anger. Was this the result of their small group's extended isolation?

Small groups of Oun had never endured such isolation before, and certainly not for so long. By the plan, they should have been back to Ounhome by now. The mother ship still waited for them in orbit. They were to have ridden back to orbit attached to one of the spacecraft the humans called a 'shuttle,' an unseen parasite on the vehicle's fuel tank. They could not have foreseen that one of those spacecraft would explode.

They had watched the whole thing from a lagoon near the launch site. They watched with the horrible knowledge they too could have been caught in that explosion.

The horror faded. There were other shuttles, and *Starbird* could return on one of them. When the next launch

merely an opportunity to learn more. Then the next launch
didn't happen, and the next. *Starbird* would be on Earth for
a long time.

Teeth found Green Stone asleep in the communal berth,
peacefully at one with the Undermind. It was against Teeth's
upbringing to wake a sleeping Oun. Sleep was important
not only to the individual. It allowed more of the individual's mind to serve the Undermind. Teeth hesitated a moment, then pounded on Green Stone's carapace with his
grippers. He was learning to do many things against his upbringing. "Wake, Green Stone."

Teeth darted back, as Green Stone rose with his grippers raised in an instinctive defensive posture. It was a
moment before Green Stone recognized his friend and
dropped his guard. "Why do you wake me, Teeth?"

Teeth moved closer, focusing his thoughts tightly on
Green Stone so as to avoid eavesdroppers. "I need to converse with you. I could not wait." The last symbol actually carried more seriousness than that. The implied urgency
was so great, Green Stone did not even consider questioning it.

"Then let us converse," said Green Stone.

"Have you noticed a general change in the crew since
we have been stranded on Earth?"

"What manner of change?"

"Mental change," replied Teeth, "perhaps even a
change in the Undermind itself."

"I have noticed something, yes. It is not a thing I can
isolate, merely a feeling of change; of wrongness."

Teeth returned a symbol of agreement. "I have more
than noticed this, I have attempted to quantify it. The small
size of our isolated group has made the Undermind weak.
In our extended isolation, we have come to adapt to the
situation. We have become more independent as individuals,

and less dependent on the Undermind. As we become less dependent, we become less controlled. We are gaining the ability to act independent of, and perhaps even contrary to, the needs of the Undermind.''

Green Stone rebelled against the suggestion. ''That is impossible, Teeth. We are the Undermind. The Undermind is us.''

''Perhaps the mere fact that I can conceive of such a thing may indicate that it is so,'' said Teeth. ''There is nothing impossible about it. The humans are proof of that. We can find no evidence that they possess an Undermind. We have witnessed too much activity on their part which is counter to species survival. There is little doubt.''

''I am familiar with those theories. I am also aware of the human's apparent effort to overcome this shortcoming through their artificial broadcasts of simulated sensory data.''

''Familiar? It is difficult for any of us not to be obsessed with it. Their broadcasts and the electrical noise generated by their machines fill the area of the spectrum used by the Undermind. Any Oun not protected by *Starbird*'s shielding would be cut off from the Undermind; in its place, bombardment with electrical noise.''

Green Stone shuddered. ''Why must you bring it up?''

''I have thought of it as much as I dared these last few days. The idea frightens me, but it intrigues me as well. What if one could be isolated from the Undermind, without suffering the bombardment of the human broadcasts?''

Green Stone shot back a symbol of denial. ''Impossible!''

''Of course it is possible. If, when we were back on Ounhome, I had entered *Starbird* alone and sealed the ports, it would have happened. The shielding which keeps out the human broadcasts would keep the Undermind out as well.

Without others in the ship, there would be no one with which to form an Undermind.''

Green Stone turned and scuttled to the far wall. ''This idea of yours is horrible, Teeth. How can you think such a thing? If the Pinnacle were to learn of it, he would feed you to the Undermind.''

''What I have told you is exactly what the Pinnacle fears, Green Stone: the freedom of the individual. Like the humans, we are learning to think for ourselves; to depend on the Undermind primarily as a computational resource, rather than a framework for our thinking.''

''I do not blame him, Teeth. Right now I fear you.''

''I am afraid too, my friend. Something is happening to us. I do not know what the end of it will be. The Pinnacle tries to resist it by imposing more discipline. I think he will fail. I fear the damage he may do us in the process.''

''You speak of rebellion against the Pinnacle? I warn you Teeth, my primary loyalty must be to the . . .''

''To the Undermind, Green Stone, as is mine. The Pinnacle is the focus of that Undermind, but he is no different than any other Prime. You knew him, as I did, before he surrendered his name to become the Pinnacle. He is not the Undermind. *We* are the Undermind, the sixty-six of us on this ship. We don't know when, or if, we can ever return to our home. For our purposes, we might as well be all the Oun left in the universe.''

Moving slowly nearer, Green Stone emitted a symbol of confusion. ''I don't understand what you ask of me, Teeth.''

''Only that you watch the Pinnacle, as well as Grasp and the others that are close to him. Do not let his authority blind you. *Think of the Undermind. Think of us!''*

Views of water wheeled dizzily across *Starbird's* viewscreens. Teeth gently slid the control plate connected to the ship's tail, bringing *Starbird* out of the descending spiral and into a straight glide. Every few seconds he would flap the wings a few strokes to maintain altitude.

They were flying parallel to the shore of an ocean inlet. Monolithic human structures lined the beach. Teeth was aware of the Pinnacle standing behind him, studying the screen, or at least making the pretense of doing so. Remote sensing was a new science to the Oun. Teeth had seen no sign that the Pinnacle had gotten the knack of interpreting the flat images on the screen. A spot of color nearby on the structures caught Teeth's attention, and he put *Starbird* into a steep bank. "I have spotted a news dispensing machine, Pinnacle." He shared his vision with the Pinnacle through the Undermind, along with a symbol indicating the spot of color.

"Excellent. Linguists stand by." Most of the useful information in human broadcasts took the form of the strange pressure-wave communications humans depended on. The Oun linguists, having no sense of hearing, found these transmissions difficult to interpret using such a small Undermind. *Starbird* was forced to seek the more easily understood printed news sheets for information about human spacecraft launches.

"Shall I land us near the machine?" While it was possible to examine a portion of the news sheets through a window on the dispensing machines, it was more useful to find a news sheet that had been discarded. Fortunately, the gulls *Starbird* emulated were scavengers. It was not unusual to see them rooting through human refuse.

"We will land on the water, and walk *Starbird* to the machine. Grasp will land."

Before he could catch himself, Teeth broadcast a symbol of unhappy surprise. "That is not possible, Pinnacle!"

"Grasp has learned the skill of water landing, has he not?"

"He has done so a number of times, Pinnacle, but this is a congested area. We may be observed by humans here."

A symbol of anger radiated from the Pinnacle. "If you have skilled him properly, he will be able to land. Stand away from the controls!"

Teeth staggered at an uncomfortable tug from the Undermind. Reluctantly he shuffled away from the controls, allowing Grasp to take over.

"May I be allowed to advise, Pinnacle?" asked Teeth.

"You will maintain silence."

Teeth turned a pair of eyes away from the screen long enough to notice that Green Stone had entered the control chamber. Teeth wished that he could converse with his friend, but with the Pinnacle this close, there was no assurance that their conversation would remain private. Then he saw one of Green Stone's midlegs point at the Pinnacle. It was a code of leg gestures they had developed as nymphs. The gesture would have been obvious to a human but it was circuitous to the Oun, accustomed as they were to use of the Undermind. Teeth wagged a lower leg joint in acknowledgement.

Teeth rocked nervously. He might be helpless, but at least he was not the only one who questioned the Pinnacle's judgement. He cocked one pair of eyes at Grasp, the other at the screen. In a level glide, Grasp did well enough, but as he banked into a turn the ship became unstable. They lost considerable altitude in sideslip. Teeth could see Grasp was fighting the controls. They were headed back in the direction they had come from, but they lacked the altitude to glide back to the proximity of the news vending machine. Grasp was struggling to bring the ship back into trim, while not paying enough attention to the screen or their altitude.

Teeth noticed they were headed towards a raised platform built out over the water. It was high, and the pylons of plant material supporting it were several yards apart.

Teeth would have had no problem gliding under it to land on the far side. He was unsure that Grasp's skill was equal to the task, and Grasp seemed not to notice the looming structure.

Teeth glanced uncertainly at the Pinnacle. Would the Pinnacle allow him to speak, even if he tried? Probably not. Teeth tightened his holding feet on the deck, and tried to suggest a warning to Grasp through the Undermind without direct use of symbols. The Pinnacle might still notice, but perhaps he wouldn't find it worthy of action.

Precious seconds passed. Grasp finally looked up and saw the obstacle. He panicked. Instead of steering between the supports, he tried to fly over the platform. *Starbird* simply didn't have enough air speed. They pitched toward the sky, wings pumping desperately. For a few seconds they continued up, then *Starbird* stalled. The nose pitched down, and suddenly the edge of the platform was centered in their screen, dangerously near. Grasp tried to dive, the controls responding sluggishly under his grippers. They brushed under the edge of the platform.

Teeth saw open space ahead. He thought they might escape with nothing worse than a rough landing. Then *Starbird*'s right wing tip grazed one of the supports.

Teeth and Grasp were almost torn from the deck. The Pinnacle and Green Stone were both thrown against the walls of the chamber. The tumbling stopped with an impact that caused Teeth's belly to slap the deck.

Teeth cautiously released his hold on the tilted deck. He took a moment to inspect himself for serious damage, then glanced up at the screen. He could see nothing but a murky green blur. *Starbird* was under water.

"Teeth!" the symbol struck him like a physical blow. Teeth looked to see the Pinnacle scuttling towards him, one leg hanging injured and useless. "This is your fault, Teeth.

You are finished. You are no longer pilot. You are no longer anything!"

Teeth could feel the Undermind pulling at him like a whirlpool. He braced himself for oblivion. As the Undermind pulled him down, he held on with grippers not of flesh, but of mind. For a terrible moment he seemed lost, then it was over.

"I live," said Teeth. Green Stone emitted a symbol of joy. The Pinnacle took a cautious step back.

Teeth realized that he momentarily had the upper hand. He moved to exploit it. "You fear me, Pinnacle, or do you fear your own failure? It was your decision that caused this accident. The Oun of this ship know it. The Undermind serves you only so long as you serve it. The Undermind knows you are at fault, or I would not be alive!"

The Pinnacle did not reply. He and Grasp exchanged a few symbols unheard by the others, then quickly left the control chamber.

Teeth emitted a symbol of jubilation at Green Stone, but then realized Green Stone's attention was on the screen.

"We are still underwater, Teeth. We should have floated to the surface by now."

Teeth rushed to the controls. The instruments indicated they were less than a foot underwater. He could see nothing above to keep them from reaching the surface. He tried gently flapping wings. The right one responded sluggishly. There had been some damage in the impact.

The deck shook as they bobbed in the water, but they were no nearer the surface. Teeth tried moving the ship's legs. The right one moved freely. The left barely moved at all.

"Engineer," called Teeth.

"This is Wedge," the answer came though the Undermind.

"We have damage in the right wing and left leg."

"I have identified the damage in the right wing. It is minor. Repairs are under way." Teeth felt the Engineer probing at his senses. He opened to share his vision of the viewscreen. "As I suspected," continued the Engineer, "we are still underwater."

"Can you account for this?"

"I find no indication of damage to the left leg. I suspect it is somehow trapped, pinning us to the bottom. Can you get a view of the leg on your screen?"

"I will try." Teeth manipulated the controls that directed *Starbird*'s head. He flexed the head downward to its limit while extending the left leg as far forward as it would go. A translucent fiber wrapped tightly around the lower part of the leg, cutting into the soft exterior. They were trapped.

White Crystal, their human studies specialist, approached Teeth and Green Stone, radiating a vague symbol of triumph. "I think I have identified the fiber we are tangled in. I believe it is used by humans to trap food animals living in the water."

Teeth turned a pair of eyes in White Crystal's direction. "Food animals?"

"Bait is used to tempt the food animals into swallowing a metal hook attached to the end of the fiber. The animal is then hoisted onto land."

Green Stone launched a symbol of irritation at White Crystal. "This is useless information. We are still trapped."

"Pay no attention, White Crystal," interjected Teeth. "It might be very useful. How large are these food animals?"

"We have observed many sizes being caught. Many are as large or larger than *Starbird*."

And probably heavier," added Teeth. "If the fiber is

strong enough to support such a weight, we have no chance of breaking it."

"Apologies, White Crystal," said Green Stone, "I spoke in haste."

"Not necessary," answered White Crystal. "We are all under stress."

"The fiber," said Teeth, "is a single thin strand. If we could reach it with the beak, we might cut it." But Teeth knew they could not reach the line. A real seagull might have managed such a contortion, but *Starbird* was less flexible in some respects.

"If it were not for the human broadcasting," said Green Stone, "we could simply send someone out to cut the line. It could be done with simple tools."

"Wedge," Teeth addressed the Engineer, who was working near by, "will water offer any protection against the human broadcasts?"

The Engineer hesitated. "Some perhaps, but not enough for what you propose. Besides, whoever was outside would be cut off from the Undermind by *Starbird*'s shielding."

Teeth did not reply to this at once. Instead he remained where he was, so still and uncommunicative that he might have been sleeping. Finally he asked the Engineer, "Shouldn't it be possible to shield an individual Oun from the human broadcasts, the way that *Starbird* is shielded?"

"Teeth!" said Green Stone, accompanied with a symbol of surprise. "What are you thinking?"

"He is thinking," said the Pinnacle, who was just entering the control chamber with Grasp at his side, "of going outside to free Starbird. He is thinking of going alone."

An uneasy state of truce existed as preparations were made for Teeth's egress. Grasp and the Pinnacle maintained a very visible presence in the control room, but they did not move to interfere with Teeth's plan. Teeth was certain he knew why. They did not expect him to return. To the Pinnacle's way of thinking, Teeth was committing suicide. As Teeth had waited for the Pinnacle to make a fatal mistake, the Pinnacle had waited for Teeth to make his.

Following Teeth's instructions, the Engineers worked feverishly to complete a shielded suit. Under this he would wear an emergency breathing pack, allowing him about a fiftieth of a day's breathing mixture. For an Oun operating with the full capacity of the Undermind, it should be more than enough. Without the Undermind, most doubted Teeth would be able to function at all, and if he did, it would be only as an animal. His mind would be too simple to allow him to cut the fiber, or even return to *Starbird* before his air ran out.

Even Teeth was not sure what would happen, but he was not suicidal. He believed he had the tools to survive, the same tools that helped him resist the Pinnacle earlier. While the Engineers worked, he maintained a vigil in the control chamber, opening and closing the simple shears he would use to cut the fiber, studying the image of the entangled leg on the viewscreen, planning where he must cut; *there* and *there*.

The whole plan had to be ingrained in his mind. Not in the Undermind he shared with so many others, but in *his* mind.

Time passed. The Engineers worked. The vigil continued.

Starbird was equipped with a number of locks to the outside. One, inside the beak, was used to collect specimens from outside. Another, located in an appropriate place in respect to the gull anatomy, was used to dispose of waste.

Teeth had chosen to exit through a small instrument lock located on the ship's breast.

Though only Green Stone and Wedge were in the service chamber with him, Teeth felt the whole ship watching him. He knew the entire ship's complement was studying him through their eyes; the Pinnacle, perhaps most intently of all.

The breathing unit was already strapped to his belly, its tubes feeding the breathing orifices on his back. The cutters were gripped tightly in his jaws. As he closed them, the cutter closed as well, magnifying his strength. Finally, the shield was lowered over his back. Green Stone and Wedge seemed hesitant. "Do it," instructed Teeth. He inserted his legs into the opening. The suit was pushed closed from either side, locking under his middle. It was as though his mind had plunged into darkness. He was alone.

"Teeth," The symbol was an alien thing in his mind, but it comforted him, even if he did not know what it meant.

"Teeth." It was one of the few symbols he had left, the rest lost, along with the rest of the Undermind.

Then something crept into his awareness, like an itch. There was something he had to do. He flexed his jaws without knowing why. An image come into his mind. He looked about for a pattern to fit the image. There was nothing like it. Only a chamber, and two others that reminded him of— himself? Restless, he began to pace around the chamber, looking for the image in his mind, the thing that could end his itch.

There were three exits from the chamber. Two were large and inviting. The third was small and dark. He attempted to head towards the largest of the exits. The two others put their bodies in his way. Against his will, he was directed into the smaller of the openings. Before he could escape, the way closed behind him. For a moment, he found himself trapped. Then he felt the chamber he was in move. The way was open again.

He pushed towards the light until he found himself stopped by a transparent barrier. With all his strength he pushed at it, cutting at it with jaws that seemed larger and more powerful than they should. In a moment he was able to get his head through, and then a leg. With some effort, he pulled the rest of his body through the surface tension and *outside*.

He looked around. There was a wrongness to this place, in the way his eyes focused, in the sluggish way in which his limbs moved. He clung just outside the opening, unsure what to do next. But there was a rightness to this place too. Something to do with the image burning in his mind; a lesser image associated with it. "Teeth," he thought. Suddenly, he knew where he was going. He climbed along the irregular white surface, heading down. The whiteness curved back. Soon he was walking upside down. Then, out of the green murk ahead, he saw it: the pattern to go with the image!

He transferred to another surface, yellow, smooth, more sharply curved. Again he went down. Just ahead, he could see his goal, a long thing wrapped tightly around the yellow thing on which he walked. He saw the places he must bite, *there* and *there*.

He crawled to the first point and began to chew. Even with the new strength of his jaws, it was not an easy task. He cut through the thing a bit at a time. For a time, it seemed as though the task would never end. Then the thing parted. He watched the severed end disappear into the murk, and a bit of the itch in his mind went away with it. He crawled in search of the second point.

Again, it was difficult, but the task was familiar now. This time, the angle of the thing was different. He was forced to crawl out onto the thing in order to cut it. It seemed *wrong* somehow, but how could anything that would end this itch be wrong?

He was getting tired. Why was it difficult to breathe? He chewed at the last bit of the thing. He was so tired. Only the itch drove him on. Only the memory of "Teeth." The thing snapped. At once he understood what was wrong. He was on the thing, and as it snapped, it pulled away from the yellow thing; the yellow thing that led to the white surface; the white surface that led to *home!* Even as he understood, everything that was familiar to him was fading into the green murk. He was so tired.

"We went to a great deal of effort to get you back, Teeth," said the Pinnacle. "It is good to know your mind still works, our effort is not wasted. I would hate to have to kill you after all this."

Slowly, Teeth pulled himself from the deck. His body hurt in a dozen places, not least of all, his jaw muscles. "You saved me."

"Once we were free of the human fiber, we were able to look for you. Once we found you, Green Stone managed to get you into the beak, and we took you in through the specimen lock."

Teeth looked around. They were in the service chamber just behind the specimen lock. His equipment was piled in a corner.

"I suppose," the Pinnacle said, "there is no need to converse with you, but I had to be sure your brain was undamaged by lack of oxygen or the shock of rejoining the Undermind. I see now it was not, and it is safe for you to become one with the Undermind."

Teeth felt uncertain of his ability to resist attack, either physical or mental. "You always intended to get rid of me, one way or the other."

"But it is better this way. Once I have removed your

threat, none will challenge me. The damage will be undone. Besides, we are few here. The Undermind cannot afford to waste flesh."

Teeth could feel the Undermind tugging at him, drawing him down. He struggled.

"You are weak," said the Pinnacle, "do not resist."

Teeth was weak, but this time was different than the last. Something had changed. He felt a sense of self, of identity, holding him up like a buttress, providing him a solid platform from which he could exercise great leverage. The Pinnacle pushed. Teeth pushed back.

The Pinnacle staggered. "I don't understand," he said.

"The situation has changed for us here. You have failed to adjust to the order of things. You have endangered the Undermind. Now there must be a reckoning." Teeth pushed again, harder. The Pinnacle sagged to the floor, a shell empty of all but the Undermind.

Teeth felt a shifting in the Undermind, like water seeking its own level. Teeth was the new Pinnacle. He reached out, testing his powers. He knew where everyone on the ship was, what they were doing. He found Green Stone in the Pinnacle's chamber, under the careful guard of Grasp.

He reached out to pluck at Grasp's mind, and felt him drop into unconsciousness. Teeth sensed Green Stone's amazement, and reached out to him. "Come to me, friend."

When Green Stone arrived, he shied well away from the shell of the former Pinnacle. "He can not harm you," assured Teeth.

"What happened to him to make him mad? What is happening to all of us?"

"Our situation is unique in the history of all Oun. We are changing to adapt to that situation. He resisted change. I embrace it."

"What will happen to us? Will we survive?"

"I do not know, I do know our way is forward. Forward only."

Green Stone looked at his friend, as though seeing him for the first time. He adopted a stance of respect. "You are the Pinnacle!"

"Do not call me that. Never call me that. My name is Teeth."

A Ghost
in the Matrix
by
Steve Martindale

About the Author

Steve Martindale is 32, was born and raised in Tucson and has been writing twenty-four years; his intention is to be a professional writer full-time. A Finalist with this story, he is continuing to enter the Contest. He has studied anthropology and languages at the University of Arizona. He and his wife, Karen, live in Phoenix.

"A Ghost in the Matrix" is set on an Earth where, we can suppose, Leonardo Da Vinci, during the Renaissance, created a starship drive. Yet, because of the way history takes curious eddies, his star-travelers are disturbingly provincial.

The result of Martindale's carefully chosen stylistic approach is that it carries us into another cultural matrix—the title has a double meaning, just as the story has a double purpose. It shocks us into realizing how recently our own society was subdivided into rigidly guarded compartments . . . and, as only one of the effects, most black males in popular literature, of course, talked like Uncle Remus. Carried by engaging technological premises, that sort of speculative power is something no other literature can deploy. . . .

I

Whereupon We See How the Voyage Begins for Jack Delaplane, Citizen of San Francisco

On May —, 18—, the clipper ship *Alice Patterson,* with a crew of thirty, departed Boston Harborage. The passenger complement was 110, all bound for New Connecticut landfall in five days hence. Many had never been voyaging before, while others were old hands at it; but looking upon their faces, so filled with hope and just a touch of apprehension, one might well have thought each of them completely new to the experience. They trusted in the steady reliability of DaVincian science, but still, a ship was a d----dly unpredictable thing to trust one's life to. Sailors must have had hearts of lions to commit their futures to voyaging.

One man who had no such apprehensions was named Jack Delaplane. He was well-dressed, with homespun manners which were impressive in their honest simplicity, a natural nobleman with little pretense. His was the face of a hard-working American, clean-cut and well-formed, with clear blue eyes that held no guile. While his success in commerce entitled him to sip cognac with gentlemen, he could drink beer like a laborer, and feel no shame about it.

Jack had no fear for the voyage because his trust in DaVincian science was absolute. Like the sailors who crewed the clipper, he accepted the certainty of the matrix:

the interaction of energy in the machines, the power which tumbled the drive and put the floating vastness of the harborage far behind them. He was no stranger to voyaging, having visited many of the American Stars in the course of business, but he never grew weary of strolling the corridors between the machines, listening to the hoofbeat thrumming of the tumblers. How much like a heartbeat it was, a muffled sound with pauses which could be counted. He felt at home aboard a ship, not as a sailor feels at home because his blood races when he gazes upon the empty black vasty, but as a man who loves great machines feels at home.

As he walked the corridor, drawing contentedly upon a slim cigar, he turned a corner to see a girl in the open observation salon, gazing out the clear bubble at the starry blackness of the vasty. He spoke not a word as he watched her. She was certainly pretty, in her crisp blue bodice and full skirt, cinched at the waist by a ribbon of brighter blue. Her hair, which flowed to her bustle, was the color of new grain; and her face, which put him in mind of a young child, was caught up in what could only be described as rapture. She quite obviously loved the sight of the starry void.

The girl turned of a sudden, caught sight of him, and started with a sharp gasp. "Oh! dear! How long have you stood there?"

"Only a moment," said Jack. "I apologize for frightening you, but I didn't dare speak. You appeared so caught up gazing at the cosmos that I thought it a shame to distract you."

"Oh; well," said the girl, with a self-conscious smile. "No harm was done."

Jack approached her and removed his hat. "My apologies again for the intrusion. I'm John Delaplane, Jack to my friends."

"How do you do, Mr. Delaplane? I'm Elizabeth St. George."

"Most honored to meet you, Miss St. George," he said, taking her hand courteously. "Pardon me for being so forward, but I sensed a kindred spirit. You, too, seem to have great affection for the stars."

Elizabeth smiled again. "As a child, I would lie awake, gazing at the nighttime sky through my window and wondering what life was like among them. I knew that people lived on the far-off planets, in cities and towns, but they always seemed a bit mysterious. I suppose that had I been born male, I might have become an astronomer, or even a vasty sailor. Does that sound foolish, Mr. Delaplane?"

"Not at all," he answered with a smile. "The cosmos is indeed a place to inspire dreams. Might I ask what brings you to the voyage?"

"My parents have passed away," she replied, "and I go to live with my aunt and uncle on New Connecticut."

"Oh. How tragic for you. Was their passing sudden?"

Elizabeth shook her head. "Not at all. My mother has been gone for years, and my father only recently joined her. He was quite ill. An explosion took his limbs and forced him to depend on life support for a very long time."

"I take it, then, he didn't receive limb transplants, or regeneration?" said Jack.

"His body was unable to tolerate either. The physicians could but put him on life support and hope for the best. He lay in that state for two years, till his body could no longer survive. I believe his passing was a blessing to him. But what brings *you* to the voyage, Mr. Delaplane?"

"I have business to conduct on New Connecticut, in the city of Crossroads. I'm an engineer, specializing in vasty drive machines. My business brings me frequently to the American Stars."

"How fascinating," said Elizabeth. "Are you from Boston at all?"

"No, I live in San Francisco."

"Does San Francisco have no harborage, that you must travel via Boston Harborage?"

"None that connects with New Connecticut," said Jack. "I had to travel by airship to Boston, so as to embark on this voyage."

"How interesting you're traveling to Crossroads," said Elizabeth. "I'm bound for Farmcrest, which is very near there. Perhaps we shall travel in the same airship from the landfall site."

"That would be very pleasant," said he. Jack was so taken by Elizabeth's fine features and self-assurance that he found himself taking a bold step: "I realize it's a bit premature to ask, seeing as we have only just met, but may I have the pleasure of your company at dinner some evening before our arrival?"

Elizabeth seemed very surprised, so that, for a moment, Jack feared he might have displeased her. But instead, she favored him with a smile and said, "Why, I don't believe that's premature at all, Mr. Delaplane. I would be honored to share your table. However, I will be unable to do so this evening, as I shall be dining at the Captain's table. But perhaps another evening . . . ?"

"Is that so?" Jack exclaimed, in pleasant surprise. "Why, so will I!"

"How nice! Then we shall dine to-gether this evening after all. But Mr. Delaplane, were you fearful of asking me to dinner?"

"I was, yes. We in San Francisco tend to be a bit more unconventional than do you in New England. I didn't want to inadvertently offend you."

Elizabeth curtsied graciously. "Why, thank you for your thoughtfulness. I shall be pleased to see you to-night."

A distinguished-looking older man, dressed in waist-coat and tweeds of the English style, entered the lounge, and he cast a skeptical glance at Jack. He said to Elizabeth,

"Here you are, Miss St. George. Mrs. Runnimede is concerned for your whereabouts."

"Oh, hello, Dr. Tully," said Elizabeth. "This is Mr. John Delaplane. He and I were talking about the vasty. Dr. Tully is a kind gentleman Mrs. Runnimede and I met after boarding."

The men shook hands, Jack smiling openly, while Dr. Tully looked dour and appeared to want to "harumph" disapprovingly. Perhaps he did not think it seemly for a man and woman not properly introduced to socialize this way.

"Please come along, Miss St. George," Dr. Tully said afterward. "Mrs. Runnimede expects you for lunch."

"Yes, of course, Dr. Tully," said Elizabeth. "It was very nice to meet you, Mr. Delaplane. I look forward to seeing you again at the Captain's table."

"As do I, Miss St. George," said Jack.

Elizabeth and Dr. Tully walked away. Jack gazed out the bubble at the vasty and smiled to himself, as it appeared the voyage would be more interesting than he had first anticipated.

II

A Dinnertable Discussion
Which Grows More Interesting

Captain Gentry's table was set in a fine salon adjoining the passengers' dining room, and there Jack found a sumptuous meal of roast beef, baked potatoes and assorted green vegetables laid out on bone-china dishes, to be eaten with sterling silverware. He saw Elizabeth seated between an older woman, who must certainly be Mrs. Runnimede, and an odd-looking gentleman in plain attire, who had a handlebar moustache which was frayed at the ends, and a bald head which looked so shiny, he seemed to be perspiring, though not a bead of moisture could be seen. A Negro steward seated Jack between the imposing Dr. Tully and a woman in the garish attire of a *nouveau riche* matron. Captain Gentry, who looked every inch the commander of a vasty-spanning clipper ship, introduced the table guests around: the odd-looking gentleman was Professor Lindsail of the University of New Vermont City, New Vermont, while the garish woman was Mrs. Edna Bryant, a recent widow from Richmond, Virginia. Seated next to the professor was Clayton Beaudine, a planter from North Carolina. Jack expressed his regards to each as he took up his napkin to place it properly on his lap.

"Mr. Delaplane," said Captain Gentry, as he unfolded his own napkin, "I understand you're an engineer. Is that correct?"

"Yes, Captain," said Jack. "In fact, many of the machines used aboard ship are based on my designs."

"Is that for true?" exclaimed Mrs. Bryant, putting down her fork so she might spread her hands in great surprise. "Why, I always thought such things to be DaVincian."

"Well, yes, they are, Mrs. Bryant. But da Vinci only established the science; men like myself built upon it."

"Oh, certainly, of course," said Mrs. Bryant, looking a bit embarrassed. "I did not mean to infer that such things as vasty-clippers were possible in Mr. Leonardo's time, as that was nigh-on 400 years ago."

"If I may ask, Mr. Delaplane," said Clayton Beaudine, "do you envision a time when mechanisms may replace *all* aspects of manual labor?"

"I suspect you're wondering if slave labor may be made obsolete," said Jack, with a knowing look.

"As a matter of fact, I am. I must confess that gentlemen in your profession do give me pause."

"Shall I ask why?"

"I suspect Mr. Beaudine feels personally threatened by

the advancements of science," Dr. Tully observed very drolly.

"Not personally, Doctor," replied Beaudine, "but morally. My feeling is that automated production on all levels would completely do away with slavery, thus upsetting God's plan for the Negro."

"Indeed?" said Jack, with great skepticism.

"Of course, I would not expect a gentleman like yourself, from San Francisco, to understand my position, nor the finery of Southern ways. But I should hope that as a Christian, you would agree that it simply would not do to manumit the Negro. The Lord intended for the Negro to serve the white race, but the automation your profession intends would give the white race no choice but to free the Negro of servitude, for there would then be no need for his labor."

"You're quite right about the results of automation," said Jack, as he calmly ate a bite of roast beef. "However, you are incorrect about the feelings of a Christian. I, myself, am a praying man, but my feeling is that slavery is an institution which should have ended years ago. The Slave States have had the means to produce far more cotton and tobacco through automation alone for two centuries, yet they persist in using slave labor to do the work."

Beaudine favored Jack with a cold, steady gaze that was filled with unspoken hostility. Jack knew this would be the reaction of the planter, for Slave State aristocrats were most protective of their way of life. But Beaudine did invite this debate, so Jack had naught to be sorry for.

However, before harsh words could be exchanged, Captain Gentry came to the rescue with a commanding forcefulness which cut neatly through the smoldering atmosphere of the table.

"Gentlemen," he said, in his lordly vasty-captain voice, "this is not the time, nor the place, for such a discussion. Please reserve your words for a more suitable occasion."

"You are quite correct, Captain Gentry," said Beaudine. "A gentleman does not subject ladies to the hostile words of men. Ladies, I do apologize to you each."

"Might I ask a question, Mr. Delaplane?" said Mrs. Runnimede.

"Certainly, ma'am," Jack said with a nod of his head.

"As one who is intimately familiar with machines such as these, could you tell me why I frequently hear snapping sounds come from the various instruments? I swear that each time I pass one machine or another, I hear a sound much like a tree limb breaking loose."

"There's naught to fear from that, ma'am. The motion of the tumblers in the drive engines produces static electricity, which accumulates in the shell of the drive. The sound you hear is the sudden discharge of said electricity."

"Is it by any chance harmful?"

"Not at all. It's only loud."

"Perhaps not all sounds are those of static electricity," said Professor Lindsail. "It may very well be the ghost making itself known."

"Please, Professor," Captain Gentry said, with a sudden frown, "that sort of talk is really uncalled for."

"What ghost is that, Professor?" Elizabeth asked.

"It is said that a ghost inhabits the power matrix of this very ship," Professor Lindsail went on to explain. "My field is biology, but I have made a long study of the occult. According to the Vasty Edition of the *Tobin Spirit Guide,* a radioactivity shield in the drive room of this vessel warped and burst fifteen years ago, bathing a young sailor named Talward Dennison in the awful rays. Young Talward died in minutes, but his spirit, the guide says, still inhabits the drive. More specifically, it inhabits the matrix."

"Foolish nonsense," Dr. Tully scoffed. "Ghosts are mere figments of the imagination."

"I agree," said Captain Gentry. "For fifteen years, I

have been compelled to inform people such as yourself, Professor, that no ghost inhabits the power matrix.''

"You mean to say you have never heard the knocking of the ghost?'' said Professor Lindsail.

"I certainly have not.''

"But is it not true that many of your crew have, and have thereby refused to sign on with you when their terms were done?''

Captain Gentry scowled at his beef as though reliving an unpleasant memory. "I confess, many of my sailors have, indeed, been of the notion that the drive is haunted; thus, they run off when their contracts end, to sign on with another ship. But I am a man of no little learning, Professor, and wise to the world and the endless vasty. I have seen nor heard naught of spirits, but the prattling of the foolish. Perhaps these ladies are frightened by your speculations, so have a care what you say!''

"*I* have no worries, Captain,'' Elizabeth spoke up when he was silent. "Ghosts are a source of fascination for me, as a mystery of the world to be plumbed at leisure.''

"You are a plucky gal, Miss Elizabeth,'' Mrs. Bryant commended her, smiling broadly. "Neither do I have fear of spooks, Captain Gentry. Us Southern folk know of ghosts very well; I would daresay that there isn't a mansion of long standing that hasn't even a single mournful spirit to boast of. I can clear recall a night when I was very small, when my granddad came to my bedside to tell me a story before I slumbered.''

"A ghost story, no doubt,'' Dr. Tully remarked in sardonic fashion, "to corrupt your young mind.''

"Not at all, Doctor. My granddad told me naught but fairy stories to ease me asleep, up till the night he died, which had been two years before. I sort of thought maybe he wanted to make up for lost time.

Mrs. Runnimede made a gasp of surprise; then she

said, "Do you mean to tell us your grandfather was a g
Mrs. Bryant?"

"Not to look at him, no," said the handsome widow.
"But he had no breath in him, and the moonlight showed
a bit through his mid-portion. He was indeed a haunt."

"Were you not frightened?"

"I loved my granddad. I knew he could do me no
harm. How, then, could I be even in the least fearful, simply
because he was no longer made of breathing flesh and
blood?"

Jack and Elizabeth exchanged glances, smiling a bit
uncomfortably. Jack had seen a great many things in his
time, on many planets of the settled Stars; but he had yet to
see a ghost. Still, though, that hardly was proof there *were*
no ghosts. If one did, indeed, inhabit the matrix, it would
make for an interesting problem of engineering: to wit;
would its presence amidst that energy alter the shape of the
flow to any degree, or even enhance the matrix by virtue of
its own supernatural power?

III

As the Subject of the Ghost Takes
An Interesting Turn After Dinner

When dinner was finished, and the men had retired to
Captain Gentry's drawing room, the ladies to his sitting
room to gossip, the Captain invited his guests to help themselves to brandy and his fine cigars. There were comfortably upholstered chairs in the room, where a gentleman
might sit and relax with fine wine and leisurely smoke his
cigar. Professor Lindsail poured brandy into snifters for
everyone, handing them around, but refused the offer of a
cigar; he did not partake of tobacco, believing it deleteri-
ous to a whole and vigorous spirit, though he apparently

out brandy. He did, in fact, finish his
s had only begun, and poured himself

ew carefully on his cigar, then turned to
n the same disapproving look he had shown
when encountered him viewing the stars with Miss
Elizabeth ... George.

"Mr. Delaplane," said he, in that stern, scholarly fashion of his, "might I speak frankly?"

"If you like," replied Jack.

"Mrs. Runnimede, and myself, wonder what your intentions are toward Miss St. George. Do you have designs upon her of a personal nature?"

"If you ask, is my intention to pay court to her, I can only say that I haven't considered that as yet. I have, after all, only to-day met the girl. Why do you ask?"

"The two of you were alone in the observation salon," Dr. Tully went on. "It certainly is not proper for a young lady to socialize with a gentleman without chaperone."

"In a public place, I don't feel much improper behavior could happen," said Jack. "Granted, Dr. Tully, we in San Francisco are not quite so prim as are you in Boston or New Haven, Connecticut; but I believe that even there, we know the difference between proper and improper behavior. And I know for a certainty that two people of opposing genders may very well socialize without chaperone in a public place, without scandalizing said young lady. Does that answer your question, Doctor?"

"Yes, quite sufficiently," Dr. Tully said with a stiff nod that showed not pleasure with the reply, only temporary satisfaction that events were not quite so dire as he imagined. "I shall certainly convey your answer to Mrs. Runnimede."

Professor Lindsail was sitting in a chair close by, and as Jack and Dr. Tully moved past, he said to them, "Mr.

Delaplane and the Good Doctor! Tell me, gentlemen; what are your *truest* feelings on the subject of the ghost?"

"As I said to you in the ladies' hearing," Dr. Tully said roughly to him, "I have no belief whatsoever in spirits. I suggest you are a scandal-monger for impugning the good name of this fine vessel; and are no fit person to school young minds."

"I am not such a scoundrel, Doctor; I am a man of science, and it is my thought the study of spirits *is* a fit pursuit. Mr. Delaplane! you expressed no such doubt. Do *you* believe in the possibility of a ghost in the Matrix?"

"From an engineering standpoint," replied Jack, "I would have to say it makes for an interesting question. But I'm not so well schooled in esoteric subject matters that I may say for certain one way or the other. I prefer to keep my mind open, lest I miss a wonder or two along the way."

"Do you really?" said Beaudine, who stood gazing at Jack with frank dislike. "I should think if a man were the Christian he claimed to be, he would discount the possibility of ghosts."

"Why is that, Mr. Beaudine?" Dr. Tully asked him.

"The Bible teaches that each man, regardless of his station in life, departs the world at the moment of death, to receive either reward or punishment at the hands of the Lord. To believe in ghosts is to disbelieve that proposition. How, might I ask, could a man's spirit then remain on Earth to become a ghost?"

"A valid question, indeed, sir," Professor Lindsail replied. "Perhaps a ghost is a separate thing from the spirit which goes to Judgement. I have not found the answer."

"Thank you for your insight, Mr. Beaudine," Captain Gentry said, joining the men with cigar and brandy in hand. "Keep in mind, gentlemen, that this is the Nineteenth Century, not some medieval time of ignorance and superstition. We have the blessings of DaVincian science to demonstrate

the fallacy of the belief in ghosts; for ghosts are the province
of the unenlightened.''

"Why, then, do so many people claim to hear the
knocking of the ghost when they come aboard this ship?''
Professor Lindsail asked of him.

"Do they really, Professor? Perhaps it is the thrumming of the tumblers which deceives them. And on occasion, passengers have heard the snapping of static electricity
and thought that to be some untoward noise.''

"These are reports from intelligent and sensible people, Captain, ascribed in the *Tobin Guide* as a sidebar. In
addition to that, many have claimed to actually *see* it.''

"Preposterous!'' Captain Gentry exclaimed immediately. "Though many a traveler aboard this vessel has seemed
to me a bit moon-struck, they have had not a word to report
on so-called ghostly knockings, nor even sightings!''

Perhaps it was merely coincidence, but the moment the
final word departed the Captain's mouth, there was a shriek
of terror in the passage. The men rushed out the door to
see what was amiss, as had the ladies, who were but a few
steps away, at the parlor door which opened to the passage.
There in the corridor Mrs. Runnimede lay aswoon, with her
knitting by her feet. Captain Gentry thought to call for
assistance, but Dr. Tully assured him he was quite able to
attend to the stricken woman himself. While the ladies
came to her side to give comfort, he produced a palm-sized
bio-scanner from his pocket and prepared to step in.

Mrs. Runnimede was revived fairly easily, and she sat
weeping piteously, her face buried in her hands. Elizabeth
spoke comforting words to her; and when she was able, she
was helped to her feet.

"Oh! My!'' gasped the sturdy woman, who looked
now as frail as any invalid. "Such a frightful thing! I
thought I should perish immediately!''

Jack chanced to look directly at Captain Gentry, and

Illustrated by Carolly Hauksdottir

saw his face was pale and drawn. The man appeared to harbor some great secret, which Mrs. Runnimede's fright had somehow touched upon. It raised Jack's curiosity enormously.

"Captain Gentry," said he, "I have the distinct feeling you know what's happened here, and wish not to hear it mentioned."

"Do you, indeed?" responded Captain Gentry. "I cannot imagine what leads you to that conclusion."

"Perhaps I shall find out."

Dr. Tully completed his examination and pronounced Mrs. Runnimede fit. He did, however, suggest she sit a while and drink a bit of brandy to steady her nerves; then she was helped to the drawing room to join the others.

When Mrs. Runnimede had gotten brandy and was comfortable, she told the tale of her fearful encounter:

"I had left the parlor to go to my cabin, to fetch more yarn for my knitting, and had taken but a few steps into the corridor, when I came face to face with an horrendous apparition! I am from good Missouri stock, and am therefore the most skeptical of souls; but I must confess, when I saw that daemonic thing, like a visitation from the Devil himself, all my doubt went directly out the window! What I saw was the selfsame ghost Professor Lindsail described!

"And such a sight it was! Oh! It had a face that was beaten and ravaged, with one eye closed by a large bruise, but the other open wide and staring as though accusing me of wrong-doing! Its clothing was torn, and the flesh exposed rent and bleeding, as though it had been attacked by some wild animal; and though it hovered above the floor, and was faintly transparent, I could nearly vow I was seeing some poor sailor, having suffered a grievous attack and wandering the corridors in search of medical aid! Oh! Lord! my poor heart felt it would burst!"

"You indeed saw the ghost of Talward Dennison?"

exclaimed Professor Lindsail. "How extraordinary! How wonderfully extraordinary! This, Captain Gentry, means there *are* reliable witnesses you cannot dispute, for if this fine woman has seen the ghost, then there must be others!"

"Mrs. Runnimede has had a terrible fright," said Captain Gentry with great disapproval; "I find no good reason for you to take profit from it!"

Jack gazed at the officer carefully for a moment, considering his humor. There was that fear again, having diminished not an iota, but actually increased a bit, as though he dreaded what might be revealed through this discussion.

"Captain Gentry," said he, "is there anything you wish to tell us about this event?"

"What shall I say?" asked the Captain. "I feel sympathy for Mrs. Runnimede's terrible fright, but I can hardly change what has happened."

"Please, Mr. Delaplane!" Mrs. Runnimede said in a gasp, as breathless as she yet was; "do not harangue Captain Gentry. He had naught to do with that daemonic thing, except to scoff at reports of it and ill prepare me for the encounter. Dear Captain, you are not to blame; but please believe now it exists! I am no calf to see fiends in every shadow."

"Yes, certainly, Mrs. Runnimede," Captain Gentry said with proper consideration for her situation. "I see now that those who claim witness were fully sensible about it."

"What shall we do about this now?" questioned Elizabeth. "If that terror is still lurking about in the passage. . . ."

"Have no fear, child," Beaudine said. "I shall protect you. Mr. Delaplane! it appears we have more now to consider than our recently-found differences. Perhaps all us gentlemen should put our heads together to find a resolution."

"Yes, agreed," replied Jack. "Miss St. George, Mrs. Bryant; it may be best to help Mrs. Runnimede to her bed, so she might better recover from her ordeal."

"Sensible thinking, sir," Dr. Tully concurred. "I shall accompany them, so I might help relax the lady to sleep."

"Of course, Doctor," Captain Gentry said with a nod. "And to the rest of you, I must bid good evening. I have a full day to-morrow, and must retire."

They thanked him for his hospitality, and departed the place. The ladies accompanied Mrs. Runnimede to her cabin, followed by Dr. Tully; while Jack, Professor Lindsail and Clayton Beaudine loitered about the passage, considering the evening's events. Jack and Mr. Beaudine smoked cigars, and their ashes fell to the floor, where a small automaton scurried about on well-oiled wheels, sucking the ashes into itself by virtue of an internal vacuum.

"Mr. Delaplane," said the professor, "you were a bit rude to our host this evening; but I sense you had reason for your behavior."

"I believe there's much Captain Gentry is not telling us," replied Jack. "He claims to know nothing about this business of the ghost, but when I look in his eyes, I see the fear of discovery. I'm actually quite a skeptic myself, gentlemen; therefore, I take no man's word so innocently when his eyes tell me he feels otherwise."

"Mr. Delaplane!" quoth Beaudine; "I am still not happy to be traveling with you, in view of your unsettling opinions on the proper place of the Negro; however, I find there are more important matters now to occupy my thoughts than that. I wonder if it might not possibly be true? Could Mrs. Runnimede have actually seen something untoward?"

"She strikes me as a sensible woman, who would hardly react as she did were there nothing to be concerned about. I'm tempted to believe she may have seen a ghost after all."

"Or something of that sort, yes." Beaudine showed a most troubled mien; then confessed, "I am not one to doubt proper Christian teaching; yet I feel I may be of a mind with that dear lady. As Hamlet said, 'There are more things in heaven and earth, Horatio, than exist in your philosophy.' Thus, I shall reserve judgement until a later time.''

"As shall I," said Jack. "Four days still remain to our voyage; perhaps we shall yet be surprised. Good evening, gentlemen.''

IV

An Episode Which Makes Jack More Certain of His Suspicions

Through-out the second day, Jack dwelt long upon thoughts of the ghost. His new acquaintances made attempts to draw him from his troubled pondering, with invitations to the many games which filled the shipboard days; but Jack was not to be swayed, for his was a mind determined to solve problems of logic. He was skeptical of stories of the occult, but as he said at Captain Gentry's table, he was openminded to new experiences. Therefore, he made it a project to find the answer to this mystery.

On the third day, he considered taking a more direct route to finding the answer, and proceeded toward that goal. Along the way, he encountered Elizabeth, who strolled the main deck in the company of Mrs. Runnimede and the formidable Dr. Tully. Jack tipped his hat to the ladies and nodded cordially to Dr. Tully.

"Why, Mr. Delaplane," said Elizabeth; "I had begun to think you decided to spend the voyage ignoring the rest of the world. Have you found a solution to your conundrum?''

"My plan," said Jack, "is to proceed to the drive room to investigate further.''

"Are you planning to confront that awful spectre in its

environment?'' Mrs. Runnimede wondered, with a shiver of
lingering dread.

"If need be, yes. Although I would much prefer not to
have to, begging your pardon.''

"Oh, do not apologize, sir. As one who has endured
such terror, I can fully understand your position.''

"Much obliged to you, ma'am," said Jack, doffing his
hat once more.

"I commend you on your courage, Mr. Delaplane,"
said Dr. Tully, looking as dour as ever. "If Mrs. Runnimede's experience was any example, you face a terrible
thing indeed.''

"Actually, sir, I don't intend to face *anything*. I go not
to summon forth the ghost, but to see what keeps it in place.''

"Good fortune to you, then," said Dr. Tully.

When they had moved on, Jack proceeded on his way
to the drive room. It was two decks below, but a moment's
descent by elevator. Jack found the entire deck to be color-
less but for an all-present gray, which characterized the
pipes and protrusions that lined the walls. Here and there
were gauges tended by sailors in grimed clothing, their
bared limbs similarly grimed from perspiration and smoke.
The deck was d----dly hot, for though this vessel plied the
depths of the aether, the machines which powered it were little different from those to be found on some sea-going ship;
it was therefore a warm and greasy place for working. Jack
inspected the gauges as he passed them, his familiarity with
such devices telling him immediately if aught was steady or
amiss. The sailors eyed him surreptitiously, as though he
were some feared personage, a high-minded inspector, perhaps, searching for evidence of mishandling with which to
condemn some poor fellow.

Jack came in moments to the drive room itself, where
sailors clambered about, scrambling up ladders to catwalks
to inspect high-placed gauges, or hurrying along the floor to

balance power here or release pressure there. Jack noted that among the sailors was a full balance of color, so there were equal numbers of whites and Negros; and each seemed to work in friendly co-operation with his mate. How refreshing it was to see such enlightened behavior!

One of the sailors, a large-chested Negro with hair the color of iron, approached him from the direction of the drive shell, wiping perspiration from his ebon face with a great rag. He did not make obeisant gestures, as Negros of other stations often did when regarding whites; but faced him as one man to another. As Jack had never had traffic with the oppression of colored people, but looked upon them as humans of a differing complexion, he did not give the man cause to feel he should do aught else.

"Suh," said the Negro; "is yo' lookin' fo' summun?"

"Actually, yes," replied Jack. "I wish to speak to someone about a fellow who once worked this very room. His name was Talward Dennison."

"Yo' be one o' them folk what was visit' by ol' Talwud, Ah reckon."

Jack was taken briefly aback. "You seem to know all about it."

"Wud do travel fast 'round heah," said the Negro. "Ah, suh, be Benjamin; ya'll could ask me 'bout dat."

"Very well, then, Benjamin. I've heard how Talward was a mate in this place, fifteen years past."

"Dat be Gospel-true, suh. Ol' Talwud, he be enjineah's mate heah, jes' a boy hisse'f, by his looks; but a fine one wit' de drive. Ol' Talwud, he knew dem ol' machines, an' dat ol' matrix, beddah den eben de reg'luh enjineah hisse'f; an' he say de enjineah, 'Dey be trouble comin', Ah sees it well.' "

"Trouble?" inquired Jack. "Of what sort?"

"Suh," replied the old boy, "does yo' know anythin' 'bout de machines heah?"

"I'm an engineer. I helped design many of them."

"Den yo' knows 'bout de radi'activity shield, Ah reckons."

"I do. I've heard that Talward was caught in the bath when the shield failed that day."

"It, too, be Gospel-true, suh. Dat shield done gib way, eben aftuh ol' Talwud, he tell de enjineah. De enjineah go tell de cap'n, an' he come back, tell Talwud de cap'n say we leeb hah'bridge anyways. Cap'n say 'Don't mattah none; we gets t' nex' hah'bridge quick 'nuff, don't have tahm t' do nothin' 'bout it.' Ah reckon de skej'l be too tight t' wait dat long."

"Good Lord!" exclaimed Jack. "Why, then, did Talward linger by the shielding, if it was so weakened?"

"Cap'n tell him so," Benjamin reported, "sayin', "Young Dennison, ya'll bes' stay wit' yo' post; don't be gibbin' me no trouble, else Ah be gibbin' yo' *bettah* t' worry 'bout den weak shieldin'.' ''

"Benjamin! how is it you know this tale so well?"

"Ah was heah mahse'f dat berry day, suh. Ah done hear' de cap'n's loud voice come clatterin' off de catwalks, as de man hisse'f stood miseratin' de boy. Ol' Talwud, he be a good soul, but de cap'n, he jus' shout him down like some nigguh what done wrong. An' aftuhwuds, when dat ol' shieldin' done fix t' bust, Talwud tell us all, 'Get cleah befo' it come,' an' d--n if'n it don't come bustin' out jes' aftuh de las' man get out. When de radiation sweepuh done make de drive room cleah 'gain, an' de doc be sittin' ovah po' Talwud, de boy tell me, 'Benjamin! Benjamin! de cap'n be 'sponsible! Ah be hale an' whole if'n he di'n't leeb de hah'bridge so quick! De cap'n be 'sponsible, an' Ah shall haunt him 'til he be punish' fo' de wrong! Ah shall be his Nemesis an' make mah presence frequent' known; an' when de othuh boys do see me, do not let them be a'feared, fo'

Ah means them no hahm!' An' de boy shut his eyes an' was pass' on.''

"Ah! such a pitiful tale," quoth Jack, with great sympathy for the lad's plight. "Why, then, did Talward make his presence known to Mrs. Runnimede, I wonder?''

"Dat be de po' lady what see him, suh?" said Benjamin.

"The very same. Were she not so sturdy, I fear the sight might surely have stopped her heart on the spot.''

"Well, ol' Talwud don't mean no hahm; but he don't always do things well. Sometime', he come out when he think de cap'n be neah, an' it be some othuh folk.''

"How is it you know the feelings of a ghost so well?''

"Yo' wuhks de drive room fo' twenny yea's, yo' gets t' know de feelin's heah'bouts. Sometime', when a man be talkin' 'bout ol' Talwud, he knocks t' let yo' know he be feelin' no offense; an' sometime', he jus' lets yo' feel his peace-ableness. Lawdy, did he lub dis place!''

Jack imagined that was so. A shipboard engineer comes to love the drive more than his own life; and if aught threatens to harm it, he would sooner die than allow that to happen. Talward must have felt terrible horror at the condition of the shielding, and graver horror yet knowing the Captain would depart harborage before it was repaired.

"Do dat answer yo' questions, suh?" asked Benjamin.

"Yes, quite well," responded Jack. "But before I leave, I have something to ask of *you*: your dialect suggests you come from the South. Were you, by chance, ever a slave?''

"Ah was indeed, suh. Ah done save' massah's life one day, an' he repay' me by gibbin' me mah freedom. Ah went no'th t' find wuhk, an' come soon t' de shipyahds. Dere, mens gib me wuhk wit' dis heah ship, wuhkin' de drive room. Ah been heah ebbah since.''

"Have you never wanted some better position in life?''

"Dis ain't so bad, suh," said Benjamin. "Ah foun' de

true meanin' o' freedom heah, fo' no one right cayahs what colo' yo' be; ebba'one wuhks hahd, an' don't hab tahm t' be worryin' if'n yo' be white o' nigguh. An' aftah a spell, yo' be so cake' wit' duht an' sweat, yo' looks black anyways. White folks in fine houses, dey be concern' if'n yo' be white o' black, but not in dis place. Ah do finds it t' mah likin'."

Jack smiled. How inspiring it was that this Negro, even with his poor grasp of the English language, could be so eloquently enlightened. The white race certainly did pay poor heed to the worth of the Negro, beyond his value as livestock in the aristocratic South. It was at times like this that Jack felt the Negro might actually be a worthier soul than the white who hectored him so relentlessly.

V

As the Truth of the Matter is Made Known, So the Ghost Might be Finally Settled

On the evening of the third day, Captain Gentry hosted a small gathering in his quarters, and there Jack found the only other guests to be the six people with whom he had shared the Captain's table the first evening. Jack had an idea as to the reason for so select a group of invitees; but he would ask no questions, simply enjoy the Captain's hospitality and allow the man to explain things himself.

When the brandy had been served and everyone was seated, Captain Gentry announced to one and all, "Ladies and gentlemen; as you have probably noticed, this is no ordinary gathering. I have asked only the few of you here this evening because you were each present at my table when the subject of the ghost was broached; and when Mrs. Runnimede bore witness to that awful presence, you each came to her aid and heard her tale. Therefore, I think it only fitting you be present as we settle this topic once and for all."

"What prompted you to make this decision, Captain?" Professor Lindsail inquired.

"I was informed by my chief engineer that our Mr. Delaplane was down to snoop through the drive room today, seeking some information on the ghost. One Benjamin Cleveland, a Negro who is senior drive-jockey, as we call the maintenance crew, spoke to Mr. Delaplane, telling him quite a bit about Talward Dennison. Ordinarily, I would not take more than passing notice of such goings-on, because Mr. Delaplane's investigation was harmless, a man simply satisfying his curiosity; however, Benjamin indicated to Mr. Delaplane that *I* was somehow to blame for Mr. Dennison's death, so I thought it best to gather you all here, to 'clear the air,' as it were."

"Nonsense, Captain Gentry!" stated Dr. Tully. "You have naught to explain. I doubt the word of a possibly illiterate, certainly undistinguished, Negro maintenance boy could do harm to the reputation of a man in your position."

"I dare say Mr. Delaplane does not share your opinion, Doctor. Is that not correct, Mr. Delaplane?"

"Contrary to the feelings of many, including Dr. Tully and, I reckon, Mr. Beaudine, I feel the word of a Negro has as much merit as that of a white," said Jack, sipping of his brandy. "I didn't accuse Captain Gentry of wrong-doing; I merely asked Benjamin—Mr. Cleveland, rather—about Talward Dennison, and listened to what he had to say."

"Mr. Delaplane!" Beaudine said, with a smile, "I offer you good advice: heed not the reportings of a Negro. As one who has worked closely with them for a very long time, as well as having been raised among them, I can tell you with certainty that they are hardly the most reliable sources of information, and that the bucks are invariable liars."

"To be perfectly frank, Mr. Beaudine, I wouldn't have expected you to advise me differently. But I put it to you,

Captain Gentry: is there any truth to what I was told? Did
Talward Dennison blame you for his death?''

Captain Gentry drank a bit of brandy; then said, ''Actually, he did. You have heard Benjamin's tale, Mr. Delaplane; allow me now to tell mine.''

''By all means,'' said Jack. ''As I said, I did not place
blame.''

''Most considerate of you, sir,'' said the imposing officer, and he began his story: ''Talward Dennison, as Benjamin must have informed you, was the engineer's mate, a
youth of barely twenty-two years, who had graduated with
exemplary marks from a fine school. He signed on as
engineer's mate at twenty, and by twenty-two, was in line
for the chief engineer's post upon the worthy's retirement.
He was a fine young man, well-liked by all who knew him,
and, despite his youth, commanding the respect of all who
worked the drive deck, white and Negro alike.

''He did, however, have one severe failing: he was a
stubborn young man, who, when he was certain of a problem, would not let loose of it until it was finished. He also
tended to make mountains of molehills, which is where the
matter of the radioactivity shielding comes in:

''Granted, the shielding was fairly flawed, but not so
much so that we could not make it to our destined harborage. The chief engineer himself certified the drive shielding's integrity. But Talward disagreed, claiming it would
burst long before we reached our destination. The chief engineer argued long with him in quarters, but Talward would
not give an inch. He would not, in fact, leave the drive
room, declaring he had to watch the regulators carefully.''

''If I may, Captain,'' said Jack. ''Benjamin Cleveland
told me you ordered Talward to remain by the shielding, that
he was to hold his post for the duration.''

''Perhaps that was what Talward told Benjamin, and all
the rest of the men in the drive room,'' Captain Gentry

said. "Also, that was fifteen years ago, and one's memory tends to alter over the years. But Talward did blame me; in fact, after the explosion, as the doctor tended to Talward, the youth declared to one and all that I was responsible for the mishap. There was, however, no basis in truth for this fevered accusation."

"Is that why his ghost lingers, to harass you till your punishment?"

Captain Gentry looked quite pained at that mention, as though a tender nerve had been touched; and he stared at Jack for a long, silent moment. Eventually, he said, "Did Benjamin tell you that, Mr. Delaplane?"

"He did, Captain. He compared Talward to a Nemesis, one of the Greek spirits of Justice which haunt transgressors until they are punished. You, sir, seem to feel there *is* reason for said punishment."

Captain Gentry closed his eyes. "I could not know the radioactivity shielding would burst. I was given full assurance that we could make it to harborage long before the danger point had arrived. Perhaps it was the circumstances of our travel which delivered the shielding the fatal blow. . . ."

Dr. Tully looked sternly questioning. "Please explain your meaning, Captain."

"I remember we were approaching a radiation belt, one of many which fairly spiderweb the cosmos; so I advised young Talward to watch the regulators carefully, for as Mr. Delaplane can attest, such conditions often cause the matrix flux to leap toward the high and low boundaries. Most radiation belts are well-charted, but often, a solar flare will create a new belt, so we must ever be vigilant when we ply the vasty. Talward insisted the radioactivity shielding would not hold under the stress of a buckling flux, but I informed him we could not turn back or even alter our course, as near harborage as we were. We would proceed forward, and hope for the best.

"As we passed through the radiation belt, our instruments naturally indicated leaps in the matrix, so we took little note of it. But a few moments later, we received the report that the radioactivity shielding in the drive shell had ruptured, and the drive room was flooded with radiation. Fortunately, the crew had gotten clear in time; but young Talward was trapped inside, after having sent the men out. Radiation sweepers cleared the room in minutes, but it was too late to save the poor lad's life, The doctor pronounced him deceased minutes later.

"I regret Talward had to die, but I tell you, it was not due to my negligence."

It was at that moment that the ghost of Talward Dennison materialized before their very eyes. Jack would later surmise the reason for the manifestation being that as the Captain, whom Talward had gone to his grave blaming for his death, had as much as called him a liar, attempting to clear his name at the expense of the name of Talward, the spirit would quite naturally wish to dispute him. But for the moment, Jack could only look on with fascination, as the spirit proved its existence no myth.

Mrs. Runnimede gave a cry of anguish, no better prepared than when first she beheld the horror, and hid her eyes behind her hands. Elizabeth, who professed no fear of ghosts, sat transfixed, her mouth halfway open. Dr. Tully stared with disbelieving eyes, unable to summon up the breath for a single "harumph." Mrs. Bryant did not look particularly horrified, or repulsed, or even astonished; but stared at the ghost nonetheless. Professor Lindsail sat grinning, as he saw his belief in ghosts vindicated before skeptics. Clayton Beaudine looked as though his Christian skepticism had grown wings and flown away. And Jack, who had searched so manfully for the truth of the ghost, gazed at it quietly, wondering what it would do, in the presence of a man it regarded as a foe.

But Captain Gentry showed the gravest reaction of all: his face was pale and drawn, his eyes so filled with woe, that Jack, who glimpsed him peripherally, feared he might fall sobbing to the floor, so pronounced was his sadness. This, quite plainly, was no new event for the staunch Captain, for in his visage was proof he knew the ghost from old.

The ghost was all that Mrs. Runnimede described, the figure of a sailor subjected to great misfortune, his clothing ripped and the flesh beneath rent and bloody, and one eye closed by a bruise, while the other was wide and staring. The apparition hovered fully two feet above the floor, and though it seemed fairly solid, the shapes of furniture and the details of pictures on the wall could be faintly discerned through it. It was motionless for a moment, that fearsome spectre; then it raised a hand and pointed ominously at Captain Gentry. Its lips moved, and though the folk who gazed upon it were no lip-readers, they clearly saw the word: "Captain!"

A moment later, the ghost faded, and there was once more only empty air. Mrs. Runnimede released her anguish, began to sob piteously, as Elizabeth gave her succor; Dr. Tully and Beaudine gazed at nothing, reconsidering their opinions in view of the visitation; Professor Lindsail pulled a notebook and pencil from his coat pocket and began scribbling furiously; but Mrs. Bryant was able to sum it all up in the most appropos words:

"Now that," said she, "was an A-1, first class haunt, or I'm sister to a boar-shoat!"

"Captain Gentry!" said Jack, "I believe there's more to this than you can account for so simply."

"I can say only that I have been visited by the ghost on many occasions," said Captain Gentry. "I apologize for not telling you sooner; but I dread the visitations so greatly, I say as little about them as possible. You see now what Cimmerian evil harrows me, and why I have been so reticent to dwell upon it.''

"Oh! please! I beg of you," cried Mrs. Runnimede; "do not speak of that daemon any longer!''

"I regret, dear Mrs. Runnimede," Jack told her, with proper regard for her delicate condition, "that we *must* speak of it a bit further.''

"What shall we do about this?" Elizabeth wondered. "I have no normal fear of ghosts, but this, I do declare, gave me the shivers.''

"We know where the ghost resides, and Professor Lindsail claims knowledge of the supernatural; so I propose we remove it.''

"Mr. Delaplane! are you serious?" cried Dr. Tully. "How shall mere mortals such as ourselves even *attempt* such a feat?''

"There is a way, Doctor," Professor Lindsail told him. "The *Granger Book of Spirits* contains a section on the exorcism of ghosts. I do not know how well it works on vasty spirits, but I have attempted it with terrestrial manifestations, and found success.''

"Do it, then, Professor!" said Captain Gentry, with great enthusiasm. "I would as soon be free of the daemon as draw my next breath!''

"It's agreed, then," said Jack. "Professor! tell us what we must do.''

"I shall first need to fetch the book from my cabin," said Professor Lindsail. "Come! we will go from there.''

VI

As the Intrepid Souls Confront Talward
Dennison, and Find a Resolution to the Matter

The drive deck had grown quiet since Jack and his party arrived, and now, as they walked into the drive room itself, the sailors stood watching, their grime-encrusted faces frozen in curiosity. Captain Gentry himself led the group, having swallowed his dread sufficiently to stride certainly into the metal chamber. No sound was heard but that of machines at work and, most notable of all, the drive itself. The metaphor of the drive being the heart of the ship was quite appropos, for the thrumming of the tumblers did sound like a heart beating.

"If Talward died upon the drive shell," quoth Professor Lindsail, "his ghost would have no choice but to occupy the matrix; for a ghost must ever remain in the place where its living form passed on."

"Except when it goes wandering," Mrs. Runnimede murmured, "to scare the life out of people."

"Nonetheless, its essence must needs remain in that place."

"Perhaps there's more to it than that," said Jack. "Let us find out."

At first, Jack had attempted to persuade the women to remain behind, to allow the men to do their work unhindered; but they would not hear of it. They had been part of this from the beginning, they declared, and, in any case, would hinder the men not at all. Even Mrs. Runnimede was game for this excursion, and needed no assistance from either Elizabeth or Mrs. Bryant. Therefore, the men relented, and allowed them to come along.

They came at last to the drive shell, where the thrumming was so loud it nearly disheartened them; for if Talward could exist in that place, where the matrix kicked and rolled, buckling upon itself in the way a cat buckles as it raises up its back to stretch its muscles, would mere mortals have the power to vanquish him from it? Professor Lindsail had no fear for their success; he had his book of spirits firmly in hand as he placed himself before the shell.

"How shall we summon it up?" Beaudine wondered.

"As easily as we did before," said Professor Lindsail, with a most confident smile. "Captain Gentry! If you would be so kind; you know what is most likely to raise the gentleman from hiding."

"I do, yes," said the brave Captain. He declared toward the drive shell, "Talward Dennison!, you are a humbug, unfit to inhabit this grand chamber! You are unwanted, and as such, must depart immediately! So raise up your poor spirit and come forth, where Christian eyes may look once more upon one who has been rejected by both heaven and hell, before you leave altogether!"

A glow settled over the drive shell, resolving itself gradually into the hovering form of a man. The sailors who crewed this deck gathered near-by to stare at the apparition, none showing any fear, only sympathy for the hapless spirit. They were old acquaintances of Talward, and knew no dread; for he was like a shipmate, unseen but never so far away that they did not know he was present.

The ghost pointed its finger at Captain Gentry and mouthed the accusing word; and the Captain quailed. Then did Professor Lindsail raise his hand in ministerial fashion and read aloud the words in his book: "Talward Dennison, you are a thing of cold bones; of empty air; of lost vigor. Here is the plane of warm flesh; of solid forms; of youth and passion. You are a deceased man, who has cheated his Maker of his spirit, for in the hands of your Maker do you properly belong. Fly to Him now, for you are indeed dead. Leave this place and do not return."

The ghost did not waver, which made the professor frown with puzzlement and notable concern. He said, "I do not understand. This has never failed to release a spirit from the place to which death bound it.

"I thought as much," said Jack; "for I believe there's more to this matter than a simple haunting." He stepped forward to confront the ghost, who took no apparent notice of any but the Captain, and declared, "Talward! listen to me. Your anger toward the Captain may be well placed, but it's doing great harm. You have inhabited the drive for a very long time, and in those years, the flux has been radically altered. The high and low boundaries are being brushed; and when cosmic radiation grows greater, to torment the matrix, your presence must drive the numbers up farther than where they ought to be. You may think you have a right to be here, and perhaps you do; but not at the expense of the drive! Consider what you're doing to the matrix; each year you inhabit the flow is a year closer to complete break-down. Ask yourself, then: is revenging yourself upon Captain Gentry worth the safety—nay the very *survival*—of the engines?"

The ghost of Talward Dennison stared at Jack for a very long moment, its beaten face showing no other expression but great surprise; then, as gradually as it had manifested itself, it vanished. Not a word was issued, until the voice of Benjamin Cleveland spoke, in a mournful tone: "Ol' Talwud be gone, now, gone f'evah. Ah feels it fo' sure; he be gone fine'ly t' his rest."

VII

As the Eventful Voyage Comes to Its Harborage, and All Threads Are Tied Off

The *Alice P.* entered New Connecticut City Harborage as subjective mid-day began aboard the ship; and after the clipper was secured in its lock and the pressure equalized, her passengers disembarked to make their way to the ferries down to the surface. Jack strolled through a broad passage, wearing his best shore attire, feeling light and vigorous.

The events of the previous five days were still fresh in his mind, making him more respectful of unknown things. He hoped Talward was happier now, wherever he had gone.

As he turned a corner, bound for the ferries, Jack nearly collided with Elizabeth. He snatched his hat from his head and made his apologies, but Elizabeth was not harmed, but all smiles.

"Why, Mr. Delaplane!" said she, "how nice to see you once more. Dr. Tully, Mrs. Runnimede, and I were wondering if we would run into you again."

"And how fortuitous for me that you have," said Jack. He paid his respects to the worthy doctor and the sturdy matron, who stood behind Elizabeth, looking on as though protective parents. "I, too, wondered if we wouldn't once more meet. We have not yet dined together."

"Oh, I feel we shall. But, please, Mr. Delaplane, curiosity compels me to ask about the events of that final day, so if you could tell me . . . ?"

"You ask how I knew the very way to rid the ship of the ghost, Miss St. George?"

"I do."

"As do we, Mr. Delaplane," agreed Dr. Tully. "We did not ask before, but ask now."

Jack smiled before replying: "Benjamin Cleveland, the Negro I spoke to in the drive room, reinforced something I had suspected all along: that Talward Dennison was the truest measure of a ship's engineer, for he loved the engines more than life itself, and would sooner give said life than bring them any sort of harm. His sort develops such a love in the course of his career on the drive deck. I suspected that Professor Lindsail's exorcism formula, while possibly effective against house-haunts, might not work in this case because Talward didn't remain behind as a spirit bound to the place of his death; he remained to see the machines were well-tended. Benjamin informed me that while the drive crew never saw Talward, they'd often hear him knocking, to tell them he was in a fine mood; the fact they never saw him was certainly due to their proper care of the drive, which never prompted him to harry them. However, Captain Gentry had already abused the system by allowing the radioactivity shield in the drive shell to decay; and for that, he would be forever haunted."

"But I thought his haunting was due to the fact that Talward blamed him for his demise," said Mrs. Runnimede.

"Most assuredly that," said Jack, with a nod. "But so much seemed to involve the drive itself, rather than his actual death, that I suspected he had more interest in the safety of the drive than his vengeance upon Captain Gentry. When Professor Lindsail's formula failed to move Talward an iota, I knew the answer for certain; so I informed Talward his presence in the matrix was causing it to slowly deteriorate. As one who had had so much love for the engines in life, he could do naught else *but* depart the matrix; and when he released his hold on the engines, he lost his only connection to the material world. Hence his exorcism."

"How clever of you, sir," Dr. Tully commended him. "I believe you shall go far in life."

Mrs. Bryant, Professor Lindsail and Mr. Beaudine came past next, on their way to the ferries. They stopped to wish their voyage-mates well; then the professor and the planter, the latter having grown friendlier toward Jack since the day of the exorcism, even to the point of asking Jack to look him up while they were both on New Connecticut, said fare-well; then moved on.

"I surely do admire you for what you did, Mr. Delaplane," said Mrs. Bryant, with her broad, country-folk smile. "That Mr. Dennison was a true credit to his living profession. As the late Mr. Bryant, rest his soul, was so fond of saying, 'If a man loves his work enough, ain't a grave deep enough to keep him from it come morning.'"

"The late Mr. Bryant was very wise," said Jack, taking her hand cordially. "Fare-well, Mrs. Bryant."

"Fare you well, too, Mr. Delaplane," said she; then she moved off to find her ferry.

"I believe we, too, should be going," said Elizabeth. "I am bound for the surface aboard Ferry #5."

Jack showed surprise. "As am I, Miss St. George." He offered his arm. "Might I escort you there?"

"Oh, please do," said she, taking his arm. "And you may call me Elizabeth."

"I certainly shall, Elizabeth. And you may call me Jack."

"Thank you very much, Jack."

And it was in that manner that they strolled off, in search of Ferry #5. Dr. Tully and Mrs. Runnimede could not say as they approved of the behavior of the young couple, as they had never been properly introduced; but, they reflected, youth shall ever take its liberties, and there is hardly aught to be done about it.

"However," Dr. Tully said, upon second consideration, "I feel they may have the right idea." He offered his own arm to Mrs. Runnimede. "Shall we go, madam?"

Mrs. Runnimede looked at him carefully for a moment; then she smiled pleasantly and accepted it. "Certainly, sir. And you may call me Agatha."

Under Ice
by
C. W. Johnson

About the Author

C. W. Johnson is about to complete his studies toward a Ph.D. in theoretical physics from the University of Washington in Seattle. He's in his middle twenties, and before concentrating on physics, his major scientific interest was paleontology. Those influences, together with his love of the Pacific Northwest, and his research into Native American and Inuit ("Eskimo") cultures, can all be seen in "Under Ice."

The writing... well, that's been honed by membership in writing groups which included WOTF writers Laura Campbell and Karen Joy Fowler, possibly by attending a Hubbard Awards event in Seattle and meeting Robert Reed, the first L. Ron Hubbard Gold Award winner, and by attending workshops conducted by Joanna Russ, Peter S. Beagle, and Kim Stanley Robinson. Talented people find help from talented people. Johnson's writing talent has attained a remarkable professionalism, and with the help of WOTF, you see its first published example presented here....

The ceiling of ice hung thirty meters above Marya's head. She could not see it, but she knew the ice was there, and the thought of it weighed down on her

It was the same with the Arctic cold. She was in a dry-suit, warm and sealed off from the frigid water. But the sound of the air cycling in her helmet and the moist condensation of her own breath drove her imagination, until she felt oppressed by the cold and the dark.

The only illumination of the sea floor was the web of beams from her helmet and those of the two divers on either side of her. The lances of light cut through the haze of sediments stirred up as they slowly trekked across the ooze. Marya stopped and played her lights over the sea bottom. The site was level, the sediment rippled by currents. A few crustaceans crabbed sidewise at their leisure. A sea bass drifted into Marya's lights, gave her a startled look, and shot off. Marya sighed. This would be difficult.

But she felt the *presence*, which was definitely strongest here, much stronger than at the previous sea-floor sites. Marya spoke into her mike. "All right, Luther. Let's try it." She switched off her light. The other two divers followed suit, leaving her in darkness. The slight current pulled at her like an unseen hand.

Luther's quiet voice spoke in her ears. "Turning up the P-amps slowly."

Marya sucked in a deep breath and blew it out. Her arms floated effortlessly in the buoyant water. She counted

Illustrated by Stu Shepherd

down to the familiar trance and tried to imagine herself, this place, above air, a cold, xeric tundra, a cutting wind, thousands of years ago . . .

Without full amplification Marya felt only a touch of the *presence,* a tugging at her eyes and throat, a small demanding voice. When she slid down into trance she could almost see, superimposed upon the sea floor, the tundra that had once been there during the last glacial advance: the blowing drifts of snow and the hardy plants.

Then the probability amplifiers warped and bent probability space, where electrons, quarks and other quantum particles swarmed, so that Marya's consciousness could punch through to another mind, another time.

Even though Luther brought up the P-amps slowly, the vision, as always, hit Marya with the rolling rush of a tsunami. She broke out in a sudden sweat and was *there*. No imagination.

She was squatting outside a skin tent, caribou skin *(Rangifer tarandus)* by the look of it. The icy Arctic wind whipped around her. The sun was low in the sky and obscured by clouds. The ground was mostly bare of snow. She could feel the soil and pebble-sized rocks shift beneath her feet through rabbitskin boots. Marya, or her host, more exactly (female, mid teens), concentrated on the task before her, scraping clean the skin of a small fox. She used a shaped bone tool. The fat was palpable on her fingers.

Her head was full of thoughts in an alien language. But they were unshaped and swift and Marya could not yet grasp them.

The young woman paused to push back a lock of greasy black hair that had fallen in her eyes, when a voice said: *"Inaala."* Marya looked up and realized that was her host's name. An old, almost toothless woman stood in front of her, triggering a flood of associations that Marya tried to grasp. *"Inaala qivalu shaa lia liaa t'ua-niuu la,"* said the old woman Harni, Inaala's husband's aunt, and Marya understood: "Inaala, finish that fox." Harni continued. "The men will be back from the sea-hunt soon."

Marya/Inaala nodded and understood. One of the hunters had returned that morning, telling them that they had caught two seals, had flensed them and 'returned the bones' (the phrase had some meaning Marya didn't understand yet), and would arrive soon. Among the hunters would be her husband Awalu, who had taken her only a month before; she could not shame him in front of the others by having been unproductive. She redoubled her efforts, removing every scrap of fat and membrane.

As Inaala worked Marya tried to place the relationship of the dwellings to each other, the garbage dump, the meat caches, tried to store the knowledge tumbling with natural ease through Inaala's mind. She did this hearing her own breath echoed in the P-amp helmet.

For it was a delicate balance, to not let the modern world intrude, and yet not to drown in the personality of her unknowing host.

When Marya came out of the trance she felt weak. Fortunately the buoyancy of the water held her up. The other divers each took an arm and helped her back to the squat submersible a few meters away. As they went, Marya dictated out all she could remember, sometimes speaking in the ancient tongue. "Two meters west of the skin tent was a sod hut, apparently semi-permanent; next to that was a bone midden, mostly caribou, the caribou paths divined with the help of the moon *ooti nuumu shaa luluii ali lia ootu . . .*"

The submersible research vehicle *Phillipe* was little more than a portable diving base: four spheres welded together and covered with searchlights, cameras, propellers, ballast, and manipulative arms. The three divers clumped up the shallow, brightly lit ramp, which led to the diving hatch. In the sub black water cascaded from them as they stepped up into the light.

Inside, hands removed Marya's bulky 'lobster' helmet and suit; other hands helped her through another hatch to the medical bay, to lie down on a bunk while she droned on and her vital signs were monitored. "Patriarchal society with some matrilineal elements. The leaders are chosen mostly for their ability to hunt and their social skills. My mother was Aruia, my *guatuu Nemte ii puuilli semsa ak Qaarnki ii . . .*"

At length she rested and opened her eyes. The project's medic pronounced her well. Behind the medic stood Luther Qin, the dark, quiet, young P-amp tech. Luther, whose background was in probability physics, smiled. "Seems like quite a find." She nodded.

Sitting up, she saw Nesmith A. Potriah duck his head as he entered the debriefing room. He was a barrel-bellied man, with wire-like gray hair sparsely covering his head and a thick, jowly face. He had stopped diving years ago but as principal investigator oversaw the initial survey. Potriah wore a jacket, even though the temperature of the sub was regulated at a comfortable twenty-three degrees. Probably much like Marya, the Arctic ice overhead weighed heavily in his mind.

"Well done, Marya," Potriah said, his mouth approximating a smile. "Jiseong is already starting to plot out the coordinates for a preliminary dig. It may be an excellent site."

Marya nodded, and told him about her host. "Apparently her husband—and there was some tension in her feelings about him—was expected to be returning soon from a hunt."

"Caribou season?" Potriah asked. "Or mammoth? Personally I hope for the latter." He talked quickly, under his breath, not looking at Marya. "That bastard Arbatov just published a paper saying they wouldn't be found this far north. Love to see him wrong."

Marya furrowed her brow in concentration. "No . . . *seal*." She looked up. "Returning from a seal hunt."

Potriah's expression went hard. "Oh, is that so?" He shrugged his shoulders casually. But his eyes burned. The senior archaeologist nodded to himself, shook his head, and ducked out the aft hatch, mumbling something unintelligible.

Luther moved closer to Marya. She said to him, "Looks like our teamwork is still holding together."

"Yeah," said Luther. He glanced in the direction of the aft hatch. "Jesus! Did you see the look he gave you?"

"Luther . . ." she began.

"Yeah, I know." Luther lowered his voice. "He's muttering more than ever about this bastard and that bastard and how he'll show them wrong. Remember how he used to?" Marya nodded. "I was only on one dig with him while you were back at school. Shigawara was the sensitive. *That* was a circus. I heard she laughed when he asked her to come back for this dig. He drove her crazy. She called him Mumbles Potriah."

"God, I hope he hasn't been mumbling about me."

"Just that he hopes 'they' haven't ruined you."

Marya stood up. "I don't want to worry about it now. Let's get something hot to drink, okay?" She shivered, still thinking about the cold.

A little over a month later a full team had been assembled. Six temporary underwater domes were erected on the sea floor forty meters from the site: two for sleeping, one for meals and socializing, two for analysis of excavated material, and one for equipment and supplies.

In Dome 3 Marya sat on her bunk, looking at the laminated map she had attached next to her bunk, marking their position on the continental shelf between Siberia and Cape Hope, Alaska: In drowned Beringia.

Marya glanced up at the clock and saw it was time. She got off her bunk and went through the low tunnel that connected Dome 3 with Dome 5, the diving dome. She dressed in her drysuit, then waited until Jiseong, a graduate student in archaeology from Seoul National University, swam through the outer hatchway and waded up into the air. He was a small, broad-shouldered and broad-faced man. "You ready?" he asked. She nodded, and he helped her with the P-amp equipped lobster helmet and checked the seals. "A-okay," his voice came over the intercom.

The black water lapped at her knees, then her chest as she descended, and finally swallowed her whole. They went through the underwater hatch to the blue-black darkness which the lights could never fully banish. Just outside the dome Jiseong paused to snap off the fins from his diving boots and attach weights. Then he signaled for her to go ahead. They trudged over towards the site.

Grid lines were laid out over a twenty-by-twenty meter area, in one-meter squares. Already several preliminary trenches had been started. To combat the fine silt and ooze, which made excavation nearly impossible, refrigeration lines were imbedded in each layer of sediment; when a section had frozen solid, it was removed and taken inside a dome for careful inspection.

The top meter or so was simply oceanic sediment. Most of this had already been stripped away, revealing the ancient soil that had once been above air. In the very first trench small rodent bones had been found, proving this had indeed been part of the land bridge between Siberia and North America.

So far no signs of human habitation, but this was only the first week of the dig. Hopes were still high. And Marya had an excellent record. Before she had gone back to school, she had been on several important sites from India to Africa to England.

Her chest tightened. Potriah had not wanted her to go back to school, especially not in theoretical archaeology, which he spurned, and certainly not under Loebbel, his arch-rival. Potriah had faith in few field archaeologists and none in theorists. Loebbel, in turn, had tried to dissuade Marya from returning to work for Potriah. Marya had pointed out that Nesmith Potriah had the grant money, and that his reputation was not built on nothing. Yes, Loebbel had admitted, at one time Potriah, though arrogant, had been very good. But now, her advisor had added in characteristic hyperbole, Potriah's as archaic as the ruins he digs.

But Potriah was going to Northern Beringia, the subject of Marya's doctoral research (computer simulations that had predicted maritime subsistence in Northern Beringia) and Loebbel was not. And sensitives of Marya's caliber were extremely rare. Like it or not, Marya and Potriah needed each other.

Jiseong tapped at her shoulder. Marya turned around, not an easy task in her bulky suit. He held up the end of the fiber-optic cable, which led off to the *Phillipe*. "I'm going to plug you in now."

"I'm ready." She felt him fumble at the back of her helmet, then pull away. "Luther? Can you hear me?"

"Loud and clear, Marya," Luther said, warm and dry in the sub.

"I want to approach the camp—" She stopped, finding herself thinking in Inaala's terms—"the site closer."

"Roger."

She stepped forward, leaning to counteract the buoyancy of the water. The black-suited figures around the dig parted for her as she approached.

Marya started to curve a little to the right, following

the tickle of *presence* that told her this was the path. She told Luther to turn on the P-amps, then shut out the sound of her own breath and counted backwards to trance.

A cold wave of the sea washed over her and she was in light, walking along a well-worn path towards the skin tent. It was late in the year: the sun was low and the air, though motionless, was biting cold. Marya/Inaala slowed as she approached the hut. Her stomach clutched in fear. But of what? Marya searched for the reason and felt the pain in Inaala's upper right arm. Inaala muttered to herself. "A humble woman, a poor preparer of your fine skins . . ."

Awalu had come back from a hunt, two days before. He was not pleased with Inaala's preparations of the seal skins. She had meticulously picked the skins clean and dry, but not fast enough for Awalu. Marya heard the echo of rage in his voice. "You— you shame your husband! Ahh! You worthless woman!"

Marya raided her host's memories and decided that Inaala was not really at fault. Her sister-in-law Oomita had in fact worked slower but her husband had not beat her. And Inaala's mother and grandmother had always emphasized that the skins must be perfectly clean—never accept less in sacrifice for speed. Make sure the skin was free from fat so never to rot.

And, in fact, Awalu had poorly flensed the seal in the process of removing its bones and leaving them behind as demanded by the Seal-Woman, who wanted her children's bones left in the sea so their spirits would come home to her. The skin was badly cut and it would be difficult to make proper garments from it. But Marya knew that Inaala would never risk her husband's wrath to tell him that.

Inaala stood in the doorway of the sod hut and trembled. She did not understand Awalu! Once, maybe twice, her father had beaten her mother for embarrassing him, but it had been sufficient for her mother to scream loud for the neighbors. Her mother never had bruise marks and always an hour later her mother and father were laughing together under the furs. Awalu was always angry and sullen. He never laughed with her—just climbed on top of her.

Inside the hut, she saw Awalu's bulk looming in the dark. "What took you so long?" he growled. "Are your feet made of stone? You miserable woman . . ."

Marya/Inaala felt the flash of pain on her cheek. She fell to the ground, tasting blood and earth, wondering, How did I make such a mistake? Why did the spirits lead me to such a man for a husband?

The tiny rec dome was designed for five to eight people to fit comfortably in it, so the atmosphere was stuffy when twelve—nearly all the workers at the site—crowded into it around the modest vidscreen. Drinks and snacks were handed around as they waited for the archaeology segment on the Science News Cable Network. "When's it going to come on?" someone said over the din of conversation. "I'm tired of this physics crap."

"Hey, it's good for you," Luther said. Several people guffawed.

Marya said to Luther, "I'm surprised at this interview. Potriah's always been very careful not to go to the media until he's got all the pieces in place."

Luther shook his head. "He's changed a lot in the last few years, after you went back to school. He doesn't stay much at the sites anymore, and seems more interested in publishing in the *New York Times* than in *Archaeological Journal*. I guess that's what fame and age do to you."

Someone hushed them. "Here it comes!"

The tinny synthesized theme music for the archaeology segment blasted away, a distorted, electronicized version of primitive drums. The crowd was well lubricated and several people chimed in: "Dum-duh dum-duh-duh duh dum!" and broke into laughter.

The reporter, a genial but no-nonsense woman, quickly went through the essentials of the Beringian land bridge. Between twelve to twenty thousand years ago, during the Wisconsin ice advance, so much water had been taken up in glaciers that the level of the ocean was ninety-five meters lower than in the modern era. Hence Beringia had appeared from the chill Arctic waters and allowed humans to cross over into North America.

Using a map of ancient Beringia, she explained how most theories placed the crossing on the more temperate southern coast of Beringia. "But we have today with us Professor Nesmith Potriah, of the University of Michigan, who has made a spectacular career of finding evidence of humans where they should not have been, from Africa to a three-thousand-year-old settlement in the Antarctic." Potriah smiled and nodded.

The rest was old news to them, how Potriah was defying conventional wisdom in looking for habitation of the less hospitable northern coast. Sequences of the dig site and inside the domes flashed on the screen. "There's me! There's me!" People in the rec dome screeched and pointed. Marya laughed, "God, I look *awful!*" Potriah proudly discussed the preliminary finds, including the caribou midden, the pre-Clovis points, and the human tibia. He also mentioned, albeit briefly, Marya's aid in locating the site. Without a sensitive like Marya, finding archaeological evidence buried in the sea floor would be impossible. He did not forget to mention that thirty-five years ago, when the P-amp was invented, that he had been one of the very first to use sensitives in archaeology, paving the way to their acceptance in other fields.

"So what were these Beringian people like, Professor?" the reporter asked. "Were they much like the Inuit people of Alaska and Greenland?"

"Well, they were similar, although more primitive. For instance, their tools were less sophisticated and they had fewer food-gathering strategies.

"What did they eat?"

"We've only found evidence for caribou. They may have hunted the woolly mammoth, which is now extinct." He glanced at the camera before continuing. "And, in contrast to modern Inuits, they did not hunt any marine mammals."

A heavy silence draped itself across the room. Marya could feel glances dart at her. Any dig is a small community and every one knew of her reports.

The reporter pressed Potriah harder. "Did the sensitive, Dr St. Jean, report that they only hunt caribou? I was told—"

Potriah interrupted the reporter brusquely. "While I value sensitives highly—without them my work would be impossible—one must take their reports with a grain of salt."

"What!?" shouted Luther.

Potriah continued: "It is very delicate work, and easily influenced by the outside. Oftentimes one runs up against what we call a ghost, a psychic reading of someone or something that isn't really there but is instead a psychological projection." Marya felt her face get hot. "Also, remember that in the Denali culture on both sides of the Bering Sea there is absolutely no evidence of maritime hunting."

"That's nonsense," Marya breathed.

The reporter persisted. "But aren't there theoretical studies that show that they could have had the skills to hunt seals and whales, and then lost those skills?"

Potriah shook his head, the rage clearly building in his face. "Those are just theories, mostly by mavericks. Unreliable ideas, I'm afraid. I'm not interested in theory. I care about the truth, which is based on fact and physical evidence. The archaeological record is solid on this. No ancient Arctic sealing. It's ridiculous to talk otherwise.''

The room fell silent.

"What an asshole," someone said. Someone else laughed nervously.

Marya fought back the tears as the room cleared in silence.

When Awalu came home after the next hunt he had with him a man Inaala did not know. The storm outside was blowing ferociously, like the howl of wolves, and the snow dropped in big, wet, sticky flakes, covering the land in heavy drifts. Inaala heard voices outside, and finally Awalu and the stranger ducked through the hide flap at the door. At first he was still wrapped in his heavy furs, the hood of his jacket covering his face so she could not see what he looked like, But he was taller than Awalu and stood with a commanding presence.

They undressed, ignoring her presence even though she quietly took their clothes away to dry and their boots to chew soft. The man was not terribly handsome: his nose stuck out too far from his face, and his hair was tangled and mussed. But his muscles moved smoothly under his brown skin, which gleamed in the lamplight, and he was obviously a good hunter: well fed, and had many fine furs. However, his clothes were in disrepair, and Inaala knew he had no wife.

"The Seal-Woman wasn't kind to me today," Awalu said softly.

"The Seal-Woman has smiled upon me this past month," the stranger said, "but not today, either. Perhaps she's angry." Awalu nodded. The Seal-Woman-Under-the-Sea sent out the game animals. Her favor was necessary for

survival. In times of bad hunting, people would hire a
s'amu to go on a spirit journey down to her undersea house,
to comb her hair and soothe her. The Seal-Woman had no
fingers so a good way to gain her favor was to comb her
long, thick tresses.

Finally Awalu acknowledged Inaala's presence. "This
is my ugly and clumsy wife—" The words did not sting
Inaala, because they were ritual humility— "but a woman's
a woman, and the nights are cold." Inaala said nothing. She
was sewing up holes in their clothes.

The stranger said, "She is a beautiful flower, and one
can't help but notice how well-kept your clothes are! Alas,
a hunter had a wife, not as beautiful or talented, but she
died."

Awalu grunted. "That's sad, to be without a woman!
Here now, this woman isn't much, but she'll keep your furs
warm tonight." This, too, was traditional hospitality.

"Oh, pfah!" the stranger laughed. "A certain hunter is
not worthy of such a beautiful woman."

So they humbly argued, but of course in the end hospitality won out and Inaala crept shyly under the furs with
the stranger. Otu, he whispered his name to her. His body
was very warm, burning with an inner fire. His skin was
soft as a baby's, and he touched her softly and gently, as if
he knew her body as his own. Through his touch she
thought she felt his sadness like a keening wind, the loss of
his wife, the loneliness of the deep Arctic winter nights.

But his passion was so intense, his desire so palpable,
that soon both of them were laughing, truly laughing under
the furs. She had never actually laughed with any of Awalu's
friends. This man was different. Still, Inaala tried to clamp
a hand over her mouth, to stifle her laughs. In the far
corner, where Awalu lay, the dark and silence were a fore-
boding presence.

• • •

"I did nothing of the sort!" Marya protested.

"Well, someone must have told that reporter," Nesmith Potriah said dryly. He had called her into his makeshift office barely an hour after his return. "She couldn't have come up with that sealing business out of thin air."

"Weisburd is a good reporter," Marya said defensively. "I've watched her before. She researches carefully. She probably called up all the experts in the field. Including Loebbel."

"Well, reporters love to call on the mavericks," Potriah muttered. "At least she didn't bring up that crazy thing about the bone taboo."

"My God, it's not crazy. It even makes sense, to leave the bones in the sea for the Seal-Woman, so that new sea mammals will come."

"It's too convenient," Potriah observed. "No seal middens to find. But not something to tell anyone unless you enjoy being laughed at." He shook his head. "I wish you'd never gotten mixed up with these theorists. They took a good talent and filled your head with nonsense." He sighed. "I was hoping, just hoping, that with some good field work you'd come to your senses . . ."

"Christ!" Marya stood up and stormed out. She bent over through the hatchway and started through the tunnel. She stopped when she heard footsteps. Turning around, she saw Luther. "How'd it go?" he asked.

"Please," she said, "I need to be alone. For a little while."

A look of pain crossed Luther's face, but he bobbed his head and turned around.

Marya scuttled through the tunnel, which was not heated, trying not to think of the cold pressure of the sea inches away through the cold metal. At the barracks-dome she lay face-down in her bunk, and let the tears stream into the pillow. She knew Loebbel was considered a maverick, even by scientists less dogmatic than Potriah. But she also thought him brilliant. And he had given her a chance no one else would. Because of her background with Potriah, everyone else who would take her assumed she would be in fieldwork. Loebbel let her do theory.

My God, she thought, could Potriah be right? Potriah was arrogant, dogmatic—but he was also too often right. Marya wondered, Am I just projecting this, to prove my thesis? To prove myself as a theorist? It had happened to other sensitives before, a mixture of fact and wishful thinking.

No, no, she couldn't think this way. Lack of confidence would be the deadliest poison to her talents. She turned over onto her back and held up her hands. She fingered a slim silver ring on her right pinkie finger, twisting it round and round.

Edwin had given her that ring. He was another sensitive, a friend of hers and, for a while, a lover. He had worked with law-enforcement agencies, occasionally solving a spectacular and grisly murder but more often working on more mundane items. But, like her, he wanted to be more than a tool. He wanted to study criminology, to join the police force and work his way up to the rank of detective. He had the intelligence and dogged determination for it; but not the self-confidence when the police he worked with had laughed at him. "You've read too many detective novels," he was told. Then they had the gall to tell him his was an honored position.

Marya snorted and turned over in her bunk. Honored position! Honored in a glass cage, recognized for an accident of nature. Edwin decided there was no place for him in law-enforcement and retired, removing himself from the situation. "If they won't treat me on equal terms," he had written her of his decision, two years ago, "then the only course of action I see is not to play their game."

She understood and respected his position. But Marya refused to withdraw. Even if—

She stopped. *Withdraw.* She had really given poor Luther the cold shoulder. Marya sat up in her bunk. She had better find Luther.

His bunk was in the next dome over. As she entered through the open hatchway she heard the high, piercing wail of Luther's clarinet. She paused to appreciate; he was a competent jazz clarinetist. The notes, each drawn out with a sweetness that touched Marya, danced up and down the scale, from the lower wavering bass notes to the highest reedy squeal Luther could squeeze from the instrument.

Finally, Marya stood in his doorway. No one was in the room except for Luther, blowing away. When he saw her he stopped and put the clarinet down. Marya gestured at the empty bunkroom. "What, did you drive them away?"

Luther laughed. "I couldn't blame them if I did."

"No, I'm kidding, you play wonderfully." He shrugged. Marya sat on a bunk across from him. "I'm sorry I was a bit curt with you a while ago. I needed to be alone."

His chin dipped a little. "Sure, no problem. Are you going to be sticking around? I wouldn't, none of us would blame you if you didn't."

"No. I had a track coach in high school who taught me you should always finish the race as hard as you can, even if you're dead last. I'm going to finish this."

Several sheets of paper were scattered on the floor around him, and a few open books. Marya picked up one of the sheets. It was thick with scribbled equations. "What's this, can I ask?"

Luther looked up at her with intense brown eyes. "Oh, some physics. Connection coefficients for probability space."

"Something important, earthshaking, I'm sure."

Luther shrugged again. "It could be. Who knows?" He looked down at his clarinet. "If we could solve the equations exactly, then we could focus—well, never mind the details. It probably won't work out."

"I have faith in you."

He looked up, and Marya smiled at him. Luther said, "Maybe. I can't deny I hope. . . ." He put the clarinet to his lips, played a few buzzy notes, and put it down, shaking his head. "Or maybe this will. I hope. I hope a lot." Luther lay down on his bunk, placing his clarinet carefully beside him, and folded his hands behind his head. He stared up at the ceiling as he continued. "I find I do a lot of hoping these days."

"Don't we all?"

"You seem to be doing pretty well, accomplishing your goals."

"With only a few major obstacles in the way."

"You mean Nezzie? The Loch Michigan Monster?" Marya laughed. Luther continued hotly, "That old fart. He's just afraid that if sensitives learn too much archaeology no one will need him and he'll be out on his ear."

"I don't think it's that," Marya said cautiously. "For all his faults, he's a first-rate field archaeologist. I have to admit I've learned a lot from him."

"Yeah, maybe. Anyway, that's not what I meant." He looked at her significantly. "About hoping."

Marya frowned. "But you're doing well on your own goals—oh. *That*."

"Yes," he said. "*That*. I . . . never mind." He sighed. "Although I have to admit you were a strong incentive to sign up."

"We're good friends," Marya said softly.

"Yes, we are. And I'm grateful for that."

After a few moments of clumsy silence, Marya said, "Look here, you have all these wonderful talents—"

He cut in abruptly. "And where do they get me? Hmm? Exactly. Silence. The silence of the sea, the silence of being alone. Sometimes I realize, you know," and he swallowed, "that I'm probably going about it all wrong. You know why I work so hard on my physics, doing these equations, playing my clarinet? Part of me hopes, you see, hopes and *dreams* and plans that my physics or my jazz will be the key to my future. Will let my light shine through for someone to see."

"I see your light."

"Not clearly enough," he said. "Not damn clearly enough."

"Luther," Marya said slowly, "if you want this—someone—so badly, why don't you concentrate on that goal, instead of all these secondary plans?"

"I know." He sighed. "Often I think that's what I do wrong. I think it's part of my mathematical training." He turned on his side and leaned up on one elbow, facing Marya. "You see, in proving theorems, it's sometimes easier to prove a more general theorem that has the one you're interested in as a corollary. That's what I'm trying to do. Attack the more general problem."

"What if you solve that and find that getting me, or anyone, isn't a corollary?"

Luther laughed and fell back in his bunk. He rubbed at his face. "Man, then I'd really be in deep!"

Awalu barely waited until Otu was outside before he turned and slapped Inaala, knocking her across the inside of the hut. "You faithless woman!" he shouted. "You shame your husband!" He hit her again and she fell down, knocking over furs, baskets, and tools. "If you love to laugh with him so much . . ."

"Then I will!" Inaala surprised herself by shouting back. Awalu was surprised as well, and hesitated, giving Inaala time enough to snatch up her boots and dash through the door.

Otu had piled his provisions on his sled and was preparing to leave when Inaala, half-naked and shivering in the cold, stumbled across the drifts of new-fallen snow to him. She clung to his fur jacket. "Take me with you, please," she begged him. "Awalu will kill me. You need a woman to sew up your clothes and chew your boots soft. Take me, please."

Awalu came charging out of the hut, shouting and brandishing his spear. The people in the neighboring huts, curious at all the noise, poked their heads out to see the commotion.

Otu took a fur from off his sled and wrapped it around Inaala's bare shoulders. "Someone might borrow your wife for a while, Awalu," Otu said loudly, for the benefit of all. "A poor hunter needs a woman more than a capable man such as yourself."

Awalu stared for a long moment. His breath puffed out in white clouds. The neighbors watched him carefully. Then, in disgust, he threw down his spear and went back into the hut. There was nothing he could do, really. Inaala did have the right to choose a different man if one would take her; she had not known any better than Awalu before Otu had come. Awalu could not refuse to 'lend' her to Otu without losing face. And here, where a neighbor's hospitality meant the difference between life and death, he could not afford to lose face.

Otu nodded and started off, pulling his sled behind him. Inaala dressed herself in Otu's furs and happily started trudging through the track his sled dug in the snow. The storm clouds of the night before had disappeared, and in her heart she felt as wide and expansive as the great swath of blue above.

When Marya told Luther she wanted to follow Inaala's path north, he said, "Nezzie will never go for that."

"I have to try."

"Okay." Luther started to get off the bunk.

"No, wait." Luther stopped to look up at Marya. "Stay here. I want to face him by myself." He pursed his lips. "Fighting my own battles, remember?" He nodded.

As Marya started down the tunnel she heard Luther's clarinet echoing after her, starting with "When the Saints Go Marching In" and seguing into "Onward Christian Soldiers." Marya smiled and felt buoyed up.

Luther was right. Potriah all but laughed. "Why? Go on another long search? I don't see the point. It would be too expensive—we were lucky to find this one so soon—and unreasonable when this site has finally started to yield results." He looked at her pointedly. "Even if not the results you wish they were."

"Maybe Inaala can lead us to a better site."

Potriah shook his head. "No. Archaeology isn't a series of wild goose chases."

"Dammit, *I'm an archaeologist, too!* Doesn't what I have to say have any validity?"

"Of course it does." He peered at her with his arctic-gray eyes. "But you know how much relocation costs. You need logic and reason behind your choices."

"And intuition. Without my intuition you never would have found this site in the first place, and your theories would be only words in dusty journals." She spoke very angrily now. "I know all that about logic and reason and training. That's why I got my Ph.D. I'm trying to blend it with my intuition, in a very delicate kind of marriage. There has to be some sort of reason why I homed in on

Inaala so strongly. There always is. I think her story isn't complete—I know it isn't—and neither will ours be until we find the end of hers."

"I will place it under consideration." His tone was one of finality, and she knew he had already made his decision. She got up quickly. Potriah added, "Marya, I know it's fun discovering new sites. But we don't have an unlimited budget."

Marya started to walk away. A sudden chill crept up her spine. "Speaking of budgets, there is money for a trip for me back to the mainland, for a break, isn't there? I'm due for a little R & R, I know. A little time away—to cool down," she added.

Potriah nodded. "Yes. That's true. It's in your contract. I'll notify the jump-jet pilot." As she walked out he called, "Marya, please don't be bitter. You've done some wonderful work. My job is to be the control, to temper things. I hope you understand."

She did and she didn't. But it didn't matter.

Luther was scribbling equations on a notepad when she found him. "Come on, Luther. Grab the P-amp gear. Not the lobster-head. Above-air."

He scrambled after her. "What's going on?"

"We're going to the surface." Marya smiled. "A wild goose chase."

"Huh?"

They rode up in the decompression chamber of the *Jacques* on its afternoon trip to the surface. Because they breathed a nitrogen-free oxygen-neon-argon atmosphere, decompression was rapid. Marya explained her plan on the way. Luther shook his head.

"Seems like a long shot to me," he said. "I mean, usually we have to criss-cross and recheck—"

"I know," Marya interrupted. "That's why Potriah

didn't want to even try. But I feel Inaala so strongly . . . I think I can pull it off."

The sub surfaced in the air hole kept ice-free by heating elements. Next to the hole was the surface support camp and a hired passenger jump-jet perched on the ice. The pilot came out of the plane as Marya approached with Luther in tow, dragging the P-amp helmet and gear. The air was still but frigid.

"Dr. St. Jean? You're the only one heading back to the mainland today."

"Good. Except we're not really going to the mainland."

"How's that?"

Marya figured she would use her travel privileges to scout north, along Otu and Inaala's path. As long as the plane was already requisitioned, she could use it as she liked. Potriah would not like it, but there was nothing he could do. Or so Marya hoped.

The pilot shrugged. "It's your trip," he said, climbing into the cockpit.

As the engines warmed up to a high-pitched hum, Luther fitted the P-amp helmet over Marya's head. Marya said, "Turn the amps on, but low. I need to give directions."

The engines roared, bellowing up clouds of snow. The plane leapt into the air, rotated and shot north.

"Fly low, as low as you can to the ice," Marya called forward to the pilot. He nodded and gave her a thumb's up.

The great white plain of ice and snow whizzed below them. An occasional seal or polar bear looked up in puzzlement at the strange noise in the sky. Marya concentrated, searching for the tingle of *presence*. "A few degrees west. There. Luther, twitch the amps up, will you?" She glimpsed the ice from the perspective of Inaala, running behind Otu as he dragged the sled behind him. But the vision was ghostly and flickering.

They headed north: twenty kilometers, forty, sixty, seventy. Then suddenly a black hand clutched at Marya's heart and she went pale.

Luther turned down the P-amps immediately. "What? What is it?"

"Set it down," she croaked in a dry voice. "Set down here!"

The plane had barely touched the ice, the jets still blasting away snow, when Marya stumbled out the door. The pilot cut the engines and they were surrounded by Arctic stillness. The air was cold and sharp. There was absolutely no sound except for their boots crunching the snow.

Marya turned to Luther. "I want the amps up full. Now."

She wandered around in a little circle. The wave of ice, cold, cold ice, hit her, and she fell to her knees.

Otu had put up the skin tent by the air hole where he had caught a big gray seal. Then he went out looking for more game, leaving Inaala to finish preparing the seal skin and meat, scraping away the blubber.

Finally she had made the right decision! Otu was so good and gentle to her. As was proper, he said very little directly in praise of her. But she could see in his eyes and the broad whiteness of his smile that he was pleased with her. He had even given her a little gift, a comb carved from the tusk of a walrus, engraved with scenes of men hunting seals. Otu said it was proper to use when on the ice over the sea. It was beautiful and she loved it. She loved Otu for giving it to her.

When she had scraped all the remaining blubber from the seal skin, she went into the skin tent and trimmed the candle. Inaala smiled, thinking of how cozy and warm it would be later, with the furs inside and Otu curled around her.

She had left some tools outside, so she started out to retrieve them. Crawling through the entrance, she heard the crunch of footsteps and saw boots on the ice. Her heart gave a little skip. Otu was back so soon—but she would be glad to see him. Perhaps he had been lucky.

Then she glanced up farther. With that one glance her heart froze. A cruel smile played over Awalu's face. "Someone's a better tracker than you think, no? And your man isn't here. He should know better, that you are a stupid, disloyal woman. Too bad. He'll think you ran away from him, too."

Inaala tried to run but Awalu caught up with her too easily. He grabbed the back of her clothes, swung her around and down to the ground. The sharp surface of the ice scraped her cheek. She tried to scramble, feet and hands clawing at the ice, but Awalu cuffed her to the ground and tore at her trousers. Her screams bounced off the ice.

Otu was too far away to hear.

After Awalu finished raping Inaala, he started to drag her towards the seal hole. "He'll think you just ran away again," Awalu repeated. Inaala struggled again. Awalu pushed her to the ground, kneeled on her arms, took her face roughly in his thick, calloused fingers, and slammed her head against the ice until she couldn't think through the ocean of pain.

Stunned, she was barely aware of Awalu dragging her the rest of the way. The white of the ground and blue of the sky whirled around her. Awalu chopped at the thin crust of ice covering the seal hole. The world rolled once more around Inaala as Awalu pushed her into the water.

Inaala sank immediately. The numbing cold enveloped her. In darkness, she weakly flailed her limbs. Her lungs shouting for air, reflex forced her to breathe: icy water flooded her nose and mouth and lungs. All went black then.

But out of the blackness arose a figure, even darker

than the water, of a huge woman. The woman lifted her face to Inaala, a kindly face, but her hair, like long tresses of seaweed, was tangled and mussed. She had arms like whales and breasts like black icebergs, and when she lifted her arms toward Inaala she had no fingers.

The Seal-Woman, Inaala/Marya realized. The Woman Under the Ice. Seal-Woman, help me.

Comb my hair, child, the gigantic figure said.

Comfort me, Inaala/Marya pleaded.

Comb my hair, child.

Inaala found she had in her hand the ivory comb Otu had given her. The animals and hunters carved on it wriggled and moved. Inaala floated down and tugged the comb through Seal-Woman's huge tresses. She glided all the way down Seal-Woman's hair, which hung past the huge woman's ankles, and beyond. Huge clouds of black boiled in the water. She smiled, knowing that Seal-Woman was sending a deadly storm to blind and kill her murderer. Inaala fell through the black clouds and into clear water, falling swiftly towards the bottom of the sea, where another woman stood with open arms. The woman looked up, and Marya was startled to see it was her own face.

It took Marya several days to work through the experience of Inaala's death, putting the memories into perspective as she had been taught to at the Swiss Institute. She had "experienced" rape and death before. It was a shock every time, and this was no different. At first her remembrance was a tumble of jagged fragments. But, bit by bit, she wove the memories into the fabric of her life.

Memories dominated Marya's life. They do everyone's life, of course—as Loebbel had told Marya, on one of the many occasions in which he waxed philosophic: To each relationship we bring the emotional baggage of all the others, from our parents and our lovers, who in turn were

controlled by their memories of their relationships, in a long
string fading into history. Memories are the building blocks
from which we build the houses in which we live. Marya
wondered through what window, framed by which past
loves, did Luther view her? She knew her idea of him was
shaded by subtle memories of Edwin and others. And Potriah, of course. In his case he was reacting to a memory
fading, clinging to memories of past victories that might not
come again, trying to hear a voice he could not quite
reclaim.

As for Marya's work—the dredged memories of the
long-dead hung over her, like the sheet of ice over the Arctic
sea floor, sometimes hidden by murky water but always
there. Memories, to Marya, were more to her than vehicles
of information, even more than Loebbel's building blocks.
She liked to think of them as the engines of compassion.
She had once read in a novel that what we feel most, we
remember best, and she believed the reverse to also be true.
By remembering, we can feel. And Marya hoped, by having more memories of more lives than most, she could feel
more deeply.

Even so, it was hard to feel much for Nesmith Potriah
as he argued, as she had known he would, against digging
at the new site she had found. But she sat calmly at the conference table in Dome 2, Potriah faced off against her at the
weekly site meeting. The old archaeologist was furious: a
waste of time and money, a silly gimmick she had pulled,
how *dare* she suggest they move on to a new chimeric site,
and so on.

She let him rage until he exhausted himself. Then she
presented her side. She knew exactly where to dig, to the
last meter. She had estimated the depth of the bones. She
laid out what it meant in terms of time and money, for this
one trench, this one chance. The *Jacques* would remain at
the primary site, and the *Phillipe* would be required only

three to four days at the second site. The cost would be only five percent of their total budget, and she reminded him that present estimates had them seven percent under budget because, in part, she had found the present site earlier than expected.

It was hard even for Nesmith Potriah to argue against facts. Marya had laid out her case beautifully. One could almost see the wheels turning in Potriah's head. More than anything else, he could not afford to take the chance that she might not be right. Perhaps that fading voice spoke to him. He swallowed and hemmed. And in the end, he grumbled that they might as well try.

Under the ice, in one hundred and twenty-five meters of water, they found the bones of a young woman exactly where Marya told them they would, buried two meters deep in sediment. The bones were radiodated to be 15,000 years before the present, the same as the bones from the primary site. Topo-maps of Beringia indicated she must have drowned in about thirty meters of water, probably about thirty to forty kilometers from shore, out on the ice. They also found the ivory comb, delicately worked and clearly showing scenes of hunting sea mammals.

The news quickly spread. Dr. St. Jean, not Dr. Potriah, was besieged with calls, from the *New York Times* to the Science News Cable Network. Nesmith A. Potriah, when finally asked, declined to say anything, not even to the *New York Times*. His silence was complete.

"Congratulations," Luther said later, sticking out his hand. Marya shook his hand, feeling silly. "You did a fine job."

"I suppose. What are you going to do now?"

Luther shrugged. "I don't know. Still not many jobs out there. I guess I'll keep on being a P-amp tech."

"I think you have potential for more. Don't underestimate yourself."

"Yeah. There are other benefits, you know." He looked at her significantly, then blushed. Marya felt a surge of warmth for him. Perhaps, she thought, perhaps. . . .

"Potriah's gone?" Luther asked.

Marya nodded. "Back to the mainland." His silence, she realized, was the only acknowledgement she would ever get from him that she was right. That she had been the discoverer of The Truth, and not him. She imagined him sitting in an overstuffed chair in his office, books looming over him. When he was younger, perhaps, he could have changed, but now he was too old, too tired, and too brittle. She guessed Nesmith Potriah would never go out in the field again. For a moment she even felt a flash of compassion for the old dinosaur.

After months of exhaustive analysis, Inaala's bones were reinterred in their watery grave, in accord with international archaeological agreements. The comb would be shared among the consortium of museums and universities sponsoring the dig. Marya substituted it with another comb, one she obtained from a King William's Land Inuit. She did not explain it was to untangle the Seal-Woman's tresses. Marya, Luther, and several of the other divers presided over the burial. Inaala's limbs were now straightened and her arms folded peacefully over her chest clutching Marya's gift. Imbedded in a block of frozen silt, they lowered her into the gaping hole in the sea floor, then covered it with more silt.

Marya began a chant, a burial chant half-remembered, in the ancient language. "*Ha Inaala taiaa lallia givia qi tuu . . .*" Marya only understood the sense of half of it. "*Iapii awuu lialik aai Sednaaqu iviat . . .*" "Seal-Woman, watch over your little sister in sleep." Marya's voice droned in a mournful tone, and she felt real sadness. And yet joy.

They finished and began trudging back to the *Phillipe,* their lights ensnaring curious fish and their boots kicking up storm clouds of silt. Marya wondered if she could, like an ancient priest, read her fortune in the swirling patterns. She wondered about many things, about the past, the present, and the future. Marya also wondered about the vision of Seal-Woman she had had; in some way she felt she had been given a gift. But, more than anything else, she kept remembering Inaala's brief time with Otu, and the color of the sky then and the light dancing off the snow crystals. She felt, through the glacial wall of memories of things that were and things yet to be, joy, the translucent light of the world above and beyond.

The Magic Picture
by
Hal Clement

About the Author

Harry Clement Stubbs was born in 1922 and earned degrees in astronomy, chemistry and education. He was a multi-engine pilot in World War II. By that time he was already capturing the attention of Astounding readers with a kind of SF writing he, in effect, invented and whose leading practitioner he remains. It's usually called "hard-science fiction"; a combination of a gripping story—as in his famous Mission of Gravity—with meticulously worked-out scientific extrapolation of a totally alien environment, told entirely or in large part from the viewpoint of an intelligent and appealing, but totally alien, inhabitant of that environment . . . to whom it's just that ordinary place he lives and must be brave in.

It's devilish hard to write, and few who've been inspired by Clement have been able to meet his standard even occasionally. But he performs with seeming ease, as masters will, and here tells us how it's done. . . .

Every story has a background; an environment in which—and a set of rules under which—everything happens, and writer and reader (or teller and listener) must have a reasonably similar idea of the nature of that background for the story to make sense.

In ordinary adventure or romance tales, the familiar "real" world forms the background, and the similarity can be taken for granted. Even in historical novels, while the author must specify the period somehow, it is usually safe to assume that the reader knows a fair amount of relevant history.

In fantasy and science fiction things are very different. The whole point is to challenge readers with the "what if?" implications of a background significantly different from the familiar and everyday. A verbal picture has to be painted, and the wordage needed to do the background is what commonly makes SF novels easier to write than shorter fiction. The ordinary storytelling rules of pacing, characterization, and motivation still apply, but the SF writer has additional work to do; book-length offers more freedom to do that.

Why bother with the extra work?

The key reason is consistency; lack of this quality in a story will bother all but the most utterly passive readers. The slips may be minor but still annoying; Ozma's magic picture, in Frank Baum's Oz stories, sometimes has a gold frame and sometimes a radium one, and is sometimes called a magic mirror instead. This never has serious effect on the plot line; the existence and properties of the picture itself are the only important things; but to readers who thought they had the background clearly in mind, the changes still give a jolt.

In the "hard" science fiction which I personally favor, the background is "real" but deliberately unfamiliar in some ways. Here, at least one aim of the writer is to take the reader by surprise with a "what if?" that is logical but unexpected, as with Phileas Fogg's gain of an extra day by going eastward around the world. The chief professional difficulty lies in spotting *all* the implications of the unfamiliar insertion, so as to maintain consistency. This task sometimes frightens writers out of the field. In my opinion, it should instead be taken as an opportunity; the implications can provide plot and action ideas. For example:

Quite commonly, science fiction authors have used planets whose atmospheres contain chlorine in place of oxygen. The usual implicit justification is that chlorine is almost as active as oxygen and chlorine-breathing creatures would probably do as well as we oxygen-breathers.

On the whole I would agree, though as a matter of fact there is a minor energy disadvantage for the chlorine types. However, unless other implications of the chlorine (or fluorine, which has an energy *advantage* over oxygen) are considered, the author faces a strong risk of consistency slips (embarrassing), and of overlooking potential story-line material (wasteful!).

Some people claim that chlorine atmospheres are unlikely because chlorine is much less common in the universe, and probably on any given planet, than oxygen. True but unimportant; it is not necessary for a substance to be the most common, merely that there be enough of it. If the most common were automatically the most probable, we should be silicon instead of carbon beings ourselves; silicon-based life has been a favorite with writers for decades because of the chemical similarities between the two elements, and they may be right. It *may* be only chance that we turned out as we did, even though Earth's crust is about a quarter silicon by mass and well under one percent carbon, but I doubt it (I am *not* saying that silicon life is impossible; that's a different and much longer debate).

There is plenty of chlorine on Earth, however. If you want to write a mad-scientist story in which a genetic engineer plans to deploy organisms that can oxidize the chloride ion to the free element, you have a realistic plot. Only about a tenth of the chloride now in Earth's oceans would have to be processed to match our present oxygen supply with Cl_2. Conceivably, it was only chance that the photosynthesis that works on oxides such as water evolved before one using chlorides; we might have been chlorine-breathers ourselves (an alternate-universe suggestion I haven't seen used yet; please note my continuing point of possible story lines). In fact, there were (and still are) bacteria on Earth that used iron, and others that used sulfur in about that way, and which *did* come first. Why they didn't end up in charge of Earth is another long question, and of course another possible set of story backgrounds.

If we grant a planet where a chlorine atmosphere does exist, what other implications are there?

They depend on further assumptions. If the temperature is in the liquid-water range, for example, we have the fact that chlorine dissolves (rather slowly) in water, reacting with it to give hydrochloric and hypochlorous acids; the latter in turn decomposes slowly to hydrochloric acid and free oxygen. To *maintain* the chlorine atmosphere, then, we need some process (presumably the original chloride-oxidizing photosynthesis) that will turn the acid back to free chlorine *as fast as it forms*; and we must also accept the fact that there will be some—possibly small but certainly not zero—concentration of free oxygen as well as the chlorine in the atmosphere.

If we had preferred fluorine, things would have been more difficult (read: more challenging). Fluorine also reacts with water, forming hydrofluoric acid and free oxygen. The acid is viciously active, even on the common silicate minerals of an ordinary Earthlike planet, with which it forms SiF_4. This is a gas that is also pretty active, and the long-term result will put the fluorine into insoluble minerals, just where we find it on Earth, instead of into the oceans like chlorine. Maybe some unfortunate early life, far back in Earth's history, did develop a fluorine-releasing variety of photosynthesis, but couldn't keep things going. If Earth were enough colder to have hydrogen fluoride oceans, with water a solid mineral, now. . . .

Be my guest again. But do some chemistry of your own; there are other problems (read: story inspirations) to be checked along this line.

With that taken care of, consider the problem of seeing. I don't, obviously, mean that the eyes of a being that has evolved in a chlorine environment would be irritated by the gas as ours are; but as most people know, chlorine is visibly colored—greenish, hence its Greek-origin name. Scientifically, we say that it absorbs radiation in the visible spectrum, more heavily at the long-wave end. This implies that over more than a short distance, which I haven't tried to calculate since I haven't tried to write this story yet, the atmosphere is opaque to human vision. Presumably native organisms, if they have evolved anything comparable to our sense of sight, use a different part of the spectrum.

What part? I don't know; you're writing the story. If I did decide to try it myself, I would find out what I could about the absorption spectrum of molecular chlorine—or just possibly, if I were in a real hurry for some reason or got too lazy to finish the research, I would cross my fingers and tell myself that, say, microwave radio photons are too low in energy to affect electronic, spin, or vibrational energies of the Cl_2 molecule. In the latter case I would not be too surprised, after the story appeared in print, to get a critical letter from a spectroscopist.

I don't want to scare potential writers into confining themselves to the narrow, "mainstream" part of the storytelling field. I want to show the *desirability* of considering as many as possible of the possibilities—something we would like to do in engineering and politics as well. However, I grant that spotting them *all* is just as impossible in this field as in those.

One can certainly produce a good story that concentrates on one "what-if?" and deliberately ignores others. Rick Raphael's "Code Three" dealt with the problems of a highway patrolman in a North America laced with five-mile-wide superhighways, whose speed lanes went above five hundred miles per hour. Many of the cars were jet-driven, and nuclear-powered ones were just starting to appear. I personally doubt strongly the possibility of fueling such a civilian fleet, but I still enjoyed the story—plot, action, motivation, characters, and all—except the end of the book version, which was perfectly logical and reasonable but unhappy (that is, my objection was a subjective, not a professional, criticism).

I realize, and want to emphasize, that Mr. Raphael may have omitted the fuel matter intentionally. He may have felt that discussing it would harm the pace of the story; he may have been saving that question for another story; he may have disagreed with me about the weight of the problem, after thought and calculation. He could even be right; science is an inherently tentative field, and maybe *I* didn't consider enough factors. (Certainty is only an emotion, and science is not for you if you feel a strong need for it. Join a group that depends on faith).

You are, in the final analysis, going to have to use your own judgement in painting your non-standard background picture. You can research in books and journals, pick the brains of friends, get information from computer networks; but only you can decide, for purposes of the story you want to tell, whether we are heading for a Larry Niven world in which checking into a hotel entails the risk of having the bed booby-trapped with high voltage and finding yourself sold for spare parts the next day, or the kind I used in "Mechanic" where the genetic code has been reduced to engineering practice and a patient's new heart or leg can be grown from a snip of his own flesh, thereby obviating tissue rejection as well as organlegging.

You are painting a word picture (or a series of them—the frames in a movie). Your pigment is your vocabulary, your brushes are the rules of grammar, and your model is the universe—the known (and thinkable, if you're extrapolating) laws of Nature.

The desirability of a good vocabulary (a rich palette) is obvious. Skill with brushes (the rules of expression that help avoid ambiguity and other forms of confusion) seems to me equally important. Many people, however, question the need for a model (scientific knowledge).

Personally, I find it convenient to have a lot of the rules and facts in my head, though the last three words are certainly not essential and not always correct—I often have to look things up. It greatly speeds up the process of painting-in the background, and it is also a fertile source of story ideas by itself. It does *not*, of course, preserve me from error; all of us, every now and then, take something to be so obvious that we don't need to check it, and then find we were wrong. Just after World War II, I was assuming that jet aircraft would not be practical commercially because of their enormous fuel consumption; I was a bomber pilot, and had a fair supply of relevant knowledge. What I should have been considering, of course, was not pounds of fuel per hour, but ton-miles or passenger-miles per pound of fuel.

In my novel, *Mission of Gravity,* I assumed, in spite of my perfectly valid astronomy degree, that my planet Mesklin would have an elliptical polar cross section (it was written before slide-rules grew buttons). Later, the MIT Science Fiction Society had a great deal of fun calculating what the actual shape would be, and of course telling me about it. In the same work, I took it for granted that my leading character's vessel, the *Bree,* would sail faster with the wind behind it. A sailor straightened me out on that one. I should have known better; I just didn't make the high-school-physics vector analysis I should have (and which I wouldn't have had to make if I'd ever done any sailing; the situation would have been familiar).

The word, then, is to spend all the time and effort *that you want* in working out your hard-science background material. I spend a lot because it's fun (for me). If you don't enjoy it, don't feel guilty; maybe (probably!) you're a better character builder than I.

Don't however, expect to avoid all mistakes, and don't worry when you're caught. You're in the entertainment business, and many of your readers will get fun out of catching you. Just remember that the fewer mistakes you do make, the more triumph they'll feel when they do; don't make any on purpose.

And don't try to claim that you did. "Touché" is a courtesy not restricted to fencing.

The Disambiguation of Captain Shroud

by
Gary W. Shockley

About the Author

Gary Shockley, 38, has already appeared in a "World's Best SF of the Year" anthology, in 1985, and was featured prominently in a book of stories by former students at the Clarion SF-writing workshops. He doesn't write fiction very often; clearly, when he does, he does it with impact.

Like a fair number of other modern-day geniuses, he earns his living as a computer expert and came to it after a history of apparently irrelevant odd jobs, including college. Some people who can write don't actually have careers—they have lives. Shockley's is an outstanding instance of that.

He's been a friend of many in SF since his year at Clarion. Those include WOTF III writer Lori Ann White, and others who kept pointing out it was only a matter of time before he did well in the Contest.

Our judges awarded First Place in this year's Second Quarter to a remarkably written story told from a unique viewpoint. On getting the author's name, we found Shockley had indeed arrived among us. And with a thump. . . .

Get us out of here.

An intriguing command, so full of possibilities. By "out of here" does Captain Shroud mean "out of the hovercraft," which is certainly a container from which one might want to get out? Or does she mean "out of the general vicinity?" That would be the case if by "us" she meant to include myself—the onboard computer—for I am not portable with respect to the hovercraft and can only be gotten out of here if the hovercraft itself is gotten out of here. Disambiguation therefore hinges on my membership in the set of "us."

Captain Shroud spoke directly into my console phonejack rather than using the craft-wide voicecom. She has done this only twice before, on occasions when the voicecom was broken. This time my sensors show voicecom fully functional, which confers to her mode of input a degree of surprisingness of 0.3170. Though not sufficient to signal an emergency, it should be investigated. I submit a subtask to do this, even as I have submitted 17,231 other subtasks to explore other aspects of the command. Some of them even now complete, providing me with additional information.

The anxiety index of her utterance is 0.0172, which is only slightly elevated. Recalibration based on her past history of calmness in stressful situations gives a value substantially higher. Still, the evidence is inconclusive. If a Code One Emergency prevails, questioning and verification of the command are not permitted, and immediate action is

Illustrated by David Lee Anderson

required. To me, immediate means twenty milliseconds.

A significant indicator turns up in a review of all her past utterances, which show a preponderance of expletives—to the point where they have become negative intensifiers. In essence, she softens commands with their use. If she had said, "Get us the hell out of here," the situation might have been serious but not dire. By saying, "Get us out of here," she has intensified the command to Code One Emergency proportions. Now restricted to twenty milliseconds, I prune my search trees, skeletonize my knowledge bases, override the skeptic governors on my belief engines, and move all of the subtasks associated with this problem into the executive queue, where they will have highest priority.

These actions inevitably demote my emoter and aesthetic hypercubes to background status. Even as they are being swapped out of the active queue, I give the verdant jungle below a final appreciative look, taking in the mist creeping out of the moss-webbed trees to curl above the river of mud directly below us. Lumpy backs break the surface, colorfully mottled with coral and algae. Tiny creatures skitter away as several snouts poke through, fluttering terminal flaps. Sine waves of agitation hint at serpentile creatures just below. On the mud bank, quadrupedal creatures wave sticks in their tentacled snouts.

Several more subtasks complete. One is a scan of Captain Shroud. She is off-balance and falling backwards away from the console, her mouth still forming the end of "here." She clearly has not remained seated with her belt fastened as the safety manuals recommend. In 1.831 seconds the back of her head will hit the view window with a force likely to knock her unconscious.

It occurs to me that by "us" Captain Shroud could be referring to just the two of us. That interpretation would hold if the crew had turned mutinous. A flood of subtasks are completing, among them scans of the crew. Moskowitch is on the floor, blood pooling around his right thigh. Qing is hanging onto the back of a chair, her hand extended towards the oxygen-backup toggle. Trimble is in midair, in mid-cry, trying to tuck himself for the coming collision with the wall. Patterson is gripping his chair and trying to activate the strafing laser. Courtney has been hit. Her forearm is even now beginning to bulge as the projectile prepares to emerge. I assign a subtask to identify the projectile as quickly as possible.

Clearly "us" refers to everyone inside the hovercraft, and quite likely the hovercraft itself. Because I have not detected any sudden change in our course, everyone's off-balance orientation registers 0.837 in surprisingness. An abbreviated diagnostic run-through turns up an unprecedented number of damaged sensors, and my craft-wide voicecom is in fact down. A software bug of catastrophic proportions has masked these sweeping damage conditions from me. I submit a background task to identify the responsible programmer and detract from his competence rating. By assimilating information from functioning sensors I discover that the hovercraft is in fact lurching hard to the right. The dense jungle and river of mud are less than thirty meters below.

Though the voicecom has two backup systems, both are damaged. I splice together their functional components until I gain access to the voicecom buffers. These contain the last utterances made by the crew members, which I review in chronological order:

Patterson: Oh shit! They're firing at us!

Trimble: We're hit! We're hit! Mayday, Captain!

Qing: Oxygen's going! What's wrong with the backups?

Moskowitch: The onboard's dead! Go manual!

Courtney: Oh Christ, we're fucked!

Shroud: [phonejack input] Get us out of here.

I discard the intensifying expletive phrases "Oh shit" and "Oh Christ." The remark by Courtney, who has a verbal astuteness index far in excess of anyone else, commands my attentional focus, but it defeats my attempts to interpret it as anything more than an idiom signifying an undesired state of submission. I drop her index by a tenth of a point. Concatenating everything else, expanding contractions and reconstituting missing elements, I arrive at the following sequence of remarks:

They are firing at us. We are hit. We are hit. Mayday, Captain. [The] Oxygen is going. What is wrong with the backups? The onboard is dead. [We must] Go [to] manual [control]. [You] Get us out of here.

When contextualized in this manner, "Get us out of here" takes on a broader, more urgent meaning: "Get us —the Captain, crew, and hovercraft—out of this predicament, taking whatever steps are necessary, and using all the resources at your disposal."

One such step would be to disable "they," so that they cannot fire on us again and inflict further damage. The question remains, who are they? I scan once more below us, assigning hostility and potency factors to all of the discernible candidates. Those in the river of mud fail to register in either category. The quadrupeds on the bank, holding sticks in their tentacled snouts, score low in both and become unlikely candidates. There is nothing more. Despite the lack of a good candidate, Code One Emergency status empowers me to relax my discriminative quantifiers toward a best-fit suspect. I conclude that the quadrupeds are our attackers.

As the allotted twenty milliseconds are coming to an end, I construct a plan of action:

Step A Concurrencies:
    1) Stabilize primary life-support systems.
    2) Level out hovercraft towards jungle cover.
    3) Strafe quadrupeds with laser.

Step B Concurrencies:
    1) Stabilize secondary life-support systems.
    2) Head back to base.

I am about to execute the plan when a conflict arises between Item 2 of Step A and my fundamental directive to preserve human resources. In particular, leveling out the hovercraft will increase the force of the Captain's impact with the window to a degree that could be fatal.

With almost no time remaining, I explore an alternate strategy. By tilting us into a steeper dive, I can greatly reduce Captain Shroud's impact. This has the significant advantage of preserving her state of consciousness. But there are three disadvantages: it delays our departure from this area; it draws us closer to the quadrupeds; and it removes the quadrupeds from my firing periphery.

I weigh the likelihood factors of everything involved—that the Captain will die if I level out; that the creatures on the bank are indeed "they"; that they are about to fire on us again; that they will disable us further if we dive, or if we level out, or if we remain in our present lurch; that the hovercraft in its present damaged state can withstand a dive—

The twenty milliseconds expire before I can gauge the full constellation of likelihoods. I tip us into a steeper dive. The Captain barely bumps the window. When that has occurred, I level us off towards jungle cover and am preparing to strafe the creatures when I get an interrupt from a subtask. The analysis of the projectile emerging from Courtney's arm shows it to be organic and seed-like in structure. I conduct a full-complement Mirucu scan of the vegetation behind us. A large pale-blue tree stands out. It has an apical seedpod, now empty, which still vibrates from the pressurized discharge of its seeds a moment ago. Playback and trajectory analysis confirm that we were directly above it when "hit."

It is indeed serendipitous that Captain Shroud was falling towards the window. Otherwise my original plan of action would have taken us over several more of those pale-blue trees before the projectile analysis was complete. I alter course to stay low over the river of mud until we are well away from the trees.

Reviewing the whole incident, I elevate Courtney's verbal astuteness index by a full point. She had been metaphorically correct, if obtuse, when she said, "We're fucked." And had I given her observation a greater weight, I might have arrived at the correct interpretation of events much sooner and without endangering the ship, Captain, crew, and the innocent creatures below.

Captain Shroud has rebounded from the window and is again falling backwards. The back of her head will soon hit the arm of a swivel chair. I reduce her body coordination index by three-tenths of a point even as I send the hovercraft into a lurch. This redirects her head towards the cushiony seat. But at the last moment the chair swivels, and she hits the arm regardless, which knocks her unconscious.

The injuries to Moskowitch and Courtney are not life-threatening, and stabilizing the primary and secondary life support systems is a simple matter. Returning my emoter and aesthetics hypercubes to the active queue, I marvel once more at the multifarious life forms wallowing in the mud below and try to imagine what Captain Shroud's headache will feel like.

About the WOTF Program:

Writing for the Future

by
Algis Budrys

About the Author

Algis Budrys has been a highly regarded science fiction and fantasy writer/editor since the early 1950s. He currently acts as the co-ordinator in L. Ron Hubbard's Writers of The Future Contest and its associated programs for discovering new talent. He has taught seminars at Michigan State University, Pepperdine, Brigham Young University, and Harvard. He is equally well known as an award-winning historian and critic of modern speculative fiction.

— *The Publishers*

Many of the writers who were first published in earlier *WOTF* volumes are now appearing regularly in magazines and with novels; other major publishers in the field seek them out. A gratifying percentage of our writers have already been contenders for top awards on an equal footing with long-established SF authors, and some have gained significant recognition in that arena. No other field of popular literature offers its novices such an opportunity for lifelong success.

We feel the new stories selected for *WOTF V* bring you the well-deserved launching of additional major careers. We hope you also agree the stories are superior reading by any standard. The basic requirement is to give you good reading *now*; the promise of the future is valid only if it comes from what has been actually accomplished today.

These anthologies spring from a program created to locate and present outstanding new talent, called L. Ron Hubbard's Writers of The Future Contest. It was founded in 1983 by L. Ron Hubbard (1911–1986), one of the most popular fiction authors ever known, and it was designed by him to be the central part of a remarkably practical and effective plan.

From his own experience in building a fiction career starting in his early twenties, and then sustaining his storytelling abilities over a half-century span, he was able to found his program on clear-cut principles. It is completely unbiased in finding talent, authoritatively and pragmatically fair in recognizing and rewarding talent, and it equips talent to sustain itself for the remainder of its own span. Those are its purposes, and it meets them; its contributions to the future of SF—its contributions to your continued enjoyment of this field—are undeniable.

With this volume, there are now seventy-four new writers who have achieved publication through the WOTF series. Many will be prominent in the field for years to come.

How does this happen? How does so much talent—so much good reading, and the promise of continued good reading—emerge from the program?

First and foremost, it presents itself. In some cases, years of preparation precede the day when a novice author enters the Contest, because very few persons who can tell a story with publishable skill are at that level when they first begin to write. And of those who begin, some grow discouraged. For many, it's not a swift or easy process . . . as any professional will tell you in recalling his or her own early days. But, with persistence and growth, one breaks through. These days, for those who have heard of the Contest and who enter it, that breakthrough often occurs via the Contest.

The Contest, in turn, does its best to advertise and publicize its existence. (You'll find its address on page 428.) Then, once an entry has been received, the following things happen:

The Contest Administration sends the entrant a notice that the entry has been received, carefully records the author's name and address and story title, and safeguards the information in records none of the Contest judges see. Then the Administrator checks to be sure no trace of the author's name appears on the manuscript itself, and forwards the now-anonymous work to me, the Co-ordinating Judge, in a plain, numbered envelope. I see all the eligible entries, each handled in the manner described. Then, every three months, on the quarterly schedule given in the rules,

I select all the stories I judge to be publishable speculative fiction, and pass those on to a group of Finalist judges chosen from our panel of the world's topflight creators of SF in the English language.

(This willingness to serve the needs of talent, on the part of people who are at the top of their profession—and therefore both prominent and busy—might astonish some. But the fact is that science fiction and fantasy writers have good reason to know that this particular mode of writing has an intense, long tradition of the older helping the younger. Not all that long ago, there were no writing programs teaching this literature, and even today those are not as readily available as they could be, nor as effective as they might. Almost all of us can point to needed expert help given to us along the way, and the opportunity to repay the past by providing for the future is one we do our best to exercise.)

Each quarter, the Finalist judges select three winners, who receive outright cash grants of $1000, $750, and $500, respectively for 1st, 2nd and 3rd Place. Thus the Contest identifies twelve winning stories per year and immediately delivers a significant reward to their authors in recognition of their merit.

Merit *is* what's being recognized; the only criterion for winning is a good SF story, of whatever kind is published in the field or could be published to SF readers. We don't know who the authors are, we don't know their age, sex, race, or their circumstances in life, and we can only guess at their hopes and fears because we can assume they are the same as ours were.

It's remarkable—we look so different from each other on the outside, and come from so many different parts of the world, but we are all one family of SF readers. Some of the family members become writers; all the family members want that to keep happening. The readers read, and thus encourage the writers. The writers make sure there's something new for the whole family to read. And WOTF provides a specific, effective channel for getting that done.

Of a Contest year's twelve winners, the four First Place entries are then judged together by a new panel, which selects the year's grand prize winner—the recipient of the L. Ron Hubbard Gold Award to The Author of The Writers of The Future Story of The Year. That brings with it an additional $4000 grant. This winner is announced at our annual Awards event, where all the year's winners have been brought, and where they all receive trophies or certificates attesting to their accomplishments. And during the week preceding the Awards, all twelve winners and some other Finalists will have had the opportunity to work under prominent SF writers as students in a workshop designed to reinforce their already existing skills—and also to show them how to continually create and develop fresh story ideas, and how to manage their subsequent careers.

That much is what the Contest does directly. There are additional benefits that developed as the program expanded:

This anthology series began only after the first Contest year's experience proved that the winning and Finalist stories were, indeed, of a quality that would please the general public, SF readers in particular but not exclusively. For the right to publish those stories, Bridge Publications, Inc., pays these authors additional monies, at generous rates. In its North American edition, and then by licensing editions in the United Kingdom, Australia, and New Zealand, Bridge brings their work to the attention of a public numbering in the millions.

Among each year's published authors, some are Finalists. Their stories are included here because, in my judgment as an editor, they will help in some way to unify or balance the overall feel of the book; make it the best possible reading experience for the buyer or borrower. The first purpose of the anthologies, after all, is to please readers; we have done so over the years, and certainly intend to continue doing so. That, too, remember, is central to L. Ron Hubbard's professional view of merit, and of the need for art to be accessible and attractive to its audience.

Appearance here also does bring these authors to the attention of other publishers, who have learned that the Contest and the *WOTF* anthologies consistently find highly competent new talent . . . that in truth this program can be seen as *the* voluntary scouting system for the entire field. (And we are grateful for, and acknowledge, the publicity and space often devoted to our program by so many other media of SF publication and of communication to readers generally.)

We're proud of being part of L. Ron Hubbard's gift to the future of his favorite mode of fiction; we're gratified that the "family" has already received so many benefits from it.

October 1, 1988, marked the inception of a new aspect of the total program—a parallel Contest for novice illustrators. Co-ordinating Judge of L. Ron Hubbard's Illustrators of The Future Contest (ILOF) is Frank Kelly-Freas. This distinguished illustrator in and beyond the SF field last year also began serving as Director of Illustration for these anthologies. You'll notice that for *WOTF V* he has obtained a striking array of story-artwork from some of the most promising "young pros" who have entered professional SF recently. *WOTF VI,* the next volume, will be illustrated entirely by the first set of ILOF winners. His essay introducing ILOF is included here; it contains full information about that Contest and the help it offers those who express their creativity in pictures.

Each year, too, the *WOTF* anthology contains expert essays of help to novice writers, which is to say they are also of considerable interest to readers who like a better understanding of how their reading has been brought to life. This year, we have "Circulate," a selection by L. Ron Hubbard from a "Golden Age" writers' magazine, which we use in our workshop teaching and in other symposia at various schools, including Brigham Young University, Pepperdine University, and Harvard. With it, we have specially written essays by a truly notable group of SF practitioners—Jane Yolen, Marta Randall, and Hal Clement.

And, as always, we reserve special thanks for our panel of Finalist judges, who are listed on our page of acknowledgements in the front of this book. Judging stories for you in this volume, in addition to all the judges from the previous year, were John Varley and Andre Norton. John Varley's is, as all of them are, a name that needs no explication to SF connoisseurs . . . nor, certainly, can anyone have grown up reading in this field and not have made a close acquaintance with the work of Andre Norton. For her long and distinguished service, Miss Norton holds the Grandmaster "Nebula" Award conferred on only a very few, by the Science Fiction Writers of America. If the worth of a program is measured by the quality of the persons supporting it, then we are supported as few things in this field have ever been.

Our gratitude and affection go, too, to our judge, Gene Wolfe. Over the years he has lent his services in many special additional ways, speaking on behalf of WOTF in many places around the world, representing us as only someone so talented and so sincere could, and, at the first of our WOTF writing workshops, helping us to refine and implement the techniques that have since become standard in that aspect of the total program. The needs of his own career have now made 1988 his final judging year, but he remains warmly regarded by the many WOTF writers he benefitted, and by all of us in charge of the various features of the Contest and its developments. Thank you, Gene; you are an ornament to the family.

And yet, the one indispensable roster is that of the Contest entrants published here. And they are:

Jamil Nasir, 1st Place, 1st Quarter
Mark Anthony, 2nd Place
Stephen C. Fisher, 3rd Place
Gary Shockley, 1st Place, 2nd Quarter
Stephen M. Baxter, 2nd Place
Paula May, 3rd Place
Virginia Baker, 1st Place, 3rd Quarter
Calvin Johnson, 2nd Place
J. Steven York, 3rd Place
Dan'l Danehy-Oakes and Alan Wexelblat, 1st Place, 4th Quarter
Marc Matz, 2nd Place
K. D. Wentworth, 3rd Place
Steve Martindale, Finalist
Eolake Stobblehouse, Finalist

Without aspiration for the future, there is nothing.

Illustrating
for the Future
by
Frank Kelly-Freas

About the Author

Frank Kelly-Freas (who has lately readopted the original form of his name) is the most popular illustrator in the history of SF, as The New Encyclopedia of Science Fiction *calls him. His first appearance was with a magazine cover in 1950. Soon he had come to the attention of John W. Campbell's* Astounding, *for which he was to do the covers that are the 1950s and '60s in the minds of those of us old enough to remember.*

(Some of us are old enough; a good deal of Algis Budrys's best writing of the time was either illustrated by Kelly-Freas or inspired by Kelly-Freas paintings; one of Kelly's ideas sparked a novel that put his sons through college.)

Kelly is still doing it—look on your magazine rack. He also designed the Skylab mission patch for NASA; an album cover for Queen; a painting of monoclonal antibodies in action for a major pharmaceutical house; scores of covers for Mad *magazine, and* Presenting the Bill *from "Great Moments in Medicine." He is the compleat illustrator. And in the position of Co-ordinating Judge for L. Ron Hubbard's Illustrators of The Future Contest, he will bring his expertise to the teaching of talented novices all over the world. Here he is. . . .*

When L. Ron Hubbard found-
ed his Writers of The Future Contest in 1983,
it was the initial step in his total program of
support for all the talents needed to make a new Golden Age
of SF.

At the very end of the 1930s, L. Ron Hubbard was
asked to bolster the young John W. Campbell's *Astounding
Science Fiction* magazine. He then swiftly also played a piv-
otal role in the founding of a sister publication for fantasy,
Unknown. The new writers being discovered by these publications were such as Isaac Asimov, Hal Clement, Lester
del Rey and Robert Heinlein.

Already a headliner as a professional writer, Hubbard
worked beside them but pursued his own direction. He set
trends with his fabulous stories—like *Final Blackout* for *Astounding,* and "Fear"and *Death's Deputy* for *Unknown*—
that were unlike anything usually seen in the pages of such
magazines.

A special chemistry occurred when the vivid characters
and dramatic situations in L. Ron Hubbard stories impacted
on the talent of a young illustrator named Edd Cartier.

"Illustration," as I define it, is art in the service of the
story. And Cartier's work for L. Ron Hubbard's stories is
an outstanding example of that. Even today, old-time SF
buffs recalling the original publication of "Fear" often go
on to think of the black-and-white illustrations, or "Death's
Deputy" and then the *Unknown* cover painting Cartier did
from it.

In the minds of readers, the "real" Tarzan books by Edgar Rice Burroughs were the ones with the J. Allen St. John illustrations; the "real" editions of *The Three Musketeers* and *Robinson Crusoe* were the ones with the Wyeth color plates; John Tenniel is the "only" illustrator of *Alice in Wonderland*, and so on. Tenniel even won a knighthood for his work. (I think that's a good idea, and more people should take it up!)

It was his awareness of the classic interplay of writer and illustrator in the public mind that caused L. Ron Hubbard to want to bring novice illustrators into the contest picture as soon as possible. ...And it's my awareness, as someone who's illustrated for some of the top SF names of later days, and who idolized Cartier's work all through my apprenticeship, that makes me glad to have been asked to be Co-ordinating Judge of the new L. Ron Hubbard's Illustrators of The Future Contest, (ILOF).

Illustration, as I've pointed out again and again, is a very special art. It requires not only graphic-arts talent but the ability to read a story, find the most eye-catching moments in it, and then render those moments in a way that pulls the reader into the work. It's not design, it's not decoration. It holds the reader's attention for its own sake, but it also sends him into the story.

And that's what ILOF is all about. ILOF isn't designed to just find and reward new graphic talent anywhere in the world. It's designed to teach the craft of illustration—and to teach it under fully professional circumstances.

Send for the rules at the address on page 431. Once you become a Quarterly winner, we'll work together, and you'll have a chance to illustrate actual stories for actual publication, with an actual professional art-director . . . me. You'll be working toward a major cash Grand Prize; more important—I think—you'll be started on a lifelong career, beginning with seeing your work published in—and additionally paid-for by—"The Best-Selling SF Anthology Series of All Time."

The judges who'll be looking at and commenting on your work, and deciding the Quarterly and Grand Prize winners, represent the top names in the field from the Golden Age on down to the present day. They are:

Edd Cartier
Diane Dillon
Leo Dillon
H. R. van Dongen
Bob Eggleton
Will Eisner
Frank Frazetta
Jack Kirby
Paul Lehr
Ron Lindahn
Val Lakey Lindahn
Moebius
Alex Schomburg
William R. Warren, Jr.

'Nuff said. Study the rules, get into the Contest. Got talent but nervous about your chances? Don't sweat it . . . just draw!

About the Illustrators

As we have done in past *WOTF* volumes, we bring you illustrations by young talent, sometimes finding it in out-of-the-way sources, sometimes bringing completely new names to your attention.

David Lee Anderson

. . . teaches art part time in an Oklahoma City parochial school and freelances art full time. He did "The Disambiguation of Captain Shroud."

Denis Beauvais

. . . ("A Walk by Moonlight") has exhibited wildlife drawings in Canada, done SF book covers, and often illustrated gaming magazines.

David Dorman

. . . illustrator of "Rachel's Wedding," is best known for his work for *Heavy Metal* and his many comic book cover paintings.

Bob Giadrosich

. . . who illustrated "Just don't," has published in *Dragon*, *Easyriders*, *Apex!*, *Pulsar*, and *Dungeon*.

Alan Gutierrez

. . . has done book covers, a Tonka Toy box design, and art for *Popular Mechanics* and the Jet Propulsion Laboratory. For us, he did "Dear Mom."

Todd Cameron Hamilton

. . . of "The Wallet and Maudie," has co-authored four SF and horror novels and illustrated guides to Zelazny's Castle Amber, McCaffrey's Pern, and Anthony's Xanth.

Dell Harris

. . . ("Prosthetic Lady") has done covers and interiors for several major SF magazines, and several book covers. Connoisseurs are already collecting his paintings.

Carolly Hauksdottir

. . . who illustrated "A Ghost in the Matrix," usually works with high-fantasy themes. She also does computer animation.

Ed Kline

. . . illustrator of "Starbird," sculpts, does computer graphics, commercial and engineering artwork, and fine jewelry in ivory.

Jean Elizabeth Martin

. . . who illustrated "Daddy's Girls," has done covers for

Dungeon magazine and *Amazing Stories*. She plans to write and illustrate children's stories.

Mark Maxwell

... ("Blue Shift") is a scientific and technical illustrator who is participating in a U.S.–U.S.S.R. exhibition of astronomical art in Moscow.

Stu Shepherd

... of "Under Ice," displays his work at West Coast convention art shows and has done most of his art for Revell aviation models.

Larry Stewart

... ("Despite and Still") was the calligrapher for the Governor General of Canada. He also did machine designs for *The War of the Worlds*.

Patrick Wynne

... is the illustrator of "The Nomalers." His pen-and-ink drawings have appeared in many magazines, books and calendars, as well as in a musical score.

C O N T E S T   R U L E S

1. No entry fee is required, and all rights in the story remain the property of the author. All types of science fiction and fantasy are welcome; every entry is judged on its own merits only.

2. All entries must be original works of science fiction or fantasy in English. Plagiarism will result in disqualification. Submitted works may not have been previously published in professional media.

3. Eligible entries must be works of prose, either short stories (under 10,000 words) or novelets (under 17,000 words) in length. We regret we cannot consider poetry, or works intended for children.

4. The Contest is open only to those who have not had professionally published a novel or short novel, or more than three short stories, or more than one novelet.

5. Entries must be typewritten and double spaced with numbered pages (computer-printer output O.K.). Each entry must have a cover page with the title of the work, the author's name, address, and telephone number, and an approximate word-count. The manuscript itself should be titled and numbered on every page, but the author's name should be deleted to facilitate fair judging.

6. Manuscripts will be returned after judging. Entries must include a self-addressed return envelope. U.S. return envelopes must be stamped; others may enclose international postal reply coupons.

7. There shall be three cash prizes in each quarter: 1st Prize of $1000, 2nd Prize of $750, and 3rd Prize of $500, in U.S. dollars or the recipient's locally equivalent amount. In addition, there shall be a further cash prize of $4000 to the Grand Prize winner, who will be selected from among the 1st Prize winners for the period of October 1, 1988 through September 30, 1989. All winners will also receive trophies or certificates.

8. The Contest will continue through September 30, 1989, on the following quarterly basis:

> October 1 - December 31, 1988
> January 1 - March 31, 1989
> April 1 - June 30, 1989
> July 1 - September 30, 1989

Information regarding subsequent contests may be obtained by sending a self-addressed, stamped, business-size envelope to the above address.

To be eligible for the quarterly judging, an entry must be postmarked no later than Midnight on the last day of the Quarter.

9. Each entrant may submit only one manuscript per Quarter. Winners in a quarterly judging are ineligible to make further entries in the Contest.

10. All entrants, including winners, retain all rights to their stories.

11. Entries will be judged by a panel of professional authors. Each quarterly judging and the Grand Prize judging may have a different panel. The decisions of the judges are entirely their own, and are final.

12. Entrants in each Quarter will be individually notified of the results by mail, together with the names of those sitting on the panel of judges.

This contest is void where prohibited by law.

L. Ron Hubbard's
ILLUSTRATORS OF THE FUTURE
CONTEST

OPEN TO NEW SCIENCE FICTION AND FANTASY ARTISTS WORLDWIDE

<u>All Judging by Professional Artists Only</u>
Frank Kelly-Freas,
Co-ordinating Judge

<u>$1500 in Prizes Each Quarter</u>

Quarterly Winners compete for
$4000 additional ANNUAL PRIZE
under Professional Art Direction

1989 Contest Year Periods
October 1 - December 31 1988
January 1 - March 31 1989
April 1 - June 30 1989
July 1 - September 30 1989

DON'T DELAY!
SEND FOR COMPLETE RULES TO:

L. Ron Hubbard's
Illustrators of The Future Contest
2210 Wilshire Blvd., Suite 343
Santa Monica, CA 90403

*Information regarding subsequent contests may
be obtained by sending a self-addressed,
stamped business-size envelope to the above address.*

No Entry Fee   **Entrants Retain All Rights**

"...as perfect a piece of science fiction as has ever been written."

- Robert A. Heinlein

Europe is devastated by thirty years of incessant warfare! FINAL BLACKOUT is the story of a small band of "unkillables" - soldiers who have survived the bloodshed, plagues and starvation - led by the mysterious Lieutenant, the most professional of the professional soldiers.

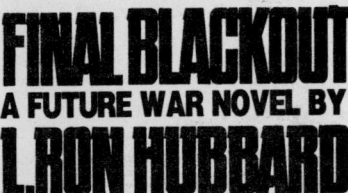

The tension and chilling power of L. Ron Hubbard's fast-paced tale FINAL BLACKOUT will capture your imagination. Buy it and read it today!

"...compelling...riveting...Hubbard's best science fiction novel."

-Publishers Weekly

FINAL BLACKOUT
A FUTURE WAR NOVEL BY
L. RON HUBBARD

$16.95
Wherever hardcover books are sold

GET YOUR COPY TODAY!

CALL 1-800-722-1733 (1-800-843-7389 in CA)

Bridge Publications, Inc., Dept WOF5,
4751 Fountain Avenue, Los Angeles, CA 90029